Little Tin Heart

Little Tin Heart

A MEMOIR

by

Suzy T. Kane

Copyright © Suzy T. Kane, 2020

Author website: www.suzytkane.com

An adapted excerpt of this work first appeared in *The North Carolina Literary Review Online 2017* as "Misadventure in Montclair."

Photographs from the author's collection

The author is grateful for permission to quote from the works listed below:

"The Love Song of J. Alfred Prufrock" by T. S. Eliot in *The Complete Poems and Plays: 1909-1950*. Copyright, 1930, 1939, 1943, 1950, 1958, 1962 by T. S. Eliot. Copyright, 1934, 1935, 1936, 1952, by Harcourt, Brace & World, Inc. with thanks to Ron Hussey at Houghton Mifflin Harcourt, New York, and permission from Faber & Faber Limited, London.

"A Minor Bird" by Robert Frost in *Complete Poems of Robert Frost*, Holt, Rinehart and Winston, Inc., New York, 1963. Copyright, 1916, 1921, 1923, 1928, 1930, 1934, 1939, 1943, 1945, 1947, 1949, by Holt, Rinehart and Winston, Inc. Copyright, 1936, 1942, 1945, 1948 by Robert Frost. Copyright renewed 1944, 1951, 1956, 1958, 1962 by Robert Frost. With thanks to Rebekah Irwin, Special Collections, Middlebury College Library; Peter A. Gilbert, Trustee and Executor, Robert Frost Estate; and Joan Ashe at Henry Holt and Company.

"Spring" by Edna St. Vincent Millay in *Collected Poems*, Harper & Row, Publishers, New York, copyright 1917, 1921, 1922, 1923, 1928, 1931, 1933, 1934, 1936, 1937, 1938, 1939, 1940, 1941, 1950 by Edna St. Vincent Millay; Copyright 1945, 1946, 1947, 1951, 1952, 1953, 1954, 1956 by Norma Millay Ellis with thanks to Frederick T. Courtright at The Permissions Company, Inc.

The Arab Mind by Raphael Patai, originally published by Charles Scribner's Sons, New York, in 1973 and 1976, revised in 1983 and republished in 2002, 2007 by Recovery Resources Press, Tucson, Arizona, with thanks to Jennifer Schneider, PhD, MD, and Daphne Patai, PhD, executor of the estate of Raphael Patai.

"Stay with Me," from *Into the Woods* with words and music by Stephen Sondheim, copyright 1988, Rilting Music, Inc., with thanks to Michael Worden at Alfred Music Publishing, Christie Lockwood at Warner Chappell Music, and Shari Molstad at Hal Leonard LLC.

Names: Kane, Suzy T., author.
Title: Little tin heart : a memoir / by Suzy T. Kane.
Description: [Wilmington, North Carolina] : [Suzy T. Kane], [2020]
Identifiers: ISBN 9798647528810 | ASIN: B0896VNH1H
Subjects: LCSH: Kane, Suzy T.--Family. | Iraqi American women--Biography. | Adult children of alcoholics--Biography. | Families--United States--20th century. | Iraq--History--20th century. | LCGFT: Biographies.
Classification: LCC HQ755.86 .K36 2020 | DDC 306.8743092--dc23

To Annie, Ben, and Zoe,

childhood's future

CONTENTS

Part One: In the Garden of Eden   1

Part Two: Growing Pains   65

Part Three: In Vino Veritas   247

Acknowledgments   295

Books That Helped   301

PART ONE:

IN THE GARDEN OF EDEN

Part One: In the Garden of Eden

*I*N *1938 IN NEOSHO, MISSOURI*, a seventeen-year-old American girl named Doris Hisaw, my mother, had finished her freshman year at Southwest Missouri State Teachers College and gotten a part-time summer job back home at Karby's Grocery Store sacking sugar and potatoes and waiting on customers for a dollar a day. Doris had pretty blue eyes and light brown hair. Her Scots-Irish skin was so white, she had to be careful not to burn it when, as a passenger, she propped her arm in an open car window. She loved music, and in addition to having a clear soprano voice, she played the piano and violin and was a member of Neosho High School's all-girl marching drum corps. A boy named Jimmy had been sweet on Doris in high school. Her mother, Lorene, took them for drives on Sunday after church and chaperoned their dates. But because she never left Doris and Jimmy alone to get to know each other, Jimmy finally gave up on dating her.

That same summer, seven thousand miles from Neosho, Missouri, in Basra, Iraq, twenty-seven-year-old Nejib Tooni, my father, and his older brother Kamil, wondered why their father, Naoum, had summoned them into the sitting room of their house. Nejib was Naoum's second son and was born in 1911, when Iraq was still referred to as Mesopotamia, an appellation left over from ancient Greek rule meaning "the land between the rivers," the Tigris and Euphrates. At five-foot-ten, Nejib was the tallest of the four boys in the family. His only sister Jeanette was the youngest sibling. In pictures in his photo album, Nejib's bright brown eyes and perfect teeth shine out of his seemingly tanned face as if they were plugged into an electrical outlet. He was good-looking in the tradition of his mother's family, whose household was known as *Bait al Hulu*, which translates as "House of the Sweet," that is, the handsome.

Just as the British community in Iraq at that time took their tea hot regardless of the outside temperature, a servant in their father's house had prepared tea for them in the samovar. He poured it into glass cups, which he arranged on a tray with a small plate of dates and brought into the sitting room. Settled on cushions on straight-backed chairs, the brothers blew on their steaming drink as they awaited their father, Naoum. Shorter than his sons, Naoum was rotund but not obese. What made his hazel eyes unusual for an Armenian was that their color sometimes looked golden. Not one for small talk, when he entered the room, he immediately got to the point, turning the serious expressions on his sons' faces into grins as he said, "It is time for you to get married."

Nejib had been attracted to an Iraqi woman in Basra named Zekiya Garabet, whose family, like his, was Christian. But her father, a Kurdish pastor of a Protestant denomination, would not countenance his daughter marrying a Catholic. He did not believe in mixed marriages.

Now Naoum was telling his sons that for them to find wives, he would give them each 500 British pounds to return to America, where they had gone to college. Five hundred pounds was a lot of money in 1938—over $50,000 apiece in the US dollars of 2018. While arranged marriages in Iraq were still common among the 95 percent of the population that was Muslim, Christians had more latitude. Their younger brother, Yusif or Joe, had followed his older brothers to college in America, but he had brought home an American wife. "Their father had been so highly gratified by the first marriage," one American newspaper would later report, "that they, too, were in search of American brides."

The first thing Nejib and his brother did after they sailed into New York was to purchase a brand new black Hudson sedan to drive to their alma mater, Hope College, in Holland, Michigan. "Boy, were we showing off!" Kamil confessed. On their way, they digressed to Angola, Indiana, to visit their youngest brother, Louis, who was studying civil engineering at Tri-State College. After Nejib and Kamil continued on to Holland, Michigan, they looked up girls they had known from their student days at Hope College before they transferred to the University of Michigan. The father of the girl Nejib contacted owned a Nehi bottling company. When he saw that the couth man who called on his daughter was American-educated, from a wealthy family, and single, he promised Nejib that the business would be his if he married his daughter. What was the father's background that would impel him to negotiate such an offer? But for Nejib, his daughter was not the girl he was looking for.

The brothers pointed their Hudson toward Newtonia, a tiny village in the southwest corner of Missouri, to meet the parents and siblings of their brother Joe's American wife, with whom they had planned a visit. Their first Sunday with the family, the brothers attended the closest Catholic church in Neosho, twelve miles away. On another day, interested in business, the brothers toured the Pet Milk plant in Neosho.

During the week, they gave a talk about Iraq at Neosho's First Christian Church, which their sister-in-law had attended. Meeting eligible girls, however, was not happening for them.

Newtonia was so small the brothers thought they would have better luck in Neosho itself, the county seat, whose population then was around 5,000. Joe's in-laws recommended a boarding house where they could stay. Once there, the first thing Nejib and Kamil asked the landlady was if she could recommend some girls they could meet. She thought of her friend Lorene Hisaw's daughter, Doris, and said she was happy to telephone the Hisaw house herself to introduce the visiting foreigners.

To purchase a box of chocolates as a hostess gift, Nejib and his brother parked their car nose to the curb on the square in front of Foster Evans Drugs, which had a soda fountain where high schoolers congregated. Entering the store in their suave sports jackets and slacks, the brothers were hard not to notice. Friendly teenage girls seated at the ice cream tables looked up from their conversations and flashed big smiles at the foreigners, whose worldly bearing set them apart. Seeing the brothers' reflections in the mirror behind the soda fountain counter, other teenage girls stopped sipping their Cokes and swirled their stools around to flirt with them. With his ready smile, Nejib beamed right back at them. Did he hear the girl who exclaimed to her friend, "Oh, he's so handsome!"?

Doris was off from her summer job the day the foreigners were scheduled to visit.

Free from work and sitting on a glider on the side porch, she was racing through the novel *Gone with the Wind*, which the librarian at the Neosho Library had let her borrow only on condition she brought it back quickly. Since the novel had won the Pulitzer Prize the previous year, there was still a long waiting list for the book. Luckily, Doris was a fast reader. Did she resent having to be torn away from Scarlett O'Hara's engrossing life to have to meet some foreigners who were coming to the house?

Doris's mother, Lorene, was sitting in the living room knitting as she awaited the foreigners' arrival; as a junior high social studies teacher, her curiosity was piqued. The only foreigners in Neosho were the Catholics. Did she expect these foreigners to arrive in native garb?

Lorene's mother, Doris's grandmother whom she called Nanny, was lying on top of the chenille cover of her bed in her room with her shoes on, not asleep but resting until the company arrived.

The twist of the mechanical doorbell and its loud ring on the front door jolted Doris out of the Civil War, which the book's protagonist confronted. From where Doris sat around the corner of the porch, she couldn't see the guests she assumed had arrived; but laying down her tome, she hurried in the side screen door to join them in the living room. After introductions all around, the Arabs, so well dressed and with such refined manners, took seats in the living room. And what a movie-star smile, she thought, on such a handsome man! They chatted affably over glasses of iced tea with Lorene, Doris, and Nanny. When Lorene commented on how well they spoke English, she learned from them that they were educated in the United States. What brought them to Neosho? The brothers explained that they had been visiting their sister-in-law's family in Newtonia and recounted their inspection of the Pet Milk plant and the talk they gave about their country to the congregation of Neosho's First Christian Church.

Nejib wondered if they might have a suggestion for something tourists could see before their visit in the area was over? Nanny said some Hollywood folks who were making a movie about Jesse James had brought an old-time train into Neosho's Kansas City Southern station. When she had gone down to see it, she met the actor Henry Fonda, who had spoken to her so nicely; but she did not know if the train was still there.

Lorene laughed. They were filming *Jesse James* in Pineville, she said, and the town had just voted to dismantle its hitching posts and lay down paving when the movie people came in, built Western facades over all the stores, and covered the roads back up with dirt. Pineville was only about twenty miles away. Maybe they would enjoy going there to watch the filming? The visitors thought Lorene's suggestion a great idea. Had Nejib and Doris all the while been locking eyes and smiling at each other? Did zing begin right there—the feeling that Doris believed indicated love at first sight? Did Nejib say to Doris, "Would you like to come with us?" or did Doris say, "May I go with you?" Whoever said what, the visitors seemed mature and upstanding to Lorene. She consented to let Doris drive with the brothers the next day to Pineville to watch the filming of *Jesse James*. An upholder of Southern hospitality, she also invited them for supper after their return from Pineville. In just a few days they would be leaving Neosho to drive back to New York and sail home to their native country.

The next day while the visitors and Doris were on the Pineville tour, Lorene made a peach cobbler for dessert. Could she ever have guessed that her teenage daughter was strolling around the *Jesse James* set arm-in-arm with an Aye-rab? She was getting ready to fry a chicken for supper when the foreigners and Doris walked in the front door. Doris got them all Cokes and joined the men in the living room to wait for supper. Were Nejib and Doris whispering to each other? Communicating silently with eyebrow semaphore, facial expressions, and nods of their heads? *Now?*

Nejib stood and walked toward the kitchen. Lorene was patting dry a piece of chicken with a paper towel when Nejib posed his question: "May I have your daughter's hand in marriage?"

"*Marriage?*"

Flabbergasted, Lorene was so caught off guard she answered, "No, but you can stay for supper." Did she think it was too rude to un-invite them? Whatever was going on in her mind, her Southern manners had kicked in as if Nejib had asked a question as neutral as "Is it going to rain?" Did she think he was crazy? Did Nejib think *she* was crazy? Seated at the table and digging into the fried chicken, was the conversation reduced to chitchat, or did they eat in silence? Did they *all* pretend Nejib hadn't asked what he asked?

After supper, once the men said their thank-yous and good-evenings and Lorene closed the front door behind them, she turned to Doris. "I forbid you to see those men again! Do you hear?"

"But mother, I love him."

"*Forbid!* Do you understand?"

The next morning, Doris sat on the cement stairs to their big front porch and, with a special key, screwed her roller skates onto her shoes and skated down her sidewalk. Her turning left to Big Spring Park next door to her house raised no eyebrows at home because Doris had often roller-skated down the long sidewalk that ran the park's entire length.

The brothers had switched their lodging to the Big Spring Inn, directly across the street from the park. Nejib had whispered to Doris at dinner the night before that he would be watching for her arrival. Now he was sitting on the bench close to the entrance of the park, waiting for her. Little St. John's Church, situated in between the bench and Doris's house, blocked the bench from her mother's view.

⁓

Believing the Arab brothers had departed, Lorene thought nothing of Doris's walking to town that afternoon with her cousin Jean, who lived in the house behind them. They stopped in at Karby's Grocery Store. The boy who shared the part-time job with Doris had a message for her. He said a man had come by with a letter addressed to her; she would find it hidden between the watermelons. It was marked *Confidential*:

My dearest Doris,

The bearer is Mr. Kirk, father of my sister-in-law, Aileen. I am waiting for you in the country and he is ready to drive you out to where I am. Come as you are—don't dress up for that might create suspicion. I don't want you to bring anything with you, for I can easily buy what you need. I am willing to marry you and I don't care who you are or what you have. I love Doris Hisaw—my dream girl & I want her to be mine always.

Darling, I love you more and more every day. Please don't break my heart. I'll take good care of you all my life. I'll dedicate my whole life towards your happiness if you only marry me now.

ana ahibecki [I love you], Nejib

P.S. Don't be afraid and don't let old women try to live your life for you.

Later that afternoon, Doris cleaned up to go to the library wearing the white two-piece crepe de chine dress Lorene had made for her. Its little blue celluloid crown buttons had been popular at Woolworth's for commemorating the coronation of Edward VIII. Doris told her mother that she had promised to have the copy of *Gone with the Wind* back to the library that day. Previously confiding in Cousin Jean, Doris entrusted her with two things she wanted to take with her when she met Nejib—her Bible, a gift from Nanny when Doris had "accepted Jesus into her heart" at age fourteen and her precious violin.

Jean had loyally smuggled both items home unobserved and later met Doris at the library with them.

Lorene and Nanny were distraught that Doris did not return from the library. As the hours mounted, did Lorene think of calling the police? When Doris finally arrived home at 2 a.m., the women were shocked to find her accompanied by the foreigners they thought had left town and even more shocked to learn that Doris and Nejib had gotten married in Arkansas, where the age of consent without parental permission was sixteen, not eighteen as in Missouri.

Lorene brought bedding into the living room for Kamil to sleep on the couch. It silently galled her that Doris and Nejib were going to sleep together in the big day bed she had to open up for them in the dining room. They interpreted Lorene's absence of criticism, however, as acceptance of their marriage and of Doris's plans to depart the next day with her new husband for a honeymoon motor trip to New York. After that, they planned to embark on the long journey by ship across the ocean to his home in Iraq.

The next morning, after Doris and the Arab brothers piled into their Hudson and left, Lorene immediately telephoned her former husband, Lloyd. She hoped against hope that Lloyd could do something to annul their daughter's marriage. Both parents feared Doris would be placed in an Arabian harem.

Movies are part of the cultural air Americans breathe. Lorene and Lloyd were of the generation that was informed about Arab culture by the silent picture *The Sheik*, which played in Neosho at the Orpheum Theater in 1922, two months after it was released. The film made a superstar of Rudolf Valentino. It tells the story in which a dashing Arab, Ahmed, does whisk a pretty British girl off to his tribal tent, and it does depict, as the subtitle amplifies, a "marriage market—an ancient custom by which wives are secured for the wealthy sons of Allah on the way to harems ... to obey and serve like chattel slaves."

An alcohol tax agent, Lloyd called the Federal Bureau of Investigation to declare that an Arab had taken his daughter in violation of the Mann Act, known officially as the White Slave Trade Act.

Nejib and Doris did not know the FBI was looking for them with the intention of preventing them from leaving the US. With Kamil, they innocently made their first stop in St. Louis, where they spent the night and next day toured the City Art Museum. The brothers then retraced their path across Illinois back to Angola, Indiana, to introduce Doris to their brother Louis and Louis to his new sister-in-law. From there they traveled on to Ann Arbor to show Doris their second alma mater, the University of Michigan, where Kamil asked that they leave him off.

The farthest Doris had ever been from Neosho was to the World's Fair in Chicago, where her mother took her at age thirteen. Now aiming for Washington, DC, Nejib and Doris proceeded across Ohio, hitting West Virginia and Maryland on the way. Doris thought that one of Nejib's friends from Basra, who lived in Washington, DC, "entertained them royally," she wrote a high school friend, by showing them around the city and taking them to Mt. Vernon. She said she had "a grand time."

From Washington they drove through Delaware, Pennsylvania, and New Jersey to get to their final stop, New York. There they took in Rockefeller Plaza and Radio City Music Hall. When they looked up a friend of Nejib in his office, the friend showed them a newspaper clipping about the Federal Bureau of Investigation's search for them. They didn't know what to think.

Nejib decided they should return to their hotel to get their marriage certificate and a letter they had received from Lorene saying all was well. (Was Lorene lying? Was she trying to trick Doris and Nejib into complacency so the FBI could catch them? And how had she known where to send her letter?) Thus armed, they headed to the Iraqi consulate in New York to get a passport for Doris before they went to the FBI themselves.

Unfortunately, the Iraqi consul had gone back to Iraq, and there was no one in the office authorized to issue a new passport or to add Doris to Nejib's passport. It would take too long to wait for a necessary copy of Doris's birth certificate to arrive so that she could apply for her own passport. So they went to the British consulate, whose consul said he had to telephone someone and excused himself. He was gone a long time and was shaking his head when he returned: "I'm sorry, but you'd better go back to the Iraqi consulate. I don't think I can help you."

When Nejib and Doris got back to the Iraqi consulate, they saw a hefty, muscular man talking with the officer they had talked to before. The hefty man approached Nejib and said, "I'd like to see you and the lady outside, please."

Nejib asked, "Are you a G-man? If you are, I want to see *you*."

Out on the sidewalk, the agent said he would have to take Nejib and Doris to the FBI. They came peaceably. When he saw that they wanted to give themselves up anyway—that in fact they were rather amused about the whole thing—he began to laugh and joke with them. He even said he was sorry to have to make a bride walk to the FBI. At the FBI office, the kidding continued, and the agent in charge told Nejib and Doris to come back the next morning for a hearing, as the St. Louis office insisted that there should be one. Nejib told them they could count on their appearing in New York's federal court the next day.

From the many often repetitive newspaper articles across the nation about my parents' escapade, I pulled the following headlines. Together, they summarize the story of their elopement:

> FRANTIC MOTHER FEARS BRIDE IS HEADED FOR ARAB HAREM,
>
> Asks U. S. to Stop Former U. of M. Student and Child Wife If They Try to Sail
>
> (*Free Press and Chicago Tribune*)
>
> ORIENTAL LOVE POTION BLAMED FOR GIRL'S ELOPEMENT WITH ARAB.
>
> (*Los Angeles Times*)
>
> BRIDE LAUGHS AT FATHER'S FEARS.
>
> (*New York Journal-American*)

SHEIK VINDICATED; LOVE WINS BRIDE: HER ARABIAN KNIGHT, A LOCHINVAR OUT OF THE EAST BRINGS ROMANCE TO THE WEST

(*Chicago Herald and Examiner*)

"Just a little bit crestfallen, G-men today learned that it wasn't an exotic Eastern love potion a handsome Arabian gave to a 17-year-old Missouri high school girl to lure her to an Oriental harem.

'Gosh,' Doris Hisaw of Neosho, Mo., corrected them in Federal court today, 'that stuff was just a bottle of Parisian perfume—the first I ever laid eyes on.'

[They] waved their marriage license to prove it was a honeymoon the G-men had interrupted, not a kidnapping.

'I think they know their own minds,' Assistant U.S. Attorney John J. Dowling told Commissioner Cotter. 'If this girl prefers Iraq to Missouri, that's her affair.'"

After the New York attorney dismissed them, Nejib and Doris accepted the invitation of a reporter to stop in a side room to have their picture taken. As they stepped through the door, an explosion of light blinded them as the flashbulbs of twenty reporters' cameras popped at once. One photographer chased behind them as they ran out of the room to collect their luggage from their hotel. They were anxious not to miss boarding their ship, the luxury liner S. S. *Manhattan*, bound for Le Havre, France. One photograph of them would take up half the front page of the *New York Sunday Mirror* beneath the headline "60,000 Nazi Troops on French Border." Did the headline make them anxious to be headed toward that very country?

Arriving at the pier, Doris marveled that a man she had never seen before addressed her by name: "Don't look so worried, Mrs. Tooni, we're holding the gangplank for you." She felt like a celebrity, as everyone they met on board seemed to know them, too.

"Did we have fun!" she wrote a Neosho friend. At sea that night a jovial red-haired Irishman with blue eyes and dimples asked Nejib if he could dance with Doris. While they were dancing, he told her he'd have something to tell back home because her elopement was in the Irish newspapers. Later an aged Englishman on board sent for Nejib and Doris to have tea with him. He took pictures of them and wrote up their story for a London paper.

Disembarking the ship in Le Havre, Nejib and Doris took the train into Paris, where they intended to take another train to Marseille, the port from which they would board a ship to Beirut, Lebanon. Because there were no available spaces on the ship leaving from Marseille, Doris and Nejib spent a week in Paris courtesy of the steamship company. "Paris is great," Doris said in her letter to her Neosho friend, "I didn't like N.Y., but Paris, oh! The people are nice, no one is in a hurry, everyone is contented on this side of the world." Until Germany invaded France a year and eight months later, the war must have seemed far away. While they waited in Paris, Doris celebrated her eighteenth birthday, toured the Louvre, and saw the American movie *Alexander's Ragtime Band* with French subtitles. When they did not go to the Folies Bergère, Doris wondered whether Nejib might either be getting low on money or believed his new bride was too innocent to be exposed to the risqué kicks of the can-can girls. Later, at parties in Basra, her new father-in-law would shelter her from the gyrations of the belly dancers.

At last setting sail in Marseille on the Fabre Line's S.S. *Providence*, Doris and Nejib had to separate, for the ship was partitioned into living quarters segregated for men and women. Bunking cheek by jowl, four to a cabin, Doris led her seasick female shipmates to the keyhole-in-the-floor latrine. Fleeing the Nazis in Germany, many of the passengers were Jews en route to Palestine, and none spoke English.

But the men and women passengers were permitted to stroll the decks and take their meals together. Nejib proudly photographed his young bride at the rail, looking out to the Mediterranean Sea and their unknown future.

The ship's first stop, in Alexandria, Egypt, was long enough for Nejib and Doris to get down and see a bit of the city. They plunged into a population costumed in *galabaya*, the loose-fitting, long-sleeved, ankle-length garment worn in Egypt by both men and women, with the men additionally in turbans or round caps and the women in *hijabs*, or head scarves and/or veils. With Doris's first immersion in a different world, she felt a long way from Neosho, Missouri. They remained on board the *Provence* at stops in Jaffa (now Tel Aviv) and Haifa and disembarked in Beirut, Lebanon, where they shared a service (pronounced the French *ser-veese*) taxi to Damascus, Syria. Since they had only a secular marriage license issued by a justice of the peace in Arkansas, Nejib wished to have proper religious recognition of their marriage. The forebears of his mother, Therouza, were from Aleppo, Syria, and she had grown up in the Syrian Catholic Church in Basra, where her uncle was the bishop. Even though Nejib's father had grown up in the Armenian Church in Baghdad, he was agreeable to raising his children in his wife's church. In Damascus, Nejib escorted Doris to the Syrian Catholic Church, where he arranged for a priest to marry them in a private ceremony. They next boarded the Nairn Transport bus for the fourteen-hour overnight drive across the desert to Baghdad. What went through Doris's mind when their bus commenced their journey, not on a real road, but on tire tracks on the desert floor? She must have been reassured they wouldn't be wandering around the desert for forty years like the Bible's Israelites when the bus pulled up in Ramadi for breakfast. Finally arriving in Baghdad, they visited cousins of Nejib before taking the overnight train to Basra.

Back in Neosho, Lorene waited in the O. K. Beauty Salon to have her hair washed and set. It had been two weeks since Doris had run off, but her daughter and the Arab were still the talk of the town: Lorene could hear voices in the next booth gossiping about their elopement. In her classroom, constantly on the verge of tears,

Lorene felt that it was torture to have to go on teaching social studies as if nothing had happened.

―

Demonstrating the power of culture, Naoum, Nejib's father, whom I called Jiddu, which means grandfather in Arabic, had arranged to marry his first cousin, Therouza, my grandmother, whom I called Bebe, which is not the Arabic word for grandmother but is a title (Bebe, as our family spelled it, or *Bibi*) that shows respect for an older woman. The marriage would take place when she turned thirteen or whenever she began menstruating. When they married in 1908, Jiddu was twenty-eight, and Bebe Therouza was twelve. There is a saying that in the West, couples fall in love and marry, and in the East, they marry and fall in love. For my Iraqi grandparents the latter appeared to be the case, as their marriage seemed stable and peaceful. At least I cannot remember their quarreling, as I vividly remember the quarrels of other family members, nor do I recall sensing any unhappiness between them, as I can recall other unhappiness.

Jiddu had taken a job as an agent for an Armenian company, Garibian Dates, based in Basra, then still a province of the Ottoman Empire, the empire formed by Muslim Turks. Just as the upper Tigris River rises in the mountains of eastern Turkey near Diyarbakir and flows with the snowmelt through what is now Iraq to the Persian Gulf, Jiddu's young Armenian parents had made their way downriver to Baghdad, where they raised their family.

But now his job at Garibian Dates in Basra was to travel by motor launch up the Tigris to supervise fourteen date-packing stations and sign contracts with the local farmers and date plantation owners. In Jiddu's era, most of the world's dates came from Iraq and were shipped out of Basra. California and Arizona, which produce almost all of the dates grown in the United States today, brought a portion of the original shoots of their date palms from Iraq.

As Jiddu worked his way up at Garibian Dates, he built a big family home for Bebe and himself with suites for each of their four sons, in hopes that one day they would all live together like good

Arabs with their wives and offspring. It would turn out, however, that none of his children, who were constantly bickering and arguing, would want to live under the same roof. The cultural anthropologist Raphael Patai maintains in *The Arab Mind* that a factor contributing to the Arab's proneness to conflict is instilled by the child-rearing practice of Arab mothers, who promote competitiveness among their children to get them to behave:

> For instance, if a child refuses food, the mother will say to him: "If you don't eat it, I shall give it to your brother," and makes a motion as if she were indeed about to give the food in question to one of her other children.

> … Or, if a child cannot or does not want to do something the Mother wants him to do, she will say to him, "Look, your brother can do this, why can't you?"

With its great hall, sweeping staircase, and fifteen rooms, Jiddu's three-floor structure was large enough to rent out to managers who ran it as the Faiha Palace Hotel. Although it is no longer in existence, in the 1930s it was considered a large hotel for Basra. During World War II, the British Army commandeered the building to house its officers, renaming it the Lord Nuffield House and paying Jiddu even better rent than the hoteliers had paid. Jiddu began investing in land that no one wanted, dividing it up, and constructing houses on some of his lots to rent out or sell for a profit.

In the meantime, Jiddu had built another house for Bebe and himself with enough bedrooms for their adult children. The walls were seven yellow bricks thick, and the windows were few, to keep out the heat. The temperatures in Basra could be extreme: in summer the servants hauled the family's brass beds up to the roof, where they stayed for more than a third of the year, with thermometers sometimes registering as high as 128 degrees Fahrenheit in the day and 90 degrees at night, made more unbearable by the 96 percent humidity. Each bed was netted in a voile-like fabric both for privacy and for protection against mosquitoes. So much dew would collect on the netting that when sleepers awoke, they had to be careful getting out of bed not to cause a shower.

In Baghdad people could stay cool during the day in their underground apartments, but in Basra, excavation always struck water. Fortunate were the well to do, whose ranks Jiddu had entered: he could afford relief from the heat inside his house with electric ceiling fans and rotating table fans. It was to this house that Nejib brought home the wife he went to America to find. Even though she could not speak Arabic and her in-laws could not speak English, Doris felt welcomed and accepted by them. In spite of the fact that Doris was Baptist, not Catholic, Jiddu said to her, "It is the same God."

Along both banks of the Shatt al Arab (the Arab River), the confluence of the Tigris and Euphrates Rivers, date palms line the water for over a hundred miles and extend into the desert for as many as five miles. "If you are on a high rooftop in Basra," reported the Hoffman sisters, American authors who lived in Iraq at that time, "a cloud of green spreads out as far as you can see."

"The date tree likes to have its feet in water and its head in hell. Southern Iraq has plenty of both," wrote John Van Ess, a missionary for the Dutch Reformed Church of America who arrived in Basra in 1912. The Shatt al Arab rises and falls from six to ten feet twice a day with the tide from the Persian Gulf. Because of all the creeks and canals that watered the date palms, Basra was often called the "Venice of the East."

"It is along the river and these canals," Van Ess said, "that the date trees flourish, something over thirty million of them. It is an impressive sight to walk through the cathedral-like corridors of a date garden on a moonlit night, or to catch the slanting rays of the sun as evening falls and touches the fronds with glory." Perhaps this is why the Garden of Eden is reputed to have been in Iraq. And wasn't Basra the homeport of the adventurous Sinbad, the Sailor? In the exotic and romantic setting of Basra, Doris felt she had slipped into the pages of both the Bible and *The Arabian Nights*.

Like Cinderella before the ball, Doris had grown up doing household chores; and, like Cinderella marrying the prince, those tasks were now behind her. Bebe and Jiddu had six servants, including a cook to do the routine cooking. But with cooking a universal language, Bebe taught Doris how to make special dishes for entertaining, such as *buraq* (little meat-filled pastries). Bebe also showed her how to string okra and shrimp to dry on the roof and how to prepare tomato paste in huge, handmade metal tubs filled with washed and cored fruit. The tomatoes were crushed in the tub, which was then covered with a gauzy cloth and brought to the roof for solar cooking. Every now and then, one of the servants was assigned to climb the stairs to stir the tomatoes. The finished paste was stored in earthenware jugs in the storeroom, where supplies were kept in large quantities—tea by the case and rice and macaroni in twenty-five-pound bags. The orange juice was always fresh. The big treat was Jell-O.

Like a human shopping cart, one servant accompanied Jiddu to the *sûq* (market) to carry the groceries my grandfather selected. The men did all the shopping, since the sûq, clamorous with bartering, was regarded in my father's family as no place for women. But the policy against women shopping in the sûq might have been peculiar to my family. As an adult, I learned many women shopped in the sûq, too.

With little spider crabs for bait, Nejib fished for *sabûr* (shad) in the Shatt al Arab when he and Doris picnicked at his father's summerhouse and farm along the river's banks. It was only a mile from Bebe and Jiddu's house in Basra. Sometimes they went by *arabana* (horse-drawn carriage) and other times in Nejib's Detroit-built Jewett car.

The husband and wife who superintended Jiddu's farm cooked the sabûr Nejib caught for their picnics, to which he and Doris might bring along a pot of *dolma* (ground meat and rice-stuffed grape leaves), some *reggi* (watermelon), and *batiuq* (cantaloupe). The superintendent's mule, Misode, was tied up to go around and around to turn a pump that brought water into the irrigation ditches; and sometimes Misode powered a mill that made date syrup, similar to molasses. Jiddu's farm produced oranges, sweet lemons, and, of course, dates. Back in Doris's hometown, Neosho, the color green was prevalent in the leaves of deciduous trees and under her feet in the grass in her yard that ran seamlessly down through Big Spring Park. In Basra she stood on ochre, with the green overhead in the fabric of interwoven fronds.

On the farm, Nejib stood in the forest of date palms, and in Doris's quirky way of putting things, he walked around "wearing birds." Rolling up little pellets of bread, her husband invited the *bulbuls*, Arabic for nightingales, to alight in his palm to eat.

Sometimes Nejib brought the portable windup Victrola and played records under the grape arbor. When he and Doris danced there, they could each reach up to pluck a juicy grape.

In Neosho, Doris had been reading since she was four years old. When Doris turned five, her teacher mother took her to school with her and because she could read, deposited her directly into second grade. Doris was an only child. Skipping the arithmetic, writing, and socialization skills learned in first grade may have hindered her academic confidence. But in Basra, as a high school graduate with a year of college, she was perceived as an educated woman. While Doris described her mother as "watching me like a hawk even in school," in Basra she felt free as a nightingale.

Not long after Doris's arrival in Basra, the *Springfield* [Missouri] *Leader and Press* headlined a gossip column "Bride of the Sheik Tells Of Arabia's High Society":

> Now Doris is writing back to her parents that being the wife of a junior sheik is for sure a good deal. And to prove it, she's including newspaper clippings from Iraq, Arabia, telling about how she gets around in the desert elite. Sheik

Senior, it seems has more bucks than McKesson had warehouses, and with it, Doris 'gave a small tea,' she wrote, 'for 150 guests.'

How did the newspaper know what Doris wrote home? How did they see newspaper articles from Iraq about her tea? Did one of her high school friends she wrote pass them on to the paper? The tea was most likely the reception her new in-laws held to introduce Doris to their relatives and friends.

Doris's grandmother Nanny had sent her the "Bride of the Sheik" gossip column and filled up its margins with a penciled note: "Your mother does not want to see any more papers .... She looks bad and has a cough. She expects to lose her school [job] over it [the scandal as Lorene and Nanny perceived it], and then what will she do?"

If Lorene was worried about getting fired from teaching before, what did she think about her job security a whole year after her daughter's elopement when she read the following Christmas letter from Doris's brother-in-law Kamil to the *Neosho Times*, which the superintendent of schools was sure to have read, too?

First, Kamil poured on the honey:

> As the universal Christmas spirit drives one to remember faraway friends, especially after hearing Christmas carols over the radio direct from America, I hasten to dispatch this by airmail, hoping that it will not be too late to wish you and all our Neosho friends the continuance of the joys of the season throughout the New Year.

And then, he slammed down the fly swatter:

> Having heard of all the fairy tales told about "harems" in my country in connection with my brother's marriage to a former Neosho girl, I cannot but laugh at the ignorance displayed by those who imagine nothing but a desert spotted here and there with palm trees with "harems" between

having heavily curtained windows shielding beautiful dark maidens. The absurdity of the pictures painted about Iraq is most amusing. If you knew that high school boys and girls over here know more about the world and America from reading English and French books, from seeing movies, hearing radios, and from taking interest in international matters more than some small town high school teachers know about this nook of the world, you would not blame the Europeans who hold the opinion that most Americans are childish in world affairs.

What was Kamil's motive in writing such a letter? "Honor is the collective property of the family: if any single member of the family incurs dishonor, the whole family is disgraced," writes Patai. Had not Doris's parents sicced the FBI on his brother and publicly questioned his worthiness? Had not they cast doubt on the stature of his family? Had not they treated his country as behind the times? Patai says being insulted damages a man's *karam*, his dignity. One-upping the insults thrown at him and "rising to the defense of his dignity," as Patai puts it, "he compels others to respect him, and thus restores his self-respect."

As an American, Lorene perceived Kamil as rude and arrogant. Preoccupied with protecting her daughter, she was unaware of how she had offended him and suffered the public humiliation of his demeaning remarks. It's not easy to tease out what is cultural and what is psychological.

───

My father did not have to be Muslim to be intensely Arab in character, for he lived and breathed the language and culture. When Nejib was born in 1911, people spoke Arabic in their everyday discourse, but his native land was still a province of the Ottoman Empire: as Turkish subjects, their official business was conducted in Turkish.

Then what is an Arab? The historian Philip Khuri Hitti says that after the time of Muhammad, no matter what their original nationality, his followers were considered Arabs: "An Arab henceforth became one who professed Islam and spoke and wrote the Arabic tongue, regardless of his racial affiliation." But Egyptian President Gamal Abdel Nasser defined the Arab simply as "anyone whose mother tongue is Arabic." Although spoken Arabic may differ in dialect from country to country, the great unifier of the Arab world is its written language.

In the montage of black-and-white photographs in my father's oldest album, he appears in his family's garden in Basra in the sensibly cool, long cotton gown of the Arabs only twice and then only as an elementary-school boy. After that, regardless of age, he seems to be never out of Western clothing: white-collar shirt, suit and tie, or sports jacket and slacks. Only the changing headgear, a kind of timeline of history in hats, signals his evolution, from the fez in his grade-school days to his high-school-era *sidara* (similar in appearance to the folding cap of the US Army during World War II) to the fedora he wore as an adult, as in a 1929 snapshot showing him in front of the Acropolis in Athens, which he toured on his way to college in the United States.

How did Nejib happen to spend his growing-up years under British occupation?

He was only three years old when World War I was heating up in 1914. Britain was disturbed that Turkey had aligned itself with Germany. Wanting to protect its Anglo-Persian Oil Company (now British Petroleum, or BP), located just across the river from Turkish-run Basra, the British launched their Mesopotamian military campaign from India during the British raj. Its army was made up of Indian troops led by British officers, who invaded southern Mesopotamia and captured Basra without opposition. The victory came so easily that the British military leaders on the ground convinced their government in England to let them take Baghdad, too. However, they underestimated the resistance of the Turks, who boxed in the British halfway to Baghdad. They were stuck in Kut because they did not have adequate roads or transportation on the Tigris for getting food and medical supplies to their troops. Four years of fighting, during which Britain finally defeated the Turks and captured Baghdad, cost 100,000 British and Indian casualties, a third of whom, if not killed outright, died of diseases and untreated wounds.

At a safe few hundred miles from the battle, the occupying British, for their own military needs, slowly brought Basra into the twentieth century by supplying it with electricity, improving its sanitation, building roads, replacing animals such as mules and camels with cars and trucks, setting up hospitals for their soldiers, dredging the river so that oceangoing vessels could come into port with supplies, and bringing the port up to snuff with an organized pilot system, dockworkers to unload the ships, and warehouses to store their cargo. Administrators for public services were no longer Turks, but English-speaking Indians, the civil servants the British sent for from India.

When my father was eight years old and the newly formed League of Nations was divvying up the spoils of World War I between England and France, Mesopotamia was officially mandated to the British, who, after expelling the Turks, stayed on. Although the mandate came with the responsibility to help improve the territory and guide it toward self-governance, some critics felt Iraq and Palestine, also mandated to the British, were really treated like colonies. Had Britain wanted to make Basra a province of India?

For his help in ousting the Turks from Arabia—a task assisted by Britain's T. E. Lawrence, of "Lawrence of Arabia" fame—the British rewarded Hussein bin Ali, the Hashemite Sharif of Mecca, by giving him and his sons their own kingdoms. His son Abdullah became king of the new country carved out of Palestine, initially called Transjordan (*trans* meaning "across" the Jordan River from Palestine) and, since 1946, simply Jordan. In 1921 the British imported the other Hashemite son, Faisal, who had been promised Syria but was ousted by the French to whom Syria was mandated. With the encouragement of both Lawrence and the Arabist Gertrude Bell, the British made Faisal king of the newly named nation Iraq, which means in Arabic "the banks of a great river for the whole length thereof." Faisal was a Sunni, who comprise 90 percent of Muslims, but the majority of his subjects in Iraq happened to be

Shiite. At eleven, Nejib was old enough to know his country now had a king.

Not all British activity in Iraq was military or political. By 1922, the archaeologist Sir Charles Leonard Woolley, in a joint British-American expedition, had spent ten years literally digging into Iraq. Finally reaching the royal tombs of Ur, the hometown of Abraham, through centuries of household trash, Woolley's expedition then hit eight solid feet of pure clay, without a trace of man-made goods, and then suddenly ran into trash again. Concluding that the thick layer of clay indicated a vast spread of water, Woolley believed he had discovered evidence of Noah's flood.

John Van Ess, the American founder and principal of Medrissa el Reja' el Ali, the school Nejib and his brothers would attend, climbed down into his friend Woolley's excavation. "With every foot I climbed a century—sixty feet, sixty centuries," he wrote. "As I climbed, I could see the remnants of more than a dozen civilizations."

Educational opportunity in Iraq did not change much from Jiddu's time to that of his children. The Jewish community and the different sects of Christians in Basra—the Chaldeans and Syrian and Armenian Catholics—maintained schools for their own congregations. My father spoke, read, and wrote Arabic, but the curriculum of the Syrian Church school, which he and his brothers attended did not go beyond elementary grades. The English language appealed to them not only because of the British presence in Iraq but also because of the proximity of "Britain's India." Since the higher grades in the Iraqi government schools did not offer English at the time, Kamil and Nejib asked their father if they could attend the American Protestant school.

Bebe's uncle, bishop of the Syrian Catholic Church in Basra, warned Jiddu, "You are going to lose your boys."

But Van Ess assured my grandfather that he had not come to Iraq to convert Catholics and that in his School of High Hope, as its Arabic name translates into English, his goal was not religious conversion—a refreshing disclaimer for an American missionary—but harmony with Arabs. The school had slowly won acceptance among the Muslim Arabs for being conducted in Arabic and was attended by such boys as the sons of Sayyid Talib, who had been Faisal's most serious rival as king, and those of Sheik Khazal of Muhammerah, a friend of the British who during the Mesopotamian campaign had kept his eye on the wells and refinery of the Anglo-Persian Oil Company for them.

When Van Ess accepted Kamil and Nejib into his school, he did make one stipulation. Even though their family home was nearby, they had to board at the school. The school had small apartments for the sons of the sheiks of Kuwait who had sent their boys to learn English; and Van Ess needed Nejib and Kamil as proctors. In Iraq in the early 1920s, a decade before there were even ten government secondary schools in the country, my father and his brothers pursued a standard American high-school curriculum of history, mathematics, science, languages, and sports.

Although the majority of the students at the School of High Hope were Muslim, Bible classes were mandatory, but Muslims are "people of the book," too. Even though Arabic was the language of instruction, English was taught so thoroughly that the boys who graduated were all bilingual. As a high-school junior, my father was already writing in English on the back of a personal photograph to describe the event it depicted, a group of about thirty boys and their teacher, George Gosselink, on an outing with the school's literary society. My father had penned in arrows pointing to the heads of those he labeled the "3 Musketeers": his brothers Kamil and Joe and himself, Nejib.

My father graduated from high school as an Arabic- and English-speaking Syrian Catholic Armenian Iraqi whose parents did not and never would speak English and who learned to speak English himself by attending an Arabic-speaking school for Muslims run by English- and Arabic-speaking American Protestant missionaries of a church started by Dutch immigrants to America!

Uncle Kamil admired the occupying British. Identifying with the aggressors, he called them "benefactors," which may account for why, in spite of his American schooling, he spoke English all his life with a British accent. His Iraqi wife, my Auntie May, had a British accent, too, but for a different reason: because of her mother's early death and her Iraqi father's job as purser on a ship on the British India Steam Navigation line, which sailed back and forth from Basra to Bombay (Mumbai), she spent her formative years in an English-speaking boarding school in Bombay. My father spoke English like an American except for two words that betrayed his foreign background.

While he stuck to Arabic for his worst invectives, my brother, Frank, and I would smile and shake our heads when in America, losing his volatile temper, he called us "ee-dee- ots" and "ning-com-poops" with a *g*.

⁓

As each of Jiddu's sons graduated from the School of High Hope, Van Ess encouraged them to go to college in America. He recommended his own alma mater, Hope College in Holland, Michigan.

"My mother, God rest her soul," Uncle Kamil said, "sold all her gold to send us to college."

Founded in the mid-1800s by Dutch pioneers who had come to America to seek economic advantage as well as religious freedom, Hope College was affiliated with the Dutch Reformed Church of America. Small and friendly, it was a good place for the young Nejib and his brother, so far from home, to start. Dr. Dimnent, the president of Hope, came to know my father well enough to write a spirited letter of recommendation for him. My father cut out a black-and-white picture of Dr. Dimnent from an alumni magazine to paste alongside his snapshots in his photo album. Twenty-eight years after my father transferred from Hope, he would go back to his 1931 Hope College yearbook to pen in the margin alongside his mentor's picture a note about Dr. Dimnent's death.

Nejib cut a dashing figure in a collegiate argyle vest and tie, standing on the steps of a classroom building with some fellow students or in a three-piece suit at his student's desk, an opposite to his blond, lounging-robed American roommate puffing on a pipe on the lower bunk. There was alacrity about my father, an obvious intelligence shining with promise. From his earliest photos of himself at eight years old to twenty-eight, he looked happy and carefree, perhaps because in fact his cares had not yet begun.

After two years at Hope College, Uncle Kamil said that he felt campus life consisted of "one religious event after another." One day he and Nejib set out for Ann Arbor to investigate the secular University of Michigan. Shortly thereafter, he and my father transferred there.

Uncle Joe had attended Hope College too, but instead of transferring to the University of Michigan like his older brothers, he stayed at Hope to graduate with a BS in chemistry. Afterward, while taking courses in petroleum engineering at Northeastern Oklahoma A&M (Agriculture & Mechanical, which evolved into Mining), he met and married a student he met there, my Auntie Aileen, from Newtonia, Missouri.

My father's natural interests in systems and inventions are evident in two little souvenirs he mounted in his photo album. The first is a paper card, no bigger than an index card that fit in his breast pocket. A flap on one end hung over the pocket edge to serve as a name tag. He had entered "Nejib N. Tooni," but an inked-in rectangle at the end of his surname suggests he had first written "Toonian" and then thought better of it. While my father and his brothers were attending college in 1932, Iraq had become an independent state and the first of the Arab mandates to join the League of Nations. Since then, Nejib and Kamil would complain to their father that because of the *ian* at the end of their name, people assumed they were Armenian instead of Iraqi. Proud of their new country, they wanted to set the record straight.

On the blank line for "Firm" Nejib had entered "U. of M. Student." Densely but legibly packed on this small card in his beautifully inked script is a fount of information outlining the step-by-step operations in making tires that he observed on a tour of the United States Rubber Company.

My father would eventually raise our family using the logical and efficient sequence of the assembly line. For my father there was not more than one way to skin a cat. There was a right way and a wrong way, with no room for error. How could he not admire the Gilbreths in Montclair, New Jersey, made famous by the 1948 best-selling book *Cheaper by the Dozen*, whose family was run on the same principle? I would attend junior high with a couple of Gilbreth grandchildren, but having seen only the 1950 movie version of their parents' upbringing, I was too young to wonder how their parents really fared under the reign of an efficiency expert.

The second souvenir in my father's album is a penny postcard held message side up by two tiny strips of paper he cut out and glued to the left side of the card for hinges. The card can be turned like the page of a little book so one can read the address side:

> Mr. Nejib N. Toonian
> 428 Cross Street
> Ann Arbor, Mich.

Again, he had crossed out the *an*. The message on the printed side of the card announced a meeting of the University of Michigan Radio Club at which Professor Lewis N. Holland was scheduled to give a lecture on the subject "Some Interesting Uses of Vacuum Tubes." The lecture made enough of an impression on my father that he wrote with his fountain pen in the margins of the announcement:

> Prof. Holland demonstrated the transmission of sound by light. He turned on a phonograph record, which was connected to a radio set which converted sound waves into audio waves and which glew [*sic*] a neon lamp and converted them into minute electric current which thru [*sic*] a radio set was amplified and produced the original music in a loud speaker.

These little souvenirs, by virtue of their having been regarded by him as worthy of saving, have the ring of innate interest.

In my father's album, too, there are several snapshots of attractive young American women. In some cases their relationship to him is made clear by an autograph across the photograph, such as "From your pal, Tony" or simply "Faye." A lineup of beauties in bathing suits in one photo was actually strangers whom he asked to stand alongside of, as one might pose beside animals on a safari. As Patai puts it, like being given the impossible task of not thinking about a pink elephant, sex is so taboo to the Arab that it becomes the prime preoccupation.

One photograph is missing in my father's album, indicated by four empty picture corners still glued to the page, underneath which the words "Wonderful You" were cut out of a greeting card and pasted, creating a space as charged with significance as the shape of space in art. Had my father ripped up the photograph in a pique? Had he pulled it out to frame? Had he removed it in deference to my mother? Probably not the latter, for he unabashedly retained a series of snapshots of "Miss Alberta Wagner," some by herself and some posed smiling and arm in arm with my father. From the changing background of winter to spring, we can deduce the relationship spanned at least a couple of months. My discovery of a diary-like entry my father penciled on the back of one of the snapshots explains:

> May 1934. It was my last year at the University of Michigan—Holland's Tulip Time comes in May & I hitch-hiked one week-end from Ann Arbor to Holland [Michigan] to see Alberta—to whom I was verbally engaged. This picture was taken just when I was returning to Ann Arbor—on a Sunday afternoon—last day of Tulip Time. All over Holland one could enjoy the sight of Tulips planted on the curbs of streets, in Parks and in front of most homes. What a wonderful time I had that week-end!

What transpired with Alberta I do not know, as the next photographs are of the swelling ocean as seen from the deck of the *Isle de France*, on which my father sailed back home to Iraq after graduating in 1934 with a degree in electrical engineering.

"When I graduated from Michigan," Uncle Kamil said, "I was a nationalist of Iraq. I was willing to fight for my country [although something about his eyesight would keep him from qualifying for military service]. "As a student," Uncle Kamil said, "I had gone around speaking to colleges about our new country wearing Arab dress. Faisal had declared upon ascending the throne, 'There is only one country called Iraq, and all its inhabitants are Iraqis. We all come from the same origin, our forefathers being Shem. We all belong to this noble race.'"

Faisal may have been sincere, but that was not the reality my father and his brothers experienced. "When I returned to Iraq [after getting my MBA] from Michigan," Uncle Kamil explained, "I applied for a job in the Ministry of Foreign Affairs in the consulate service of the Iraqi government, where they had vacancies. They practically laughed at me because I was Christian; otherwise, with my education, I would have been appointed a minister or a counsel. One Christian we knew did change his religion to become something. Your dad could have been director general of telephone and telegraph for the whole country if he had been a Muslim."

Instead my father and Uncle Kamil went down to the Port of Basra, which was run by the British, and met Sir John Ward, the director general of the port and the first man to employ them. Uncle Kamil was hired to manage the electricity and water supply, and my father, the telephone and telegraph. Between them, they ran all the utilities in Basra.

The British community in Basra had its own daily newspaper and, with connections to British Army radio communiqués, was impressively current with detailed accounts of the daily air actions over England. England declared war on Germany in September 1939. In Bebe and Jiddu's house, the family gathered around the radio in the evening for crackly news broadcasts from the BBC, which their sons translated for them.

"Naughty baby! Naughty baby!"

Haiganoush, the Armenian midwife who had lost her family in the Turkish genocide, strode into the room in Maude Memorial Hospital in Basra, where the English doctor and his nurse had gotten my mother settled. The doctor had originally been summoned to my grandparents' house, where my parents were having tea. My mother's water had broken, but as she had no pains, the doctor sat down for tea, too, and tea switched over to Scotch. Finally, my father and the doctor drove my mother to the hospital. Believing it would be a long while before she delivered her first child, the doctor sent my father home and told my mother he was going to the club.

Alone in the hospital room, my mother had turned on her side that Sunday, December 3, 1939, at 9 p.m., and there on the bed, "You just came right out," she later told me. Five and one-half pounds.

"What did you do? Did you pick me up?"

"No. I rang for the nurse, and I could barely reach the bell. You did not stop crying."

Striding into my mother's room, Haiganoush had expected to explain to my mother in her faltering English that sometimes it can be a long while between breaking water and delivering a baby. Instead she discovered the mess of my birth on the bed.

"Naughty baby! Naughty baby!" the midwife clucked.

In my father's Iraq, a man learned his wife had given birth to a boy when he was told, "Praise the Lord, you have a son," but he knew he had a daughter when he was greeted, as my father was, "Praise the Lord, the mother is well."

I was the first grandchild, but not the preferred male heir. It was my uncle Kamil, still a bachelor at thirty, who brought his twenty-eight-year-old brother, Nejib, back to the hospital to see his new daughter and my uncle who carried the present of a big doll.

"When you were born, Suzy," Uncle Kamil told me, "the nurse brought you out and wanted to hand you to me. She thought I was the father. Your father was so afraid, he would not come up to your mother's room." I never learned why my father feared hospitals.

My mother, an only child who had had no experience with babies, was seven thousand miles from the females in her family who did. She had just turned nineteen.

⁓

In none of the photographs of me in my first four years is my mother holding me. My father picks me up to pose; various relations and family friends hoist me in their arms; but in pictures with my mother, I am usually sitting next to or standing alongside of or in front of her. Even in the formal portraits, I hold my mother or lean against her while my baby brother, Frank, born two years after me, sits with my mother's arms around him in her lap.

"You never wanted to be held," my mother explained when, as an adult, I questioned her about the photographs. "You would always run away."

"When did this begin?" I asked. "From the moment you were born."

⁓

In 1939, malaria was still Iraq's Public Enemy No. 1. According to an Iraqi government report at the time, it killed directly or indirectly from fifty thousand to seventy-five thousand people a year and was undoubtedly responsible for Iraq's high infant mortality rate of 20 percent. Infant mortality soared to 30 percent in districts like Basra, with its marshes and irrigation ditches for the date groves that created a particularly fertile breeding ground for mosquitoes. Iraqis then were just learning to tuck the mosquito nets draped over their beds under their mattresses, to mosquito-proof their doors with screens, and to construct their doors to open outward, so that mosquitoes resting on them would not be brought inside. My father kept handy a Flit gun loaded with insecticide. Pumping the long handle in the metal tube connected to the can, he sprayed the Flit mist around our beds on the roof.

My mother had malaria when she was pregnant with me, doctoring it with Atebrin, which made her skin turn yellow. I had malaria attacks myself on and off from the age of two to four. When I was an adult, amazed at my own survival, I asked my mother how I had made it.

"I don't know. I guess like Topsy," she quoted *Uncle Tom's Cabin*, "you just 'growed.'"

But it was not the malaria that almost did me in. My mother tried to breastfeed me. Two weeks after I was born, Auntie Aileen, Uncle Joe's wife, observed my distended belly—which my mother had interpreted as a sign of satiation—and declared, "This baby is starving to death!"

My mother always claimed my father responded, "If this baby is going to die, she will die on a full stomach!" A pot of milk was on the stove for tea, and my mother maintained my father proceeded to heat it and feed me from it, thereby saving my life.

Knowing what I know about my father's squeamishness, and knowing how I instinctively trusted Auntie Aileen, I tend to believe my aunt's version of the story: it was she who looked up my symptoms in a book, claimed I was starving to death, and went to the stove to do something about it. Whoever saved my life, my near death by starvation is not contested. My mother told me that soon thereafter my father bought a cow, arranging with a nearby farmer to board it and bring its milk to our house each day. Even with the danger of hookworm, the farmer went barefoot, as did most of the *fellahin* (peasants) and servants. According to my mother, the soles of the farmer's cracked feet were as thick as leather. He delivered the milk in old whiskey bottles, castoffs of the British.

The danger of germs factored into my everyday consciousness. The cook washed our fresh vegetables like lettuce in a solution of purple permanganate. Auntie May, Uncle Kamil's wife, told me when I was an adult that her father's drinking water was under lock and key.

"It was so easy to catch something," Auntie May said, "typhoid, malaria, the plague, cholera, tin poisoning [from spoiled canned food]. All water was out of the Shatt al Arab, so it had to be filtered and boiled and put into whiskey bottles in the refrigerator."

The only time she remembered her father ever striking her as a child was when he caught her taking a swig from his water bottle.

Jiddu and Bebe had invited relatives and family friends to meet my mother shortly after her arrival in Iraq. After the old women filed in to plant kisses on Nejib's new American bride, Jiddu muttered, "Germs! Germs!" and instructed my mother to wipe her face with eau de cologne. Although our family had a refrigerator, food did not keep easily in the hot climate. Years later my parents would learn that Bebe's uncle, the bishop, had died reputedly from drinking milk that had spoiled. Whenever we went out visiting after Frank was born, I would prevent him from eating anything until my mother tasted it first. In America, as I started being invited to eat at my friends' houses, it took me a long time to let go of my role of surreptitious inspector of food, glasses, and silverware. If my friend Betty asked for a bite of my apple, I let her keep it.

With his retinue of young priests, the bishop baptized me in my grandparents' house on the eve of the New Year of 1940. The house bustled that day for the big New Year's Eve party my grandparents hosted annually and for which guests reputedly started preparing their costumes in November. Although in other years my father would go as a pirate or Mickey Mouse, this night he wore only his tuxedo; but under his nose he had penciled the twirling mustache of a magician or impresario. My mother dressed as someone about to dance the bolero. Pre-party, long afternoon naps were de rigueur because, with its table groaning with food and its great tiled hall resounding to the live orchestra's *dumbuk* and *oud*, the party would last until 6 a.m.

One summer evening in 1940 the British consul's wife and her helpers sponsored a fundraiser on the grounds of the consulate to support Britain's war effort. Nejib and Doris were invited. The 150 guests who attended comprised almost all the members of Basra's British community. An orchestra from Shaibah, the Royal Air Force base, played for dancing. Between the dances, the committee had organized hidden talent for entertainment. There were a humorist who spoke in different dialects, a piano soloist, and some community singing. Two Scots played the bagpipes so rousingly they inspired their fellow Scots to spontaneously commence an eightsome reel, which, in spite of the heat, they danced to the end. And Doris played her violin, responding to the hearty applause with several encores.

My first conscious experience was not only nonverbal but pre-verbal—*mysterium tremendum.* My first summer in Basra, when my father carried me up the outside stairs to our beds on the roof of Jiddu's house, I gasped in awe, eyes wide and breath stopped short, because the spectacle of the sparkling stars packed into the night sky was literally breathtaking. Another memory I have from that time is of lying in my arabana (baby carriage), which had been rolled under a palm tree, and being fascinated by the dappled light that shone through the fronds and netting.

According to my mother, I cried often those first months of my life and slept only a half hour at a time. One night my father was especially vexed by my cries, which must have disturbed not only him and my mother but also my grandparents and the aunts and uncles, all of whom had their netted beds in various sections of the big roof. Drained of patience, my father jerked me out of my crib and shook me. "That's *it*!" He must not have known that shaking a baby could break its neck. "It was the last time you cried in the night," Auntie Aileen said. "He wanted you perfect." When tears produce such dire consequences, we learn to suppress them and the emotion that caused them as well.

My mother and Auntie Aileen often sat together to sew and knit, play cards, and read the American magazines their mothers sent them. Although my mother had not known her before, Auntie Aileen, blond and slim, had also graduated from Neosho High School. Having grown up with a baby sister, Auntie Aileen taught my mother how to bathe me in a dishpan as they sat on the kitchen floor, so I would not have far to fall if, soapy, I slipped out of her hands.

Toilet training is a kind of litmus test of culture. Supported by American child-rearing manuals that her mother also sent her, my mother was proud to have Frank and me out of diapers by age one. One such handbook of the day advises the mother to start infants on a chamber pot when they are just a few months old, before they can even sit up. Recommending keeping charts on the baby's "rhythm," the book purports that "one of the easiest ways to begin training, along about the tenth or eleventh month, is to put him on the toilet just before the chart shows he is likely to urinate." Unlike the baby care books today, which recognize crying as vocabulary in the baby's language, a college text of my mother's time observes:

> The natural desire of a young mother to "enjoy her baby" often leads her to do anything that pleases him. Soon he cries if the indulgences are not repeated; he cries to be rocked, to be taken from his bed, to be carried about, to have a light in the room, to have a pacifier. The one sure way of teaching a child to cry is to give him everything for which he cries. The only way to break such a crying habit is never to give a child, under any circumstances, what he is crying for.

This book regards grandparents as the worst offenders, "especially the grandmother." Perhaps this is how my mother felt about Bebe Therouza, who doted on me, her first grandchild, calling me *aini* (my eye—as in "as precious as my eyes") and *galbi* (my heart) as she rocked me in her lap with her arms around me, kissing my neck and exclaiming, "*Shamatuq!*" (I could inhale you!)

Jiddu owned enough property to be able to give a lot to each of his sons on which to build his own house. When we moved out of Bebe and Jiddu's after our own house was built, my mother made sure I had my own room. I remember standing in my crib, looking out the window to see the Japanese lanterns strung across the backyard of Uncle Joe and Auntie Aileen's house for a party. I started to cry when I understood that my mother and father were leaving. "Don't be silly," my mother said. "Lie down and go to sleep. We'll be right next door."

Early one February morning, a big, black raven persistently banged on my parents' bedroom window. Someone from a different culture might perhaps read the raven's appearance as a symbol that required interpretation: the raven might have something to say to the one it visited. Anticipating the raven's return, my father, the complicated man who let bulbuls alight on his shoulders, was ready for the bird the next morning. When the raven banged on their window again, he shot and killed it.

Because the raven is a scavenger, my father's culture might have considered the bird unclean. Later, when we were growing up, my father never kept a gun in the house, and he would warn us to stay away from guns. Perhaps he felt badly to have robbed the raven of its life.

When I first heard the following joke as an adult, I laughed and only later realized that it was an unconscious laugh of recognition. Ever since Freud we know that what we laugh at can be as revealing as our slips of tongue. Why does one joke strike a person as funny and another not? Persisting in my memory is a joke about a husband hitching his horse to a buggy to take his new bride for a ride. As the buggy pulls away, the horse stumbles. The husband stops the buggy, climbs down from his seat, and, looking the horse in the eye, says, "That's one." Returning to his seat in the buggy, he sets off again. Before long the horse once more trips. Again, the husband descends the buggy, goes round to look the horse in the eye, and says, "That's two."

Getting back in the buggy, the man starts off when the horse lurches yet again. He jumps off the buggy, faces the horse, and declares, "That's three!" Pulling a gun from his coat pocket, with a single shot, he drops the horse dead in its tracks.

Appalled, the new bride clambers down off the buggy and exclaims, "Why on earth did you do that?"

Fixing her with his eye, the new husband retorts, "That's one!"

In the case of my father and me when I got older, I would feel that, as with the raven, he never even granted me two and three.

My mother did not like joining the British women for "elevens," their morning coffee klatches, nor their afternoon teas. She said they always "parked their children with nannies." We usually went to Bebe and Jiddu's for tea, where there were always dates and bonbons and plentiful *fistuq*, the pistachios for which I had an unbridled appetite. When my mother was ready to go home after tea but I wanted to stay with Bebe, I would throw such a tantrum that, unable to catch my breath, I would turn purple. My mother would start up my breathing by throwing a glass of water in my face. Bebe was worried I had epilepsy and should see a doctor.

Even though Iraq was a member of the League of Nations as a sovereign state, two years before independence, Iraq had signed the Anglo-Iraqi Treaty, which kept it bound to Britain for another twenty-five years. As historian Geoffrey Warner reports, the treaty promised Britain use of Iraq's "railways, rivers, ports, [airports], and means of communication" and entitled them "to maintain two RAF (Royal Air Force) bases on Iraqi territory," one near Baghdad and the other near Basra. Warner says the treaty included the condition that if Iraq needed foreign military instructors, they would be British, and that Iraq's military equipment would be the same as that of the British: thus began Iraq's modern army. "For Iraqi nationalists," Warner concludes, "1932 was less the date of independence than that of the substitution of indirect for direct British control."

When King Faisal died in 1933, his inexperienced twenty-one-year-old son Ghazi, who had a passion for cars, succeeded him.

In 1938 just months before Nejib left Iraq to find an American wife, he had attended the gala 700-invitee reception King Ghazi threw after he ceremoniously opened the new Basra Airport with its art deco cocktail bar, which brought the port city into the twentieth century. The British designed and built the grand facility, which, not incidentally, the RAF also used for a base. Just over a year later in April 1939, the young king, who supported the nationalists, was killed in an automobile accident. In her *Baghdad Diaries*, Nuha al-Radi says that her great-uncle Sa'ib, as chief surgeon and head of a hospital, was called on to autopsy Ghazi's body and issue a death certificate. "He did not think that the hit on the head was in the right place for the way the king's car crashed into the pole. He was sure that the British were responsible for his death." Her great-uncle did not want to sign the death certificate. But by not saying that her uncle refused to sign, al-Radi implies that he signed anyway.

When the royal car collection was sold, Nejib bought the late king's big yellow Packard sedan in which he enjoyed riding around Basra, beaming, before he resold it at a profit.

Ghazi's four-year-old son, Faisal II, succeeded his father, with his uncle Amir Abd al Ilah appointed as regent until the new king attained his eighteenth birthday.

When Britain declared war on Germany in September 1939, Iraq broke off its diplomatic relations with Germany. But Italy, a partner with Germany in the Axis, still had an embassy in Baghdad. In 1940 Rashid Ali al-Gaylani, a nationalist who had opposed the Anglo-Iraqi Treaty, became prime minister of Iraq. Prodded by four nationalistic Iraqi army officers who called themselves the Golden Square and wanted to throw off Britain's control, the prime minister called on the Italian minister in Baghdad to feel out where the Axis stood on true independence for Iraq and to see if they could give Iraq any help toward achieving it.

The British got wind of Rashid Ali's intrigue, however, and put economic sanctions on Iraq. Saying that they were availing themselves of a provision of the Anglo-Iraqi Treaty for passage of troops, they also brought a brigade of Indian troops into Basra as well as four hundred airborne infantrymen into their RAF base. A company of Gurkhas, the crack British-trained Nepalese soldiers who had the reputation of being fierce warriors, was quartered next door to our house. My mother would take me out in the arabana, and the soldiers always greeted us with nods and smiles. On the roof of their quarters, my mother once spied a Sikh let down his long, wet hair to dry in the sun.

It was at this time that my father was drafted into the Iraqi Army and sent to Baghdad to "military college," as his six-week officer training was called, from which he emerged a lieutenant. To be near my father, who would visit whenever he could get away, my mother and I and a young servant girl named Bahreah went to Baghdad, too, where we stayed in a house loaned to us by a lawyer friend of my father's. While we were in Baghdad, my mother took me for a medical checkup to allay Bebe's worry about my having epilepsy. From a culture not known for empathy with children, the British doctor who examined me concluded, "This child does not have epilepsy; she is just a brat" and prescribed a drug to calm me down. I was eighteen months old.

The British refused to recognize Prime Minister Rashid Ali's anti-British cabinet. When they informed the prime minister of the arrival of a second batch of troops from India into Basra—not in transit to somewhere else, as the Anglo-Iraqi Treaty specified—Rashid Ali refused them permission to land. This reaction so alarmed the British ambassador that he ordered the evacuation of British dependents from Baghdad.

While the Indian troops poured into Basra without incident, the Golden Square ordered two of their infantry brigades to occupy the heights overlooking the RAF base near Baghdad. Seizing the opportunity, at dawn on May 2, 1941, British aircraft struck the Iraqi positions, and war between Britain and Iraq began.

That evening in Baghdad, the loud explosions of bombs scared me and made me cry. My father held me up to the window to see the streams of light from the bombs and anti-aircraft guns: "See, aren't the lights pretty? They aren't going to hurt you." It was good my father wanted to comfort me, but how is a child to trust her own feelings if they are not affirmed? Wouldn't it have been better if he had said, "Yes, I think the bombs are scary, too" or something like that? Instead I felt there was something wrong with me to be frightened.

Decades later, on the opening night of the US-led war on Iraq in 1991, I watched the news on CNN in horror as one airman described the explosions and tracers over Baghdad as "lit up like a Christmas tree." The fear I had tamped down so long ago resurfaced. Intensely identifying with the Iraqi children surely frightened under those bombs, I felt I was one of them.

In the middle of May in 1941, Hitler, having been preoccupied with plans to invade Russia, finally sent Iraq a Luftwaffe commander and a squadron of fighter bombers (painted with the Iraqi insignia to disguise their origins)—"too little too late," as historian Geoffrey Warner observes. The Germans could not send the ammunition the Iraqis requested because it would not fit the British weaponry the Iraqis had agreed to use in the Anglo-Iraqi Treaty.

Caught in Baghdad, where all foreigners were being interned, my mother could no longer risk speaking English outside or leave the house without being wrapped in an abaya with a headscarf and veil. The night my father's officer training was completed, he furtively bundled us into a taxi to a dock on the Tigris, where a launch he had hired was waiting to transport us downriver to Basra.

On that same day in Basra, Uncle Joe was doing seismographic work for Iraq Petroleum Company, a branch of Standard Oil, and was caught in the desert with British and American oil company personnel. By rounding up abbas and veils to disguise the foreigners as women, he saved them from the Arab nationalists and was awarded the George Medal, a British honor established by King George VI for civilians in recognition of their acts of bravery.

Because the British took Basra in the first two or three days of fighting, passage in and out of the city was barred, and we were detained in Amara, a hundred miles from home. A doctor, a bachelor friend of my father's who had just built a house on the river, loaned it to us. Although the rooms were empty of furniture, the doctor's neighbors and friends brought in things that we needed. My mother had a recurrence of malaria. When my father managed to get a message to Basra, my grandparents sent one of my father's linemen to cook. Each morning the British planes would drone overhead, dropping bombs. Refusing to come out of her room, the frightened servant Bahreah did nothing but cry. My mother was annoyed that Bahreah was acting so silly. After the planes left, if the bombs hit the river, the Arabs would dive in for the fish that bobbed to the top. Auntie May said that in some riverboats the British loaded big pipes used in the oil pipelines to make the vessels appear to be equipped with cannons, causing the Arabs who saw them "to run for their lives."

Historian Geoffrey Warner cites British Prime Minister Winston Churchill's belief that Hitler, by sending his airborne troops to Crete instead of Iraq, "cast away the opportunity of taking a great prize for little cost in the Middle East." With Italy and Germany's ability to wage war limited by oil shortages, Warner wonders at the different outcome access to Iraq's oil supplies might have meant to them.

The armistice between Britain and Iraq was signed May 31, 1941, just a month after the revolution had begun. That day anti-Jewish rioting and pillaging began in Baghdad. Between 170 and 180 Jews were killed and many more wounded. The Jews had been in Iraq for three thousand years and had an important role in Baghdad's social and commercial life, but that did not protect them from the fury of the mob fomented by anti-Jewish propaganda on Radio Berlin and the influence of malcontents like Haj Amin al-Husseini, the Mufti of Jerusalem, exiled from Palestine and given refuge in Iraq. My father later bought a sewing machine in Basra for my mother that had most likely been looted.

All four officers comprising the Golden Square were eventually tracked down and hanged, while Rashid Ali escaped to live in exile. Iraq officially declared war on Germany in 1943 and for the remainder of the war cooperated with Britain.

Once the hostilities were over, our family was free to leave Amara and go home to Basra, where our lives returned to normal. My father resumed his job with the telephone service and, like his father and brothers, engaged in a number of other business activities. The women in the family spent their time at home or in visiting other nearby relatives and friends.

One of my father's cousins and his family were our neighbors; and their daughter, Samira, who was my age, two, came over to play. I have a photograph of our fumbling to hold each other's hands as we attempt to make friends. My mother was not so fond of Samira because, according to her, she used to "devastate" my toys. I have a distinct memory of being left alone in a sitting room one afternoon until I had cleaned up the mess of my toys that I had made by myself. I was on my fanny on the floor, crying, reaching for toys around me and angrily flinging them one by one into the bottom of the big mirrored wardrobe where they were kept. My insolence so incensed my mother that she stormed in, her jaw jutting, and yanked me up by the arm. She said she would give me "something to really cry about" as she vigorously spanked my bottom and, when she missed that, the backs of my legs. She told me I could not come out of the room until the job was done. I could not catch my breath for shuddering. Wouldn't it have been great if she had picked me up in her arms and held me until I had calmed down? If only she had said, "What's the matter? Are you OK? I know it's a big job. Let me help you. We can do it together." But that's not what happened.

Another distinct memory at this age is gustatory: relishing orange sherbet at the Basra Airport, as I sat at an outdoor table with my parents and the British major I liked, who had a mustache. He was at our house for tea or drinks with our family one afternoon when everyone was sitting in the garden. A bulbul was hopping around on the ground outside our circle of chairs around a table. Handing me a saltshaker, my mother told me I could catch the bird if I put salt on its tail. *I can*, I confidently believed, tiptoeing up behind the bird, which kept hopping out of reach, and then running after it as it flew off. When I turned around, the adults were all laughing. Although I did not know the word then, it was my first conscious experience of embarrassment.

We had three servants. Muhammad, the cook, who was from Baluchistan (now a province of Pakistan), lived with us. He brought me a tiger cat as a present and often little candies in a cone of newspaper. For some reason, my mother did not like Leila, who came to clean daily, but she could not complain about her work. And there was Ossria, a descendant of African slaves, who was hired to come every day to take care of me. My mother liked her pleasant disposition. A devout Muslim, Ossria, who did not speak English, would sit me on her lap and tell me stories in Arabic from the Bible, which Muslims honor as well as the Qur'an. My mother, a Southern Baptist who knew her Bible stories, denigrated Ossria's stories as "all mixed up," but I could feel Ossria's delight in me as she raved about how smart I was. She always told me she loved me.

One afternoon, Ossria wheeled my brother, Frank, in the arabana while I walked alongside her. She told me she was going to show me where she lived only two blocks away. It was a hut made of palm branches with a kerosene light and a charcoal brazier for cooking. The women who lived in the huts washed their clothes in the river. Later, when I asked my mother why Ossria didn't live in a house, my mother scolded Ossria for taking us there. Maybe my mother thought Ossria had given me too much to think about.

The war and the presence of both the British and the American armies opened up many business opportunities for Jiddu and his sons. Jiddu's new company, N. F. Tooni, Incorporated, provided both armies with labor. The British were literally digging in in Iraq, preparing in case Germany's armored tank division, which Field Marshal Erwin Rommel was leading across North Africa, reached Egypt. Jiddu's labor company off-loaded ships, loaded trains, and transported goods. The trains would bring supplies and dump them in the desert, where workers would move them to different depots. With shovels, the laborers would hand dig enormous pits to bury drums of gasoline, or with grapples and ropes they would stack railroad ties. The British in Iraq were preparing, if need be, to hold the Germans back from marching across Iraq into their India.

Jiddu's company had a camp in the desert beyond Az Zubair, where two thousand laborers lived with their families. My father drove to the camp with bags of cash to pay different gangs, sometimes sharing a meal with them in their tents and sometimes spending the night, when he would sleep on the roof of his station wagon. What a view of the stars!

Even before the Japanese attack on the American fleet in Pearl Harbor brought the United States into World War II, the Federal Maritime Commission had stepped up the construction of new merchant ships, many of which were built to help the British, who had suffered severe losses at sea from German U-boats (short for *Unterseeboots*, or submarines). At first the merchant ships were called emergency ships, but eventually they were renamed Liberty ships.

"Often when bulky items, such as tanks and other vehicles, were shipped," historian Robert Kilmarx says, "there was a great deal of space between the items. In US shipments to England's Middle East campaign, ship owners filled these gaps with items that were totally useless to the British war effort. The British attempted to persuade the US government to pressure US ship owners to discontinue this wasteful practice, but not before some forty-one thousand tons of useless items had been dumped in the desert." Once, supervising the unloading of a Liberty ship, my father came home smelling like peppermint. A shipment of hard candy had broken, and all the laborers had grabbed as much as they could to sweeten their tea.

Arriving in Basra on one of the Liberty ships was an American officer assigned as a naval observer. He turned out to be from Nevada, Missouri, the basketball and football star of Neosho's biggest rival high school. He and a couple of other officers, one from Kansas City, rented one of Jiddu's houses. Hiring a cook and servant, they would have my parents over for dinner, and my parents would host them for dinner, too. "Uncle Joe would bring home for dinner Americans he met on the street," my mother said. "Then he was always wanting us to come over to help entertain them." Uncle Joe was putting in practice the high value Arabs place on generosity and hospitality.

As a telephone and telegraph engineer, my father supervised the first long-distance line that went across the desert from Iraq to Iran. After my father built our house on the nearby property Jiddu had given him and we had moved out of my grandparents' home, he hooked up telephones just between our two houses.

My father always had several projects going. He built benches into the sides of his station wagon, which he worked as a taxi as well as a bus service for a little hotel he owned called the Royal Palm. His taxi drivers were two of his telephone linemen. My mother did not have to cook, clean, wash, or iron at home; but occasionally, for the Royal Palm, she helped iron sheets. With her Southern Baptist upbringing, my mother was embarrassed one day to recognize an English nurse who had stayed overnight in the Royal Palm with a man who was not her husband.

My mother never knew when my father might send a lineman home to wash the floor. Payment was in food or quinine for malaria. The linemen would sit in the kitchen in the middle of the floor and deftly eat with their hands, polishing off a tray of rice.

For Jiddu's company, Uncle Kamil would make up the bills and, together with the receipts for goods, take them to the British officer in charge of the depot to sign. Once the bill was signed, it was as good as cash, for Uncle Kamil would then take it to the paymaster, who would issue Jiddu's company a check for the amount.

One day a British major in charge of one of the depots invited Jiddu and Kamil to his office. Over Scotch and sodas, he told them he wanted 10 percent of their gross.

"How can I give you 10 percent," Jiddu asked the major as Uncle Kamil interpreted, "when we don't make 10 percent?"

"You bring a receipt," the major answered. "My supervisors all know you do it for me. You take a receipt for one thousand tons and you make it two thousand. I'll give you 10 percent of our profits."

"No," Jiddu said. "You come home with me, and I'll give you curry and rice, but I can't give you what you ask."

The British major found another Iraqi not as honest as my grandfather. Uncle Kamil knew the man and also knew why he became a millionaire.

One day Uncle Joe's nationalist neighbors saw a British Army van pull up to his house and deliver two bags of cement he needed for some repairs. His being seen accepting gifts from the occupiers caused resentment and anger from some other members of the Basra community. Uncle Joe was blacklisted by the nationalists and besmirched the family name. Later, at a party, a girl refused his invitation to dance because of the blacklisting. Angry and having had too much to drink, married Uncle Joe impetuously grabbed the front of the girl's dress to pull her onto the dance floor and ripped it. The family settled out of court to the tune of one thousand dinars (the equivalent then of one thousand pounds sterling, or over $60,000 in 2017 US currency), and Bebe personally placated the girl with a gift of a diamond bracelet.

Uncle Kamil said the Iraqi governor in Basra hated him. One day he called Uncle Kamil into his office: the governor was going to put him in jail. "He had ordered a blackout," Uncle Kamil said. "We had a party, and the servants forgot to cover the windows." Although the commandant of police was present, the governor had not been invited.

Disobeyed and slighted, the governor might have been further antagonized by a party where liquor was served, for the sale, purchase, and consumption of alcohol is prohibited to Muslims.

"Who the hell do you think you are?" the governor roared. "Do you think you own the electricity and water in Basra?" It was only because of a telephone call from Sir John Ward, my father and uncle's boss who ran the port, that the governor tore up the papers for Uncle Kamil's arrest.

The same governor slapped my father's face when my father reported to him that he could not meet his deadline for getting him a telephone. The governor did not understand that having a working telephone involved wiring for telephone lines outside as well as inside.

Uncle Kamil said that at this point in time, they read the handwriting on the wall: as Christians in a land 95 percent Muslim, they were second-class citizens. He felt that he and his brothers were not going to get anywhere with their jobs; it took three years to get a promotion of just five British pounds. Their British benefactors would eventually have to leave Iraq, and communism was creeping into the country. It was time to depart their native land and emigrate to the United States.

The first of the family to leave Basra were Uncle Joe and Auntie Aileen, who, like my mother, was an American citizen. Her parents sponsored them. Uncle Joe got exit visas by offering the necessary officials cases of liquor and having Bebe and Jiddu throw them a big party complete with *artistes*, cabaret girls whom they had also invited to entertain them with belly dancing. Our family was next to leave. My American grandmother in Neosho had written her senator, Harry Truman, to help get her daughter and family out of Iraq. All of the necessary papers and passports for my parents were in order. There was only one hitch: as a lieutenant in the Iraqi Army, how could my father get away? One night he took to the cabaret a certain Iraqi Army clerk, who, upon being amply fed and entertained, assured my father that his file would be misplaced. There is always risk in such assurances. In case everything did not go as planned, charges of being away without leave were still a possibility—the reason why my father wanted to keep our departure for America secret. I was not told we were going until the very last minute that November of 1943.

Frank and I had to leave all our toys behind, for my parents packed only our personal clothing. As soon as we had a permanent address, Jiddu would ship us our silver and rugs by Liberty ship. We kissed my weeping grandmother and teary grandfather goodbye. I believed them when they said we would see them again in America.

Finally, we revealed our departure to the servants. Ossria wept copiously to learn the news. But as keening Ossria hugged and kissed me while I was crying too, my mother, to whom such a display of emotions seemed both hyperbolic and unseemly, stoppered my tears. "Don't be silly, Suzy," she said, "we'll come back to visit. Maybe Ossria can come to America to visit us. You'll see Ossria again."

Many years later, when I was working with a psychotherapist, she suggested I try going once a week to a dancer who did bodywork. For several sessions, one of the things the dancer had me do was simply to stand in front of her while she looked at me as if she were waiting for my body to say something. She encouraged me to "just let your body do whatever it wants to do." Each time I stood there, after a minute or so, my right foot would inexplicably roll in as if it wanted to walk on its side.

"Does that mean anything to you?" the dancer asked.

"No," I answered. I was emotionally blank and didn't have a clue, until one afternoon at home, as I was talking on the telephone with my mother, she unwittingly proved it true that the body remembers. I asked her about her life in Iraq, and she brought up Ossria. "She was crazy about you," she said. "You know she had a clubfoot."

The trip we embarked on by bus on the asphalt road that crossed the desert from Basra to Transjordan ordinarily took twelve to fourteen hours. But because of the Tehran Conference, the first meeting of Franklin D. Roosevelt, Winston Churchill, and Joseph Stalin, our bus was detained for ten days halfway across the desert at Rutbah, where wells had been dug and a fort and rest house had been built along with radio and telephone stations. We bus passengers, including some political prisoners being returned to Palestine, were put up in cabins, but everyone's luggage stayed strapped to the roof of the bus. In a small zippered canvas bag, my mother had brought us each a change of clothes and an extra pair of underwear, which she had to rinse out every night.

My parents' anxiety was contagious while we waited for the delay to be over so we could be on our way. One night an army officer knocked on our cabin door and said the customs officer wanted to see my father. I could feel the increase in their worry. My father whispered to my mother, "Keep your fingers crossed and pray hard." Of course, I did not know he was AWOL and would not have understood even if I did. When he returned to our room, he was grinning: the customs officer turned out to be an old school chum who just wanted to say hello! Whatever was going on, I felt relieved, too.

In Transjordan the customs officer was asleep, and his underlings at the customs post did not want to let us through. One of the passengers, a crone, pretended she was pregnant. My mother told the clerks she had a sick child and threatened to report them to the American Embassy if they didn't let us through. It was true. I was feverish, and my teeth were chattering with another malaria attack. I don't know if the man permitted our passage because of my chattering teeth or my mother's threat to report him, but we finally arrived in Transjordan. The following day we made the short drive across the Jordan River to Palestine. That December of 1943, I turned four in Jerusalem, where we stayed a week before traveling on to Egypt.

My father did not know that everything in Jerusalem was rationed, even the water.

When we had our first meal there in a little restaurant, he learned that he had to have special stamps to pay for dinner. The people at the neighboring tables all chipped in to come up with the stamps my father needed, which he gratefully paid them for. Before we left Jerusalem, my father hired a guide to show us such holy sites as the Wailing Wall (now the Western Wall), the Garden of Gethsemane, and Golgotha, the site where Jesus was crucified and buried. Walking where Jesus had walked seemed especially significant to my mother.

Once in Cairo, we stayed at the stylish Shepheard's Hotel while my father made the rounds of the embassies to try to find places for us on a ship bound for America. But after a few days, when the length of our stay started looking more indefinite, we switched to less expensive lodgings, although my parents often returned to Shepheard's for dinner. It was where my mother from the Ozarks ate her first spaghetti.

The hotel we moved to did not allow children in the dining room for the evening meal. Frank and I had our big meal at noontime and our last meal before bed at teatime. My mother always put us down early, and then she and my father would leave. "Don't be silly," she said if I started to cry. "We're only going for dinner." When my parents closed the door on our darkened room, they hung a Monitor sign on the doorknob to alert the hotel personnel that there were children inside. Frank always went to sleep, but I stayed anxiously on guard, worried that something might happen to my parents and they wouldn't come back. Sometimes a bellboy would open the door to our blackened room and call in to see if we were OK, and I would call back, "*Aye*," the Arabic yes.

One afternoon we toured a pyramid. My father took me with him inside it, while my mother waited outside with Frank. We started off in the thick darkness behind an Arab in a white galabaya who led the way carrying only a candle. As we went up the narrow, open steps carved out of the side of the wall, I got scared and cried, and my father had to take me out to stay with my mother and Frank. We have a photograph of us in front of the Sphinx, with me smiling warily from the saddle of a kneeling camel. We are posing with a group of Polish soldiers in British uniforms. With a government in exile in London, Poles fought in many campaigns with the Allies. Censors razored out the head of the Sphinx from the photograph because it identified the soldiers' location too specifically.

Another afternoon we went to the Giza Zoo, where I could not wait to see my first elephant. A beautiful word, I thought: *el-e-phant*. "Don't call me a monkey anymore," I told my parents. "I am an elephant." It was adorable Dumbo from the picture book I had in mind. When I saw real elephants, I was deeply disappointed. (As an adult, however, I came to admire them.)

Just a little more than a year before, Rommel's forces, pressing toward Cairo, had advanced as far as El Alamein, where the British Eighth Army held them back only seventy miles from Alexandria.

After three weeks in Cairo, we moved to Alexandria in time to spend Christmas in another hotel. We were finally scheduled to sail on New Year's Day, 1944. We comprised four of the ten passengers who had booked passage on the Norwegian freighter SS *Fernplant*, the flagship of a convoy of twelve ships, which included tankers and an escort of destroyers. Allied planes buzzed protectively overhead.

We were standing on the deck of the *Fernplant* as it sailed out of the harbor when suddenly it let out a blast from its smokestack. I jumped and tried to contain my brimming tears. The sound was so big that it filled my whole body.

"Don't be silly," my mother responded to my fright. "It's just the boat."

My father laughed and, imitating the ship's sound, resonated his deep voice into his cupped hands: "vvvt-vvvt." I got interested.

"Like this." He showed me how to line up my thumbs alongside each other and "vvvt-vvvt" through the crack between them into my own cupped hands.

"Vvvt. Vvvt." I imitated the ship's smokestack, feeling better now that I could be in charge of the sound.

No one had explained to me that German submarines were prowling the Mediterranean, sometimes as many as eighteen at one time. A month after we sailed, the Joint Chiefs of Staff of the Allies devised Operation Swamp, in which the Allies forced down German U-boats until they had to come up for air and, when they surfaced, attacked them. Before the convoy system, merchant ships, alone and freely using their lights and radio equipment, were easy prey for U-boats.

On the *Fernplant* my parents heard a rumor that the convoy ahead of us had been sunk, but as our convoy made its way across the Mediterranean from Alexandria to Gibraltar, they heard another rumor that the German submarines had been called in for repairs. Where were these rumors coming from? But now my father was smiling, and I could sense the whole *Fernplant* riding higher in the water, buoyed by the sight of Gibraltar and lighter with the release of apprehension, which had been as palpably cast overboard as cobblestones no longer needed for ballast.

"Show me." I reached out my arms for my father to pick me up.

"There." He pointed with his free arm as he hoisted me up in the hook of his other one.

"Where?" I saw nothing but a few spots of light on a dark mass of land that seemed to slip by against the twilight sky, even though it was really we who were slipping by.

"There. See the lights? That's the Rock of Gibraltar." Still smiling, he said to my mother, "We'll be picking up an American flagship now."

I liked the lights. They meant people and safe ground. My mother had promised Frank and me that when we got to America, we could play in a park. A pretty park with green grass, she said.

My father set me back down on the deck and spoke to me in Arabic, but I ignored his words as if I could not understand his language. "I am going to America," I had announced to my parents when we had to leave Basra. "I am going to eat apples, and I am never going to speak Arabic again."

Exasperated, my father switched to English. When he said, "Suzy, move away from the door," I stepped to the side of the bulkhead.

My mother later said that while I was always "so tense all day," Frank and I seldom cried on the voyage. She and my father had impressed on us that we were in a war and we had to be quiet in order to get to America. I had not always felt well, with recurring bouts of malaria, which my parents treated with tiny chocolate-covered quinine capsules, dispensed from the drawer of a little cardboard box. I liked the chocolate. All in all, Frank and I were very good. We had managed not to cause the Germans to bomb us.

On the *Fernplant*, we had lifeboat drills on deck every day; my mother was in charge of Frank, and my father, of me. The adults had to practice getting into their rubber suits. One day my father watched us both so that my mother could wash her hair. Her head was covered with suds when the alarm sounded, and she panicked, thinking the attack was real. Luckily, it was only a drill.

In our tiny two-bunk cabin, I shared one bunk with my father, and Frank shared the other with my mother. With our life jackets handy, we slept in street clothes reserved just for sleeping. In those days, I later learned, the sailors had a rule of thumb that determined how you slept. Since a ship loaded with iron ore would sink like a stone, you slept on deck for a fast dive overboard because if a torpedo hit you, the ship would founder in less than a minute. You could sleep below deck if the ship carried general cargo, but you had to sleep with your clothes on and the door open, so you would have time to escape. (The hold of the SS *Fernplant* was full of copper, which is denser than iron.) But you could undress, close your cabin door, and enjoy a good night's sleep if you were in a tanker carrying aviation gas, because if you were hit by a torpedo, then it was instantly all over.

With the *Fernplant* following its new American flagship, our convoy continued from Gibraltar on its slow passage across the Atlantic. We passengers used the lounge of the *Fernplant* as we would a living room in which we all gathered in the evening. Besides our family of four, the other passengers were two male Turkish students and a Canadian missionary couple and their two children. The two students would play their records while my mother crocheted and chatted with the austere Canadian missionary and his wife, who were on furlough from someplace in the Middle East and going home. The "Puritan wife," as my mother characterized her, wore black clothes and pulled her hair back severely. Her hands looked raw. Frozen foods were just coming into the news, a point of interest for my father, who was always looking toward future possibilities. The Canadian woman told my mother that her mother had always made an extra pie to bury out back in the snow and dig up later when they wanted it. I do not remember the Canadian children at all, but the word *languor* comes to mind.

That winter of 1944, I wish I could say the Statue of Liberty symbolically welcomed us, for all his life my father would dream the American Dream. The *Fernplant* docked instead in Baltimore, but at least Baltimore was America. We had been at sea in our tiny vessel for one month and living out of suitcases for more than two months. When we crossed the threshold of yet another hotel room, however, I cried.

"Now what is the matter?" my mother wanted to know.

"I thought I was coming to America to eat apples and play in a park."

But I cried even harder when my parents started to leave Frank and me alone in the room; and with no one to monitor us, I did not stop until they took us with them.

Our arrival was probably not what my mother expected either. In the six years she was gone, America had changed. For the first time, she saw girls on the street in rolled-up blue jeans, bobbysoxers who swooned over Frank Sinatra. My mother felt dowdy in her old-fashioned clothes, worn out from travel. We went shopping for new outfits before we set off for Neosho.

What must have been going on in my mother's mind with her reunion with her family so imminent? Why was my father growing increasingly irritable? I knew about my mother's relationship with her family the way I knew about German submarines, which is to say I knew nothing except that my body told me some strained, secret something was going on.

From Baltimore, we had to board a big Greyhound bus stuffed with soldiers for the long ride from depot to depot, places with strange names like Pittsburgh and Indianapolis and St. Louis. Because of the war and the rationing of fuel and rubber for tires, the speed limit was restricted to a maximum of forty miles per hour. The time seemed interminable to cross the eleven hundred miles to the middle of America, where the grandmother and great-grandmother Frank and I had never met were waiting for us.

Sometimes the bus would make a rest stop, and we could get down and stretch our legs and go to either an antiseptically smelly or a malodorous bathroom. If the toilet was clean, my mother would lay strips of toilet paper on the toilet seat. Cautioning me not to touch anything as I backed up to the seat, she lifted me under my arms to help me up. But if the toilet was dirty, I refused to go and would hold it. Sometimes, having almost forgotten how to walk, we had to leave our rented pillows and stagger down the bus stairs in the middle of the night to transfer to another bus. Sometimes we would sit at a depot counter on interesting stools whose seats could twirl around, and we would nibble on something foreign. My mother said she had missed hamburgers and hot dogs and Cokes the most. Although I readily adapted to chocolate milkshakes, I did not like the way most things tasted and was suspicious that fare as innocuous as ham and cheese sandwiches bore germs. Why couldn't I be like Frank, who happily gobbled up everything? But what did he know? He was only a baby.

My mother would glower at me. "Don't wipe yourself all over the window," she would say as I knelt in the bus seat to peer out at the telephone poles flicking hypnotically by in the passing landscape. Even though I tried not to touch anything, my hands and elbows and knees felt soiled, and my clothes appeared as tired with travel as I felt. Sometimes my mother would look at me and frown.

"Just a minute," she would say. "Let me get my hanky." And I knew one of her spit baths was coming. She would fish around her purse for a white cotton handkerchief, usually with little flowers embroidered in one corner, and working up some spit, she would dab the handkerchief on her tongue.

"Sit still," she would hiss, and with the wet part of the handkerchief wrapped around her index finger, she would mercilessly rub my cheek or forehead to erase some particularly stubborn smudge.

After my parents had fallen asleep, I felt I had to keep watch. Lucky Frank on the bus to Missouri with his head in my mother's lap—he seemed able to sleep all night.

Why did I seem to take on the job of watchman? Did I not trust my parents to think of me? Did it start at the hotel in Cairo where I had been left with Frank while my parents went out for dinner? It was exhausting to stay awake as long as I possibly could. Why did I feel so responsible?

Consider child-development pioneer Arnold Gesell's description of the lively and expansive four-year-old, bursting with motor activity: "racing, hopping, jumping, skipping, climbing" and bubbling over with what he calls the "abandoned use of words." After more than two months of confinement to buses, hotel rooms, ship cabins, and more buses, when my mother finally turned Frank and me loose in my grandmother's backyard in Neosho, we did not know what to do. With the whole Big Spring Park before us, we just stood there.

But it wasn't long before Bebe Lorene (my grandmother liked our calling her that) was referring to Frank and me as the Katzenjammer Kids, after the popular cartoon strip that featured two incorrigible children: she discovered that I had pressed the clay she bought for us to play with onto a corrugated white shingle on the outside of the house. I think it was hard to get off.

Bebe Lorene and my great-grandmother, Nanny, cooked a big fried-chicken dinner and invited my mother's cousins, Jean and her sister, Lee, whose husbands were away at war, to come see Doris, back from Iraq with her family. The cousins were pretty and fun. A photograph of us all gathered on the front steps of my grandmother's house in our coats shows them kidding around with us. My mother and Nanny are not in the picture, and my father, who is, looks like he'd rather not be. It is hard to describe his expression. If his mood didn't look so dark, I'd say he was doing a slow burn. But he was saved by the bell: he couldn't stay in Neosho.

A letter arrived for my father announcing that he'd been accepted for a job he had applied for at Federal Telephone and Radio Laboratories in Newark, New Jersey, whose classified work at that time was mainly to help the war effort. Federal Labs, as everyone called the company, wanted him to start work as soon as possible. I was disappointed to learn that war work didn't mean he would be wearing an Army uniform, because I thought he would look handsome in one. I also wanted him to grow a mustache and smoke a pipe instead of cigarettes.

My father told my mother that he would send for us as soon as he found a house.

After he reported to his new job, he wrote her a letter to say that a man in his office recommended nearby Montclair as a good town to live in because of the excellent reputation of its public schools.

We don't know what turn the story will take while we're living it. If we knew, maybe we would not want to go down that road, but then what would we learn? Nejib and Doris were about to plunge into yet a third culture that neither of them belonged to. But it was hard to tease out what was culture and what was psychology ... or something else.

Nejib at fourteen.

Bebe and Jiddu in Basra, Iraq.

Jiddu's house becomes the Faiha Palace Hotel.

Part One: In the Garden of Eden

Collage of elopement news.

Doris at seventeen.

Nejib and Doris en route to Basra.

Nejib and Doris at Jiddu and Bebe's house in Basra.

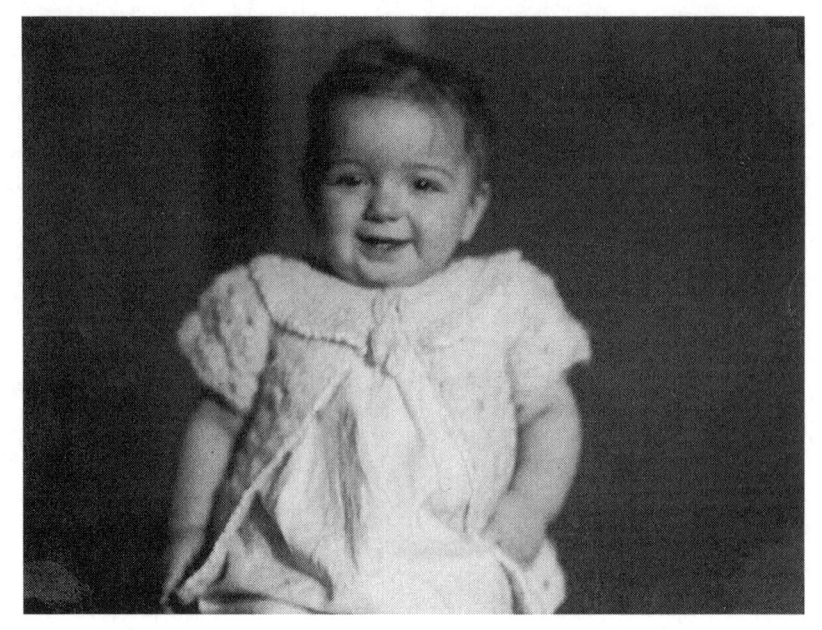

Suzy, age one.

Suzy and Frankie with Doris.

Nejib in his new house in Basra.

Suzy and Frankie with Nejib en route to America.

Suzy and Frankie arrive in Neosho. New overalls for Suzy to grow into.

PART TWO:

GROWING PAINS

I WAS IN THE FRONT HALL OF OUR HOUSE on Brunswick Road in Montclair, New Jersey, when I felt the first stirrings of the idea that there might be more to life than meets the eye. I was lying on my stomach on the Persian rug, fascinated by the pictures in a clever children's book the previous owners of the house had left behind. My mother had suggested I look at the drawings through a little square of a red cellophane candy wrapper; when I did, hidden images in special ink not noticeable to the naked eye became visible. I held the red square up to my eye and panned the room, longing to have anything hidden similarly revealed.

Dr. Blackburn made a call to our house to look Frank and me over to see if we were healthy. He asked my mother a lot of questions. After he pressed a wooden depressor on my tongue and looked into my mouth, peered into my ears with a light, and put a stethoscope in his ears to listen to my heart, he said to her, "Madame, when you cross a Missouri mule with an Arabian horse, you are bound to get something that will last."

School was already underway when my mother walked me to Miss Wynkoop's kindergarten class at Edgemont School, a graceful colonial brick public school. Among the odds and ends the former owners had left behind in our new house on Brunswick Road was another children's storybook, this one with photographs, called *Mac Goes to School*. It was written by Miss Wynkoop, the kindergarten teacher, and starred her black Scottie dog, Mac. Some of the faces that appeared in the book I would later recognize as belonging to the big kids in the upper grades—literally in classes on the second floor— the fourth, fifth, and sixth grades. The lower grades were on the ground floor, as were the principal's office in the middle of the long marbled-floor hall, the auditorium/gym in a wing on one end, and the big kindergarten room in its own wing at the opposite end.

Miss Wynkoop, a brusque, athletic woman, with wavy salt-and-pepper hair clipped short, met my mother and me at the kindergarten door. Having just arrived in the middle of the school year from Basra, Iraq, via Neosho, Missouri, I did not know a single person in the whole room. The other kindergartners all knew each other, and everyone was engrossed in play. I could not help it: when my mother turned to leave, my bottom lip curled down and my face crumpled without my consent.

"She will be all right, Mrs. Tooni. Don't worry about a thing," Miss Wynkoop reassured my mother, hurrying her out the door. Miss Wynkoop was right. After taking me on a tour of the room, where groups of children were huddled around blocks and cars and trucks and miniature tea dishes, she asked me what I might like to do. I said I would like to draw. I equated writing with drawing because my first aesthetic experience was loving the shape of the small script English *r*. Most likely I first saw it in my mother's signature, *Doris*. I longed to be able to write a small script *r* myself. I remember sitting at a table with my mother in Basra as I drew on a paper with a pencil. Perhaps I asked her to write her name. But when I asked her to teach me how to make a small script *r*, she answered, "No." She felt I should not know such things "ahead of time" but should wait until I was in school, when the teacher would show me the proper way. Although my mother would often remind me that she was reading herself by the age of four, she felt reading precociously had never done her any good. I didn't know then the possibility that she was trying to protect me from her fate of always feeling behind in school because her mother had her skip first grade on account of her ability to read.

But that day Miss Wynkoop launched me on a satisfying long-term art project that I enjoyed making—a thick book of the flags of the world, a project that I realize in retrospect she sensitively selected to help me recognize that it was acceptable to be from another country. Each page of the book was a sheet of manila paper filled to the edges with a carefully crayoned individual flag. The

Italian flag, with its three simple vertical bands of color, was easy to draw and color; but copying a pattern as complicated as Britain's Union Jack was difficult or to tell the truth, impossible. I was proud of this project, and Miss Wynkoop expressed her pleasure in what I had accomplished. When I brought my book of flags home, finally completed, I could tell by the expression on my mother's face that she thought it was good, but she purposely avoided praise. She feared if I knew I was smart, I might become conceited. The pattern of withholding praise to protect me from myself prevailed throughout my schooling. If my father had any comments about my flag book, I do not remember them, a pattern that also continued.

One day we all grouped our little chairs in a semicircle around Miss Wynkoop, who had descended to sit in one of them, too. She told us a true story that amazed me. If you fill a milk bottle with water—milk was delivered in bottles by the milkman to our door in those days—and if the temperature dipped down to 32 degrees, she said as she moved a wide red ribbon down a giant thermometer painted on a white board, the water would get *hard*. It would *freeze*. She asked us to guess what would happen to the bottle. It might crack and break! Recently arrived from a subtropical climate, I found her talk gripping. When Miss Wynkoop gathered us in to tell us about something as important as *tem-per-a-ture*, she splayed her long legs astride her little chair to keep her balance, which meant that you could see her underpants.

Every classroom in Edgemont School, including the kindergarten, had a cloakroom, a long, skinny, usually windowless and thus dark room with hooks along the wall for our coats. You entered the cloakroom through a heavy swinging door at one end and exited through an identical swinging door at the opposite end. The whole seven years I spent at Edgemont School, I never saw a single cloak. But this is the kind of conversation you might overhear in the cloakroom as we filed through to get our belongings, also sometimes referred to as our "wraps":

"Did you see Miss Wynkoop's underpants?"

"Oooh, Gordon, I'm going to tell Miss Wynkoop you said that."

One day all the female kindergartners filed through the girl's room door for "lavatory." A classmate was looking at me as I dried my hands on a paper towel. She brushed the hair away from her eyes and asked, "Where did you get your dress?"

"My mother made it," I answered, proud to have a mother so clever.

"Are you poor?"

"No!" I answered indignantly. But the girl's remark stung and made me self-conscious for the first time about my appearance and social status; my dress did look homemade. I think I hurt my mother's feelings when I asked her if from then on I could buy my clothes in a store. I did not want to be different.

We were seated at the dining room table, where we ate our Sunday dinner together. The wartime meat did not smell so good, and it tasted funny. My father threw down his fork and exploded: "Horse meat! I thought so!" He bawled out my mother for wasting the food stamps and his money.

"It's not my fault!" my mother cried.

"You should be able to tell the difference!" he shouted.

I felt sorry for my mother and did not think it fair that my father was mad at her and not at the butcher who deceived her.

I was standing in the front hall when I watched my parents grab each other and whirl around after hearing on the radio that the war in Europe was officially over—Nazi Germany had unconditionally surrendered. The next thing I remember is being in downtown Montclair on Bloomfield Avenue with people lined up on the sidewalk in straggly bunches, waving little American flags, which you could buy from men who were selling them as well as orange paper poppies. I think people simply did not know what to do with themselves after such a momentous announcement and came out on the street to share the news communally.

A letter my father wrote, published in the *New York Times* dated September 2, 1945 (coincidentally, the date of Japan's unconditional surrender), shows him as not as enamored of the British as his brother Kamil seemed to be. Here are my father's own words:

> Why, may I ask, should the British continue to use their control over the sterling to prevent the thousands of importers in the sterling area from buying in the United States?
>
> I was in the Middle East during this war and I know how the people there have been anxiously waiting for cessation of hostilities in order that they may be free again to import goods from the United States. Those people have a strong faith in American goods and American business standards. They have also accumulated large sums of money from this War and a lot of this money came from services rendered to the American armed forces. But their desire to import goods from the United States has been suppressed by the British who have exchange controls in practically every country in the Middle East. It is beyond doubt that this situation will force those people to buy mostly British goods. This will mean fewer jobs for Americans.
>
> The Americans did not fight this war in order to give the British control of trade of the people living in the sterling area. Those people should have the freedom they had before the war to buy and sell wherever they please.

Frank and I were not allowed to keep toys in our rooms. According to my father's irrefutable logic, that's why they were called *bed*rooms. But he did fix up a playroom for us in the basement, the only room in the house where we could act like kids—up to a point, that is, for we had to keep it neat. So that our rear ends would not freeze, my father spread on the cold cement floor a big blue-and-white fringed

Arab rug, the designs of which are often surprisingly similar to the weavings of some Native American tribes. The walls were whitewashed. As you came down the basement stairs and turned right into the playroom, across the far left-hand corner you could see a plywood platform my father had built, on which Frank's electric train ran round and round an oval of track.

When we got tired of playing in the playroom, we would whine, "There's nothing to do" and come up from the basement to hang around my mother in the kitchen. Once, she consented to letting us use a couple of blankets to make a fort in the playroom by draping them over the child-size table and chairs that Bebe Lorene had given us. But before long Frank and I started getting "rambunctious" (my mother had a good vocabulary from all her reading), and from the kitchen she would call down a warning: "Don't start." If we got too silly and our giggling got out of hand, she would come downstairs with the slitted eyes and jutted jaw and, yanking us up by the arm, give us each a good spanking to calm us down. If we'd been on the second floor, she would have come after us with the back of her hairbrush. Usually, Frank and I both cried. Nothing made her madder, however, than when she spanked me and I laughed. Laughter is so close to tears.

When she stomped back up to the kitchen, Frank and I might play our favorite game with the identical beaverboard dollhouses that Bebe Lorene had sent us for Christmas. Each was a four-room colonial sporting a columned front porch whose roof formed a balcony off the second floor. On the rug we set up our dollhouses with their front doors facing as if they were across the street from each other. We had little plastic people, and we took turns inviting each other's dolls over.

"Hi. Come on in."

"What a nice house."

"Let me show you around ... This is the living room."

"What a nice living room."

"This is the kitchen."

"What a nice kitchen."

"This is the bedroom."

"What a nice bedroom."

By now, our dolls had worked their way to the upstairs balcony.

"Let me show you the balcony ... Come closer. It has such a lovely view."

And with that—"*Aaaah!*"—we would shove the little guest over the parapet.

My father's desk, which faced the window that looked across our driveway, the hedge, and the side of the Tracys' house, was the only piece of furniture in the front hall. The bookcase with the leaded glass doors and the seat against the stairs were built-in. On the desktop the dark-green tooled-leather accessories of blotter, calendar, and letter opener were watched over by a lamp whose base was the black-and-white ceramic head of a zebra. When not in use, my father's portable typewriter, which was forbidden to us, stood at attention in its black case alongside the desk. I would not dream of touching it.

One day, while my father was at work, out of curiosity I pulled out the big bottom drawer of his desk. Disappointed that it was full of files, I opened the smaller drawer above it. It had some stationery in it and a jar of ink. I picked up the jar and, wanting to look inside, unscrewed the lid. The jar was full to the brim. Because I was holding it at an angle, ink spilled onto my father's files below.

When my father got home from work that night, he spanked me with his enormous hand really hard, but his punishment took a second to what happened not long thereafter.

Nobody told Frank and me what was the matter with my mother except that suddenly she was sick and had to go to the hospital. (I didn't learn until I was an adult that she had to have an ovary removed.) At the time, I was worried that my mother was never coming back.

My father hired a woman named Mrs. Montague to take care of us while he was at work. She was lean and had thin, white hair, rimless spectacles, and a conspicuous case of plastic in her ear that was a hearing aid of those times. She moved tentatively, as if having to test the reality around her before stepping into it. I tried not to notice her diffidence and carefully explained to her where my mother kept everything in the kitchen and what my mother usually made us for lunch. Mrs. Montague's doing everything differently made me miss my mother all the more.

But timorous as she was, Mrs. Montague was also kind, and after lunch Frank and I walked with her to the grape arbor whose lattice stretched across the back of our property. We sat on its built-in benches, my brother and me on either side of her, while she read us a book.

After a time, I thought I heard a strange sound coming across the backyard. "Mrs. Montague, I think I hear something funny in the house."

"I don't hear anything, dear."

"It sounds like a frying pan sizzling."

"Well, maybe we'd better go have a look." She took Frank's hand on one side and mine on the other, and we walked up the driveway to the back door. The closer we got, the stranger the sound: it was difficult to determine what it was. When we entered the kitchen, we were appalled to discover water all over the floor. Even worse, the plaster had fallen out of the ceiling over the stove, and in between the exposed laths, a stream of water steadily poured down onto the stove, trickled across the slightly slanted floor, and made its way down the basement stairs.

Mrs. Montague was a trembling wreck and, of course, had to telephone my father at work. I don't remember whether she realized that the source of the stream was the upstairs bathroom faucet, which had been left running with the stopper in the sink, or whether she waited for my father to discover it. I only know that after he rushed home and saw the mess, he humiliatingly bawled her out and told her he was going to get someone else to take care of us. I felt sorry for Mrs. Montague because leaving the faucet on could not possibly have been her fault. She had not even been upstairs. Frank and I both had washed our hands upstairs before lunch and didn't remember who had left the faucet on. It was an accident.

"*Bûma!*" my father exploded in Arabic, turning his attention to Frank and me after Mrs. Montague left. Patai observes that an Arab's anger easily flares up, and "once aroused, his wrath has no limits."

"*Bûma!*" my father shouted repeatedly, calling us "owls," which in Iraq are noted, not for their wisdom, but for their stupidity.

"*Kuzzer-kut!*"

It didn't matter that we didn't know what it meant. He was steaming, and it felt like he was calling us the lowest of the low, as he went crazy and pounded us both to a pulp. That was the beating that got first prize.

That day was my watershed for consciously trying to be good and not make any mistakes.

When I was six, my mother took Frank and me to the movies with her on what she called her "night off." My father did not want to go. We caught the bus at the bus stop on Valley Road, which ran perpendicular to the top of our street, right to the Wellmont Theater in downtown Montclair. My mother had to take us along: since my father worked all day, he did not want the job of babysitting at night when he got home. That is also why he did not drive us to the movies after he got his aqua four-door Studebaker sedan with the bullet nose. Frank and I sat through a string of Humphrey Bogart, Sydney Greenstreet, Veronica Lake, and Rita Hayworth movies at an early age. I could usually hold it, so that I would not have to go to the bathroom in the middle of the movie and annoy my mother. Even though the show was mostly grown-ups talking and I did not always get what was going on, I liked going to the movies, and I liked being with my mother. Frank usually dozed off in his seat. Afterward, we waited in the night in front of the bank for the bus at the stop across the street from the theater. While we waited, Frank and I peered down the grate in the sidewalk, sometimes spotting a shiny nickel or dime with buying power then, certain it could be ours if we only had a string and some gum. Sometimes if Frank and I got tired of standing, my mother would lift us up to sit on the cold marble ledge cut into the facing of the bank.

But when she took us to see Walt Disney's *Snow White and the Seven Dwarfs*, I was riveted to my seat. Poor Snow White! I held my breath every time her cruel stepmother stepped up to ask, "Mirror, mirror, on the wall, who is fairest of them all?" and the mirror lied that she was. And when the witch came to the dwarves' cottage to proffer Snow White the poisoned apple, I was afraid she would eat it and die. But when the witch with slitted eye and jutted jaw flew up the stormy mountain in a rage, I cried in terror, and my mother had to take me out into the lobby.

"Don't be so silly, Suzy; you're spoiling the movie!" my mother said. "It's just a story."

I stopped sniveling and collected myself, and we went back to our seats in time to see the prince kiss Snow White, waking her up from the dead to live happily ever after.

After that, in bed at night, I had a frequently recurring fantasy: I was lying in a little open coffin, and all my classmates filed by to look at me.

One afternoon, about that time, my mother tossed me an offer too good to refuse. "How would you like to earn a nickel?"

"Sure!"

"You could do some dusting for me."

"Sure!" Not only was this an opportunity for financial gain, but I was also delighted. I had never dusted before, and here I was being asked to do a real job. As I received the dust rag from my mother's hands, I felt she was bestowing on me a mantle of adulthood.

In our household a dust rag was always a dust rag with the word's hard connotations, not the euphemistically soft "dust cloth" to which I would catch rare references in the houses of my more affluent friends, who would also say "washcloth" for the cloth used for the bath or "dish cloth" for the one found at the kitchen sink. A linguist could discover in our family's dust rags, washrags, and dishrags vestigial evidence of the frugal, waste-not-want-not passage of my maternal forebears through the Depression. In spite of Nanny's healthy inheritance, her daughter, Bebe Lorene, would say of her childhood, "We were poor, but we were never hungry."

"Now calm down," my mother said. "Don't open up the dust rag like that in the house. You'll get dust all over the place. When you've finished dusting, I'll show you how to shake out the rag outside. T-shirts make the best dust rags," she added, correctly interpreting the question on my face as I realized I would be wiping the table with my father's undershirt. "Old flannel pajamas are good too."

I nodded trustworthily as I absorbed this esoteric knowledge.

"But, of course, you always take the buttons off, so you don't scratch the furniture."

I was being taken into the trade. I was being included in the business of the world. "OK, let's see. Why don't you start with that little table? How would you do it?"

Easy, I thought, as I swiped around the things on top of the end table by the side of the couch (why did we call it a "couch" and some people, a "sofa"?). A cinch, I thought, as I ran the dust cloth over the empty second shelf and around the magazines on the bottom shelf.

"Whoa! That's not dusting. You have to dust under everything. Here, let me show you."

I watched my mother take the glass ashtray off the top of the table and set it on the Persian rug (why did we call it a "rug" and some people, a "carpet"?). From the table she also removed a cylindrical silver object from Iraq, shaped like a minaret and around which hand-etched camels stood under palm trees. I never knew what the object was for, as I could never get the top off. Then she gave me a look to be sure I was paying attention.

"Now I don't expect you to pick up the lamp," she said. "You might break it, so you can just dust around it."

She wiped the tabletop, making a point to poke the dust rag in the fancy cutouts of the little border that ran like a fence around the top of the table. With her finger in the dust rag, my mother dug in along the curves and curlicues.

"See? You have to be sure you've wiped the dust off all the little places where it can collect." My mother even dusted the ashtray and the little silver minaret before she put them back on the tabletop. After improving on my efforts to wipe off the empty second shelf, she removed the magazines from the bottom shelf and set them on the rug, dusted the *Saturday Evening Post* on top and the bottom shelf itself, and put the magazines back.

"See?" she asked, standing back with a little frown as if she were appraising her work through the eyes of my father. "OK?" She looked at me.

"Yes!" I snapped smartly, the eager soldier reporting for duty.

As she left the room, I set to work on the matching table at the opposite end of the couch. It was thrilling to be able to pick up the jaunty Hummel figurine of the little boy in his lederhosen and feathered green cap, his cheeks puffed out in a whistle, which I had not been allowed to touch before. I placed him on the rug and carefully removed his companion, a Hummel figurine of a Swiss girl in a pinafore and apron, and set her down alongside him.

"Hello."

There was a matching glass ashtray on this end table, too, which I also deposited on the rug. Then, as I had watched my mother do, I carefully dusted the top of the table, going around the lamp, making sure to dig into the corners. Wrapping the dust rag around my index finger, I poked into all the cutouts in the trim before I arranged the little boy and girl to peek coquettishly around the lamp at one another and returned the ashtray. The next shelf held only a short stack of cork-bottomed coasters, which I held aloft until I finished dusting under them.

The bottom shelf was easy to dust because it had nothing on it. Next I tackled the coffee table in front of the couch. It also had an ashtray on it, which I moved to the rug, and a brass cigarette box from Iraq. Opening it, I found it empty but enjoyed smelling the cedar lining with its residue flecks of tobacco leaves. There was another silver doodad from Iraq on the table, but I did not know what it was, either. It resembled an apple and was about the size of one and had two delicate silver leaves on stems that stuck out from the top of it like antennae. I tried to open it, but the top was stuck. I put these things on the rug and dusted the big rectangle of glass that fit flush into the top of the dark wood frame. Then I carefully put everything back where it belonged on the coffee table and looked around.

I walked across the rug to the big radio/phonograph console, which I was ordinarily not allowed to touch because I might break it. We were almost the same height, but I could see over its top and stretch my arm across it well enough to dust it.

"I'm finished!" I announced to my mother in the kitchen. She came into the living room looking surprised.

"You've finished the hall and dining room, too?"

"The hall and dining room?" A forest of chair rungs multiplied before my eyes.

"Don't forget I'm paying you."

That was incentive, but the work was tiresome and beginning to look like it was not worth it.

When I finished the job, she showed me how to shake out the dust rag on the back porch steps and hang it on a nail in the broom closet.

"Here's your nickel. Now go on upstairs and wash your hands."

On the way up the back stairs, I was smiling, thinking about the five movie star cards I would buy the next time we walked to Greenberg's stationery store.

A few days later, my mother asked me again, "How would you like to earn a nickel?"

"Doing what?"

"You could dust for me."

I shook my head. "No, thanks."

"Don't get smart, young lady." My mother pressed the dust rag into my hand. "It's time you pitched in around here. I had to dust when I was your age, too, and I didn't even get paid."

Dusting, I celebrated my rite of passage into the unrelenting routine of daily life in our household. But as my mother pointed out, I lived there, too.

One fine afternoon on curly-headed Johnny Slocum's back porch, tired of playing store, I asked him if his mother had any scissors.

"Yes."

"Well, do you think you could get them?"

"Well, I think so."

"Well, would you?"

"Well, all right, but I don't think my mother is going to like this."

When Johnny brought out the scissors, we played barbershop. And later, when an upset Mrs. Slocum called my mother on the telephone and asked her if she knew what her daughter had done to her son's beautiful curly hair, as if I were a hoodlum and my mother did not have any control over her children, my mother turned to me in utter consternation.

She said, "Why, Suzy!" as if what I had done was so bad she was speechless. I got a good spanking, even though I did not think I had done that bad a job. Johnny was, after all, my first customer—and, as it turned out, my last.

The first time we saw Bebe Lorene after we left Neosho to move to Montclair, she came to visit us for two weeks in the summer. For some reason my mother seemed to be only pretending to enjoy her visit, even though my father cordially drove my grandmother all around Montclair to show her our town. But the whole household seemed on edge.

After reading *The Arab Mind* as an adult, I wondered if Bebe Therouza breastfeed Nejib until he was two or three while his sister was weaned at one or two, as Patai describes the experience of other male and female Arab babies at that time. If so, my father would have been old enough to verbally demand the breast and, with his mother at his beck and call, would have gotten instant gratification. Patai says that this practice may be the source of the "characteristic Arab male attitude to women: that the destiny of women in general, and in particular of those within the family circle, is to serve the men and obey them." If these were my father's early childhood impressions of life, they would explain a lot about him. He was also used to having servants.

Maybe it was the way my father bossed my mother around that made my grandmother say, "You don't have to take that, Doris. You can come back home and live with me." At those words, my father headed for the guest room and started putting Bebe Lorene's things back in her suitcase. I didn't understand what was going on and wanted my grandmother to stay. She told me she was leaving because she was homesick. My father then drove my grandmother to Newark's Pennsylvania Station to catch a train back to Neosho.

Even though my father smoked two packs of Pall Mall cigarettes a day, he did not allow himself to smoke above the first floor of our house. His reason was not to keep the bedroom air fresh, but to prevent his accidentally falling asleep in bed and setting himself and the house on fire. My father had a phobia of fire. He would often read aloud to us from the *Newark Evening News*: "Listen to this—'Whole Family Burned to Death.' You see what can happen when you play with matches?"

One afternoon, my mother discovered a hole the diameter of a cigarette end burned into the white linen doily on the arm of one of the big scratchy armchairs in our living room. Worse, a faint curl of smoke issued from the hole, which indicated that the fire had insinuated itself into the stuffing, where it still smoldered. She yelled for us, and from wherever we were in the house, Frank and I fell in at attention beside the armchair as my mother ran from the kitchen with a glass of water, which she carefully trickled down the hole. Maybe my mother herself had put the hole in the chair with her look.

"I didn't do it." I was quick to defend myself.

"Just wait until your father gets home," my mother said, turning to Frank and, without touching him, commenced his daylong torture.

My father interrogated us that evening. "Who was playing with matches?" It was like God calling, "Where are you?" to Adam and

Eve in the garden, when, of course, he knew perfectly well where they were.

"Do you understand that the spark that went down into this chair could have burst into flames and set the whole house on fire while we were asleep?" Smoke issued from my father. "And killed us?"

He did not have to say much more. There was the black-edged hole spoiling the arm of the chair, and even a child could understand what might have happened.

"Who was playing with matches?"

Frank's face screwed up, and he started to cry. "I did," he bawled. "I'm sorry. I won't do it again. I'm sorry."

"Just so this never happens again," my father explained, as if he had not already impressed on us the seriousness of the dangers of playing with matches, "come here."

Frank stepped forward, still sniveling. I knew he was going to get it, but I did not expect what happened next.

"Hold out your hand," he commanded Frank.

Frank stuck his hand out. Withdrawing the cigarette dangling from his lips, my father branded a circle on Frank's wrist the same size as the one on the arm of the chair.

───※───

One morning, before he got his Studebaker, my father was waiting for a bus on Valley Road at the top of our street to go to Newark, where he was working for Federal Labs. After the war, few people had cars. A big, smiling man with a high voice who was also waiting for the bus started talking to my father and introduced himself as Happy Mitchell. He asked my father where he was from and was so fascinated by the reply that he invited my father then and there to bring his wife to dinner. My father could be very charming.

That is how my parents met an entire neighborhood of people about a half mile from our house—the Mitchells, the Lynches, the Scovilles, the Hugheses, those are the ones I can remember—and became members of a monthly men's poker club and women's sewing circle. The men took turns at one another's houses sitting around tables in sports shirts, eating cold cuts, and playing poker under a blue haze of cigar and cigarette smoke; on a different evening the women took turns at one another's houses gossiping over dessert while they darned socks pulled over wooden eggs. The monthly dues of the sewing circle went into a kitty, which one time got earmarked for a day at the circus at Madison Square Garden. And that is how my mother happened to take us somewhere besides the movies without our father.

 The time Frank and I went to the circus with my mother and the sewing circle, I fit right in. I asked to go to the bathroom, and five or six other children in our group had to go at the same time too. I wasn't the only one craving cotton candy, and nobody said, "You don't need it." When it came time for a souvenir, everybody got one. Even though it was as useless as a doodad on a stick, nobody said, "It's a waste of money." My brain bubbled over with images of the tightrope walker who slipped on the wire and almost fell to his death, the troupe of trapeze artists swooping down to daringly swap swings in mid-air, the party of little dogs that could twirl and dance, the tall parading man whose pants rose up with his long strides to reveal his stilts, and the impossible crowd of clowns that endlessly spilled out of a midget car.

I read on the back of a comic book that you could win prizes and get rich selling seeds for the Lancaster Seed Company. My mother did not like the idea of my selling things door to door. Selling potholders I had made with colored cotton loops woven on the teeth of a square metal frame to our next-door neighbor, Miss Crane, was one thing; but what would the neighbors think, my mother worried, about a little girl out selling? It was not ladylike or nice. My father, however, was all for it. He helped me mail the form I cut out to sign up as a Lancaster salesman, and soon I received a carton of twenty-five packets of assorted seeds to be sold at twenty-five cents a packet.

 I pounded the pavement. *Ding-dong.* "Would you like to buy some seeds?"

When I ran out of prospective customers on our square block, my father consented to let me ride my bike as far afield as Erwin Park two blocks away—farther than where we heard that a boy named Franklin, riding his bike, had been hit by a car and killed. I sold all my seeds, and when it came time to fill out the form to mail in to collect my winnings, I had an option: cash or a prize. My father said I should go for the cash, but the illustrations of the available prizes were drawn seductively, with rays coming out around them like sunrises. I had my heart set on the beautiful silver bracelet from which little silver hearts dangled, and I counted the days until the mailman delivered the small brown package from the Lancaster Seed Company. The bracelet was a piece of junk. My father lifted his eyebrows and shrugged his shoulders. He did not have to say, "I told you so." It was my first conscious experience of disillusionment, and it cured me of door-to-door selling.

Down the street from our house lived my first true friend, Brent Paul. We would become the kind of friends Antoine de Saint-Exupéry might describe as being, not absorbed in each other face to face, but "looking outward together in the same direction."

In the Pauls' backyard was a magnificent white ash tree, whose graduated branches provided ringside seats overlooking the world below to every child in our neighborhood, regardless of age. Trees seemed to me to have personalities. The ash's lower branches were attainable by us younger kids, and its dizzyingly higher branches were for the older daredevils. On one of these lower branches, Brent and I sat side by side, nibbling on graham crackers to make them last and pointing to the parade of all the changing animals we could see in the cumulus clouds that sailed across Brunswick Road over the fields of the Montclair Athletic Club, which all the neighborhood children insouciantly referred to as the A.C.

In the 1940s, the summer air in our backyards glittered with a veritable confetti of butterflies: swallowtails, monarchs, red admirals, mourning cloaks, as well as the small white or copper or occasional tiny blue butterflies that flitted around like airborne forget-me-nots. Brent and I crashed through this paradise armed with a bottle of deadly nail polish remover to fill out our butterfly collection. We would pin our dead victims to the pieces of cardboard that came in laundered shirts and add them to our museum, a warped and rickety card table set up on the side of our garage my father did not use. Brent said it did not hurt the struggling butterfly one bit when he covered its head with a wad of cotton soaked in nail polish remover and its body went still. But I wondered then what had gone out of the butterfly? Brother butterfly, I am so sorry.

I had to choke down untold cups of Ovaltine, the malt powder pretending to be chocolate that my mother stirred into our milk, before she would relinquish the jar's label. It was necessary to include the label with my quarter to send off for the Captain Midnight ring I wanted; it had a secret compartment and glowed in the dark. By the light of this ring, I attempted reading a comic book under my covers when I was supposed to be asleep. The problem was that in order to get the ring to glow, I had to hold it up to the light bulb in my bedside table lamp. Turning on the lamp, of course, was exactly the risk I was trying to avoid. That is, until Brent's ingenious invention.

One afternoon, on the workbench in his basement, Brent showed me how to make a flashlight with parts he supplied, and he let me keep it. Imitating him, I used his mother's bandage adhesive tape to wrap a length of soft soldering wire to the side of a fat battery. I made a little U with the end of the wire that could touch the bottom of the battery and wrapped the other end around the threads of a small bulb positioned at the top of the battery. When the wire contacted the bottom of the battery at the same time the bulb touched the little knob on top, the filaments reddened and glowed. I felt like Thomas Edison.

Although it was a bright afternoon, Brent and I ventured outside to look for unexplored darkness. We crawled under Miss Crane's big front porch with our handmade torches cutting satisfyingly through the dark. Hunched over, we cast lengths of light up to the cobwebby rafters above us and down on the old planks stashed haphazardly on the dirt floor. We scared our black-and-white tomcat, named Peeshu, who bolted out through the lattice at the other end of the porch above. My mother had a funny expression on her face when she told me Peeshu meant "salt and pepper" in Arabic, but I believed her, as I accepted most everything she said. I was startled to learn as an adult that "salt and pepper" is *filfil ou mela*. Was she pulling my leg, or was she trying to make me think that she spoke Arabic?

Brent asked me to spend the night on his screened porch so we could flash our lights around. Even though Mrs. Paul said yes, my mother said no because she did not think it was nice for boys and girls to spend the night together. I wondered what it was that could be wrong and felt oddly guilty that I had begged to go. But I sneaked my homemade flashlight into my bed to read comics under the covers. What *is* light? When the bulb sputtered as the battery finally faltered and died, there was nothing to look at but the zillion little red dots on the inside of my eyelids.

After school in second grade, my mother let me have a birthday party that I thought was a great success, but she said, "Never again!" If there was something my mother hated, she said, it was packs of females. For all the countless times in grade school I was invited to my friends' houses to lunch and to play, my birthday party was the only time I can remember inviting friends inside our house on Brunswick Road.

"Hi, Jim!" I greeted the crossing guard who stopped the traffic for us so that we could get across busy Valley Road to school. Valley Road is a main artery running from Upper Montclair to downtown Montclair.

"OK now, miss." Jim touched his hand to his cap, which had a silver badge on it like a policeman's, although his gentle bearing was more akin to that of a faithful doorman. His uniform was a worn suit jacket over a blue wool cardigan buttoned up to the fat knot in his necktie. He looked to each side to be sure that none of the cars he had halted started up before we children had run or skipped safely to the opposite curb. I was on my way home for lunch.

The day was particularly dazzling, the sky blue and the sun beating down blindingly. I was astonishing myself that I could count to one hundred. Imagine that! *One hundred!* I staggered with the numinous realization of how long it would take to count to one thousand. I was overwhelming myself wondering not only how long but how to count to one million when I stubbed my toe on a slab in the sidewalk that had heaved up. I went sprawling, badly gouging one of my knees. I picked myself up and ran home crying, thin rivulets of blood running gloriously down my leg.

"Why, you must be made in Japan." My mother assuaged my tears with a little joke. In the 1940s, after World War II, items with "Made in Japan" stamped on the bottom had the reputation for being tacky and likely to fall apart. (Who could have anticipated Toyota and Sony?)

My mother had me sit on the lid of the toilet in the upstairs bathroom while she washed my wound with soap and water and got me generally cleaned up. She explained everything as she went—for instance, that the soap would prevent infection. And before she painted the wound with a little glass wand that she had dipped in a bottle of Mercurochrome, she told me to expect the liquid would sting a little, and it did. But not as much as iodine would sting, she said, and furthermore, Mercurochrome did not stain as badly. Too bad we had no iodine, I thought. Then she cut a length of gauze from a roll kept wrapped in blue paper in a blue box with a red cross on the side. Folding the gauze into a square, she anchored it on my knee with two strips of adhesive tape that she cut off a metal spool.

"Your knee is going to feel stiff by the time you go back to school," she predicted.

"Gee, Mom." I was truly impressed with her knowledge and calm capability. "You should have been a nurse."

"I did think about being a nurse one time," she said, not looking at me but at the roll of gauze she was wrapping back up in the paper.

"Did you really? You would have been good. Why didn't you?"

"Oh, I don't know," she answered in a dreamy way. "Bebe Lorene didn't want me to be a nurse. She wanted me to be a teacher. Now go eat your sandwich, or you'll be late for school."

It was strange for me to think of my mother having had a life somewhere before I even existed and of her wanting to be something besides a wife and mother. And there was something about her having wanted to be a nurse and knowing that she'd have been good at it—but not becoming one—that made me sad.

I limped proudly back to school, acting as if my conspicuous bandage was akin to a wounded soldier's emblem for bravery instead of a symbol for falling flat on my face.

My mother treated toothaches with a tiny over-the-counter poultice that she kept with the first-aid supplies in the upstairs linen closet. Saturating one of these poultices with several drops of potent, numbing oil of cloves, she would pack it against my pulsing gum. The strength of the smell was so overwhelming that I forgot about the toothache. If the poultice did not do the trick, however, the last resort was a long trip by bus with my mother to Dr. Cooper's office in Newark. Dr. Cooper had officially retired as a Montclair dentist, but he still practiced dentistry in Newark. I think my father preferred Dr. Cooper's fees, which apparently had retired, too.

There were several things that were good about the trip to Newark. I always enjoyed looking at the people riding the bus and walking around on the sidewalks; each one of them was like a story. Dr. Cooper's office was in a tall building, so we got to ride an elevator up to his floor. Then, because we usually had to wait, I had time to read a couple of funny jokes in *Reader's Digest*.

But there were several things that were not so good about the trip. First, Dr. Cooper was old and hard of hearing, and even to my untrained eyes, his bulky equipment looked primitive. But he was cheerful and friendly, and before he started drilling, he would say, "Now you just let me know if this hurts."

There was nothing subtle about his drill, which ground into our teeth like the jackhammers used for breaking up cement in the street.

"Mm-aa-rr-gg!"

"What's that?"

"Mm-aa-rr-gg!"

"Just a minute." Dr. Cooper turned off his drill. "What did you say?"

"You said to let you know if it hurt."

"What's that? I can't hear you."

"YOU SAID TO LET YOU KNOW IF IT HURT."

"Oh. Right. It's sensitive, aye? Well, it won't be long now; we're almost finished."

Several times, after shooting Novocain into my gums with a giant hypodermic needle, Dr. Cooper simply gripped his wrench and uprooted a big molar as if it were a tree.

I developed a mental technique for making my situation bearable. As Dr. Cooper drilled away, I would intensely picture a soldier all shot up but still alive, lying in a trench with his bloody, twisted leg dangling by a tendon. Having my tooth repaired by Dr. Cooper then seemed like a luxury. I didn't learn until I was an adult that this technique did not serve me well when the pain was psychological, that is, not allowing myself to suffer my own pain because it was not as bad as the Holocaust.

One time, my father drove me to Newark to see Dr. Cooper because on the way home we were going to shop. Nanny had sent me money for my birthday, and I needed a new bathrobe. But leaving Newark, my father did not deviate from the route he had taken coming in—that is, he did not take me to a nice department store. He said only to call out when I saw a dress shop along the way. I announced the first one I spotted. He pulled up to the curb and sat at the wheel with the engine running while I ran in. The little store did not carry robes, and I jumped back in the car. The second shop I spotted did, and I had to move fast.

"*Yella, yella!* Hurry up! Let's go!"

That's how it was with my father. What I chose off the rack would be, not the best robe, but the least worst one: it was quilted, floor-length, and blue, with tawdry flowers all over it as big as fists. And we bought it a size too big, so that I would grow into it. It wore out, however, before I got any bigger.

In America the transfer from the Syrian Catholic Church to the Roman Catholic Church made sense for our family. My parents tried to go to the Immaculate Conception Church, a large Roman Catholic edifice in downtown Montclair, but in pre–Vatican II times, the liturgy was still in Latin and unfamiliar to both my parents. The liturgy in my father's church in Basra was in ancient Syriac. Also, in the cavernous sanctuary of Immaculate Conception, the heads of the women were often cloaked in black mantillas, and worship seemed a more private than communal affair. My mother had grown up on Southern hospitality. When we were the new family in town, she observed, no one at the Catholic church had even said, "Boo."

So my mother tried the Baptist church in Montclair. After the service, as she was putting her coat on in the vestibule, a parishioner bade her good morning and asked what church she was from. When my mother answered, "The First Baptist Church in Neosho, Missouri," the woman replied, "Oh, we are not *that kind* of Baptist!" That was enough for my mother.

My father's colleague from work who had recommended Montclair for its excellent public schools invited my parents to the Montclair Heights Dutch Reformed Church, which he attended. He thought my father would be interested to hear the guest speaker, a visiting missionary from Iraq, who, with his wife, was back in the States on furlough. My father accepted his invitation on behalf of our family. The missionary turned out to be George Gosselink, my father's English teacher at the School of High Hope in Basra! The friendly congregation went all out to make my parents feel welcome. This is how it came about that even though I was christened Catholic, I was raised Protestant.

Now the Reverend and Mrs. Schenck of the Montclair Heights Dutch Reformed Church were having our family to dinner. The Schencks had no angles or lines but were, rather, composed of a series of circles: round heads, round cheeks, round chins, round breasts for Mrs. Schenck, and a round stomach for Mr. Schenck; and both had arms that could warmly encircle. They had been missionaries themselves in Japan, they told us, and had a glass cabinet full of Japanese souvenirs—little carved fat-figured men and chopsticks and fans. The dinner they invited us to in the manse was served on delicate blue-and-white Japanese dinnerware, but all I remember about the meal was a clear Japanese soup, served in the shallow blue-and-white bowls. The flavor, I thought, came from either the design in the bottom of the bowl or the inside of the cabinet in which the dishes had been stacked. My parents expressed their admiration of the porcelain, cocking their heads with interest, which I could not understand. I think they did not want to hurt the Schencks' feelings that their dishes had obviously been made in Japan. I was proud when Mrs. Schenck asked me to help clear the table. As I carried the plates through the swinging dining-room door to their kitchen, I think the skin under my mother's fingernails went white.

Mrs. Schenck introduced me around the Sunday school using my given name, Suzette, which I hated and which no one called me, not even my parents when they were mad. "Suzette," she said, introducing me, "is from Eye-rack." I was received with polite smiles pasted beneath eyebrows arched with mild curiosity. None of the children I met at the church went to my school, Edgemont.

In Sunday school, time passed so slowly that our bodies ceased to age as we fidgeted in rows of squeaky wooden folding chairs. All the grades met together in a downstairs assembly room for devotions and an offering. Then we dispersed in a noisy stampede, folding and dragging our chairs over the wooden floor to our various classrooms, spaces that were partitioned off along the sides of the room and upstairs around the balcony. We colored pictures. Some of the boys threw spitballs. Most of us giggled ... hour after hour after hour. I don't remember learning a shred of Scripture. Even my mother remarked, "These people don't know their Bible stories."

Years later my mother took on the job of teaching the fifth-grade Sunday school class and eventually became superintendent of Sunday school. She took the preparation of her class seriously and was creative in the kind of craft activity she planned to complement her lesson, which was always based on a Bible story. She was the kind of no-nonsense teacher I would have liked to have had.

One spring Sunday, it was so delicious outside that even our teacher could not stand being in Sunday school any longer. Instead of holding class, she took us for a walk in the big cemetery adjacent to the church. It was the first time I had been in a cemetery.

As the others in my class did upon being sprung, I ran up and down the grassy aisles. But stopping to read a tombstone here and a tombstone there, I soon sobered up as I calculated the ages of the deceased and wondered about their lives and how they had died. I was shocked to see there were even graves that belonged to children my age.

Indeed, the big cemetery was nothing but a field of dead bodies! How could this be, with the buds obliviously bursting and the birds obliviously chirping? Years later, I thought of our outing when I read Edna St. Vincent Millay, who wrote that as long as "under ground … the brains of men [are] eaten by maggots," it was not enough to her "that yearly … April / Comes like an idiot, babbling and strewing flowers."

One evening the church sponsored two films for families. The first was a Disney nature movie full of birds nesting, buds blooming, and butterflies emerging from cocoons. Seeing nature through the perspective of time-lapse photography did not make me want to go to church, but it did inspire my sense of wonder.

The second movie was Cecil B. DeMille's silent film *The King of Kings*. Even without sound, the story of Jesus engaged my interest. What was it about him? What longing did he awaken? What hope? Nobody in church seemed to take Jesus as seriously as the people in the movie did.

I always woke up before the rest of the family. On weekend mornings I had to stay quiet in my room until my parents started moving around. To occupy myself I would peer into the world of my marble that I kept in the drawer of my bedside table. It was my favorite marble because it was not opaque, but made of clear glass and peppered with constellations of tiny bubbles through which swirled a milky cloud suspended like a distant galaxy. I wished I could enter it, travel around inside it, and meet its people. I suffered from a kind of cosmic homesickness, longing for the world where I really belonged.

⁓

I was in the second grade when the steady stream of Iraqi immigrants began to flow through our house on Brunswick Road. We had plenty of room. In February 1946, Uncle Kamil and Auntie May were the first of the family to arrive. They stayed in our guest room on the second floor for two or three months while Uncle Kamil looked first for a job and then for a place to live. As if they were still on honeymoon—for they had been married less than two months—Uncle Kamil would sometimes take Auntie May out for dinner in the city after job hunting in New York.

With the high cheekbones and penciled arched eyebrows of Claudette Colbert, the American movie star my Iraqi aunt was often told she resembled, Auntie May was habitually cheerful and laughing—or "lahf-ing," as she would say in her British accent, tossing her wavy auburn hair. A cigarette often dangling from her full, lipsticked mouth, Auntie May always had a good joke to tell, but when my parents would raise their eyebrows and cock their heads toward us children, she would switch to Arabic. It wasn't until I was a teenager that I was privy to her humor, as in this old Iraqi folktale I heard her tell in English:

"Hassan ibn Hussein was stuffing himself at a feast in his village when the unthinkable happened: he 'noised the Noise [forbidden flatulence] … which none can make without lasting disgrace.' Hassan ibn Hussein was so ashamed he immediately returned to his home, bundled up his possessions, slung his bundle over his horse, and rode off.

"As the years passed, Hassan ibn Hussein became increasingly homesick. After fifteen years had gone by, he thought his act would be forgotten and he could safely return to his village. As he approached its outskirts, his horse was thirsty; and he stopped at a stream, dismounting to let his horse drink. He overheard a youth talking with a woman who was bent over the stream washing her clothes.

"'Mama, the men in the village were asking me today how old I am.'

"'Let's see.' The woman stood up. 'You were born the year Hassan ibn Hussein noised the Noise.'"

"Upon hearing this, Hassan ibn Hussein immediately mounted his horse and once more galloped away."

Auntie May was the kind of woman who knew arcane cosmetic tips—the Turkish method of hair removal, for instance, reputedly originating with Turkish royalty and similar in principle to waxing. Sugar is cooked with a few drops of lemon oil to the consistency of thick syrup and, after it is cool enough to handle, smeared over the body area from which you wish to remove hair. Then you peel the sugar paste off and bathe.

Auntie May swore that if you use this depilatory long enough, the hair gradually stops coming in at all, and the skin stays smooth. She said she had always heard that the Muslims and Jews used this method *everywhere* in preparation for their wedding night.

During the time Auntie May and Uncle Kamil stayed with us, my mother did all the cooking and cleaning. I think she felt underappreciated preparing meals for people who loved Iraqi food and had had cooks to prepare it. Foods that had been rationed during the war, such as meat, canned fish, butter, cheese, and sugar, were becoming more available, although sugar was still rationed. Frank and I were fed at the built-in breakfast nook in the kitchen and put to bed before the adults ate together in the dining room. Even though I was two years older than Frank, we were both tucked in at seven o'clock. I got an extra half hour on Saturday nights so that, for Sunday school the next morning, my mother could roll up my hair in leather-covered wire curlers, a process I hated. Since I had curly hair to begin with, rolling it up only made me look as if I'd stuck my finger in an electrical socket. At least during the preparation time my mother would snap on the radio, and I got to listen to *The Lone Ranger*. If I had known any state secrets when my mother combed out the frizz, I would have blurted them out.

"Ouch!"

"Sit *still!*"

During dinner, while Frank and I sat across from each other in the kitchen, we would swing our legs under the table, sometimes kicking each other over whose turn it was to get the solitary cherry in the canned fruit cocktail. Or with our cheeks working like washing machines, we agitated red Jell-O in our mouths until it turned liquid and then squirted it between our teeth, an activity that made us laugh uproariously. But on the nights my mother served us creamed peas made with canned Pet milk, which Frank gobbled up, he bounded away from the table long before I did.

I would not be excused until I had cleaned my plate. While I sat there gagging on my peas, my mother sometimes stood at the sink to wash the dishes, or she would go into the living room and curl up in an armchair to read, waiting for me to finish. As I struggled to fend off the peristalsis that rippled threateningly into reverse in my throat, the great plain of linoleum from the breakfast nook and across the kitchen to the hall door and finally into the living room seemed a vast, desolate landscape and I, a mere particle in it. Hiding as many peas as I credibly could under the rim of my plate, with my fork I would spread out the cream sauce, trying to disguise its unchanged volume.

"I'm finished," I would call out.

My mother inspected my plate, exasperated by my finickiness. Casting a disdainful eye on the lack of sufficient flesh on my nervous frame, she sighed as if personally affronted.

"What are you going to do with someone who counts the peas on her plate?" she asked the air.

After I fled from the kitchen, at least she did not call me back to make a thing of the ring of peas on the table she discovered when she lifted my plate.

While the dictionary says *gag* means "to cause to retch," it also means "to prevent from free speech" and "to be unable to endure something." The theory that behavior is a language that can be decoded is borne out in my early fascination with quips and jokes and cartoons—which are also, of course, called gags. My first original public gag came straight from my mouth one morning in fifth grade, as I was standing around in a cluster of my classmates in the bike shed waiting for the school bell to ring. I was fiddling with a tiny blue plaid doll coat I had asked my mother to make for a plastic doll that stood only two and a half inches high. I believed my mother could sew anything. The coat had a snap at the neck and perfect little sleeves and for some reason had wound up in my pocket. I turned around for a minute and, without anyone seeing me, wadded up the little coat and stuffed it in my mouth. When I turned around again, I waited for just the right moment to spit the wad out into my palm. "Blaaah."

"Ew! What's that?"

"I must be sick!" I wobbled as I conspicuously unfolded the little garment and held it up for all to see. "I have a coat on my tongue!"

I'm not sure my peers got it.

One day Uncle Kamil read in the paper that the newly organized United Nations was opening a New York office at Hunter College. After going into the city for an interview, he was hired as a finance officer in the Office of the Comptroller and became the first Arab hired by the UN Secretariat. So began my uncle's twenty-four years with the UN, where eventually he became chief of the Commercial Management Service. He was in charge of all the UN's moneymaking operations, such as the Delegates' Dining Room and the United Nations store, as well as the United Nations stamps and postal services. He would always send my father the first-day issue of UN stamps, which my father and Frank collected.

After Uncle Kamil and Auntie May left our home for their new house in Bellerose, Queens, my mother was pretty mad when she discovered that Auntie May had helped herself to her precious supply of sugar to take the hair off her legs.

⁓

I was moved into our guest room so that when my father's sister, Auntie Jeanette, the baby of the family, and Uncle Bob arrived, they could stay in my room and have the extra space of the adjacent sun porch for my baby cousin. Their stay with us did not seem long. One evening I was about to go into my old room to watch Auntie Jeanette feed her baby, who was sucking away at her breast. My mother happened to pass by in the upstairs hall. Horrified, she yanked me by the arm back out the door.

"But why?" Auntie Jeanette, who seemed genuinely puzzled, asked my mother. "It's only natural."

"She is only a *child!*" my mother insisted, sealing in my mind that breasts had less to do with nurture and more to do with something vaguely forbidden. I had been summarily shut out, too, the afternoon I had gone upstairs to look for something to do. As I was about to wander into my parents' bedroom, my father suddenly loomed in the doorframe like a satyr, nude and eye-poppingly erect. "We're busy! Go downstairs!" The words seemed to hang in the air as I stared in fearful confusion at the slammed door.

⁓

That fall, Bebe and Jiddu, who at sixty-six had retired, arrived in a Trans World Airlines airplane at La Guardia Field (which became La Guardia Airport the following year). My father had made the third floor of our house into a studio apartment for them, complete with bathroom and kitchenette

One Saturday, my father and mother and Frank and I squeezed into the Studebaker with Bebe and Jiddu to make an off-season trip to Atlantic City on the Jersey shore. There we all tromped through several eerily vacant boardinghouses and small hotels for sale, which Jiddu considered buying. But my father, and later Uncle Kamil, who referred to their father as "the old man," talked him out of it.

At least we got to walk the deserted boardwalk, watch the waves crash, and buy a box of saltwater taffy before the long ride home.

Uncle Kamil and my father would dissuade Jiddu, too, from investing in properties that had caught his eye in Montclair and even in New York. What did the old man know about the New World? He did not even speak English. Never mind that he did not speak English in Iraq, either, when he did business with the British and Americans. America was his sons' territory now. But there was not a property Jiddu picked out that did not later appreciate.

I do not remember much else about Bebe and Jiddu's stay with us—my mother told me not to bother them—but I did make a few forays to the third floor for a fistful of fistiq, the pistachios I craved from my early years in Basra, which they miraculously kept on hand in America, too. Where did Bebe and Jiddu manage to get them? We never had any. I don't know when and how they shopped, but probably my father drove Jiddu.

"*Ta-ali*, Suzy," Bebe beckoned me to come.

I crossed their living room area dutifully to kiss her.

"Hi, Bebe." I did not know what else to say. By then, I no longer spoke Arabic and had grown as stiff as my mother had predicted. My mother also reminded me that I didn't like to be touched. My Iraqi grandmother, so simple in her generous affection, and I were awkwardly estranged. Even though we could no longer communicate in words, Bebe never abandoned her love for me. When she looked at me, she would always smile and say, "Hi, Suzy, *shamatuq*," and rock her head from side to side, indicating, I felt, some inner dance of approval.

Jiddu bought a two-family house in Jamaica, Queens, not far from where their eldest son, Uncle Kamil, and Auntie May lived. Bebe and Jiddu lived in the downstairs half of the house, and for a while Uncle Joe and Auntie Eileen lived in the upstairs half, during a period when they were both in splendid uniform for the US Army. I wanted to be a WAC like Auntie Aileen.

After Uncle Kamil and Auntie May had settled in Bellerose and Bebe and Jiddu in Jamaica, our family began our frequent treks from Montclair to one or the other location for Sunday dinner; we were less frequently the hosts. One Sunday, however, rather than convene around somebody's dining room table, the whole family met in New York City's Central Park Zoo: Bebe and Jiddu; Uncle Kamil and Auntie May, who still seemed to be extending their happy honeymoon; my parents; and Frank and me. I liked the monkeys the best, but even they did not make me glad enough to hop, skip, and jump the way I noticed other children unselfconsciously doing. I found it impossible to lose myself in play with my parents around. Also, I felt sorry for the animals. The buildings they lived in were so smelly I wondered how they could stand living in them. It did not seem right to me that we were on the outside staring at them as if they were inferior while they paced around in prison. I wasn't able to articulate how I felt then, but the zoo made me sad, for I felt something was wrong.

We found the refreshment terrace at Central Park, pulled two tables together, and arranged ourselves on the wire café chairs while my father and Uncle Kamil went inside to buy coffee, tea, and Cokes for everybody. After my father and Uncle Kamil returned, distributed the cups, and sat down themselves, their babbling Arabic sounded as if it were being broadcast over a ball field. How could they all be acting so *foreign*? Perhaps I hadn't noticed it before when, as we moved from cage to cage, we were so spread out.

But now that we were all concentrated together, I wanted to disappear. Many years later, when I worked in the city myself, I discovered that of all places in America, every language in the world seems to be spoken in New York.

That summer, I played with my red-haired, freckled-faced friend Betty on the days she came from a neighboring town to visit her grandmother, Mrs. Lopez, who lived on the corner of our street. Mrs. Lopez was a grandmother from central casting, with a white apron tied around her wide waist and her white hair pulled back in a bun. She was kind and gave us the run of her neat and clean house. She even let Betty crank up her deluxe windup Victrola by herself to play old recordings of Enrico Caruso arias. There were black-and-white photographs of Betty's relatives everywhere, but a portrait of her uncle upstairs was particularly memorable. It hung on the wall that faced the bed on which one afternoon we decided to play hospital, an activity for which we took turns removing our underpants and lying on top of the bedspread while the nurse inspected between the patient's spread legs with her finger, back and forth in the moist cleft, a feeling of too-much-ness.

"Did you see that?" I said, getting up from the bed and fixing my clothes.

"What?"

"It looked like your uncle's eyes moved. See? Wherever we go, he seems to be watching." We walked slowly one way and then the other in front of the photograph and agreed that his eyes seemed to follow us. Years later I thought of that photograph when I realized how our superegos, the rules that our parents and society make for us, keep eyes on our every move.

The next time Betty visited her grandmother, she walked down the sidewalk to our house, where I was sitting on our front steps petting our sun-sleepy cat, Peeshu. "I can't play hospital any more," she said immediately—not that I wanted to anyway. Her priest, she said, had told her never to play it again.

"Your priest!" I was incredulous that Betty had told anyone, but nothing else was said about it. Handing me an old tennis racket that had belonged to her uncle and carrying one of her own, Betty and I walked over to one of the A.C.'s dirt courts, which seemed abandoned, and attempted to volley an old, bald tennis ball. Mostly we chased "mountain balls," that is, balls whose trajectories described mountains.

On another visit to her grandmother's, Mrs. Lopez allowed Betty to invite me for dinner and to spend the night.

"You're not going to like spending the night at somebody else's house," my mother said confidently. Why did she say this? Was she trying to prevent me from liking somebody else's house better than my own? But she consented.

As a special treat, Betty's grandmother made us each a baked apple for dessert. I had never tasted one before. I could tell my friend and her grandmother were disappointed that I was not as excited as they were to eat the hot, collapsed apple. I had trouble swallowing the first mouthful.

"What's the matter, dear?" Mrs. Lopez asked me. "Don't you like it?

"Thank you, but I'm full."

"Well, now, don't you worry. You don't have to eat it."

We played with paper dolls before we went to sleep, but my heart wasn't in it.

Playing hospital was not on my mind. I was bored and homesick.

"I knew you weren't going to like spending the night at somebody else's house," said my mother when I told her about the dessert.

⁓

Jimmy lived next door and was big for his age, which was the same as mine—seven. One afternoon he and I agreed to meet in his basement for mutual viewings. He sat on a little stool by the workbench, while I stood. "You go first," he said.

"No, you."

Jimmy obligingly reached into his fly and pulled out his penis. It did not look at all like Frank's. First, it was erect, and second, it was the first American penis I had seen. I did not know then about circumcision. "Go ahead, touch it." The skin at the tip of his penis was surprisingly silky.

"It's your turn. I showed you mine. Now let me see yours." I was wearing a dress.

When I took down my underpants, he roughly touched my vulva.

"I have to go home now," I said, pulling up my pants and turning for the stairs.

The next day my mother called me into our kitchen. Her eyes were slits, and her jaw was jutting, and she was trembling with rage.

"Is it true what Mrs. Tracy told me about you and Jimmy?" Jimmy's family lived with Mrs. Tracy, his grandmother.

"What do you mean?"

"Did you play dirty with Jimmy in his basement? Yes or no?" How Mrs. Tracy found out and what her intentions were in telling my mother I'll never know.

"Well, yes," I said, but before I could add anything, my mother grabbed me by my arm and hit me as hard as she could with her open hand on my backside.

"Don't you *ever, ever* play dirty like that again, do you hear? Nice girls don't do that!"

"I'm sorry! I promise I won't! I'll be good!"

After I stopped crying and my shudders finally subsided, I asked if I could go to the playground at school by myself for the first time. Punished, I felt strangely renewed: my slate had been wiped clean. What would my mother do if she learned about Betty? I was not about to tell, but my guilt and the fear of her finding out were burdensome, until time finally suppressed them.

Confident that I, a wild horse, had been broken, my mother said yes, I could go to the playground. Once out the door, when I twisted around to look at myself where it hurt, I could see the outline of her whole hand raised in a welt on the back of my thigh. I wasn't worried that anybody else would spot it, though, because school was closed and the playground was deserted. At the top of the jungle gym, I hooked the inside of my knees over the bar and hung upside down. I think I just needed to be by myself. After that afternoon I slipped into the respite of latency, a period when sexuality seems to go dormant. Without much more maternal spanking, when I surfaced a few years later, it was usually my father who went out of control.

―

Before setting off for a Sunday dinner with Bebe and Jiddu in Jamaica, Queens, my father stopped at the Gulf station on Valley Road in Montclair. (I didn't understand why a gas station was named after a sport.) While a friendly older man my father seemed to know filled the Studebaker up with gas and washed the windshield, my father took out a pencil and a little spiral notebook he kept in the glove compartment and jotted down some things. I asked him what he was doing, and he explained that he was recording the mileage and gallons so he could figure out how many miles to the gallon the car was averaging. I did not understand him, but I thought he was a genius.

As the man opened the hood and pulled out a stick that showed if there was enough oil in the engine, my father told us the man owned the gas station. The man then checked all the tires to see if there was enough air in them. He took the money into the gas station that my father had handed him out the window, and when he came back with my father's change, he reached into the back seat to give Frank and me each a lollipop. As we pulled away, I was touched when my father said the man and his wife loved children but didn't have any of their own.

After we got on the road, my father flicked on his car radio for some music, alternately keeping time to it by clicking his diamond ring against the steering wheel and loudly snapping his fingers to the rhythm. For some reason this embarrassed me.

I remember, after a Maxwell House coffee advertisement came on between songs, cracking an early original joke.

The slogan in the advertisement was "Maxwell House coffee is good to the last drop."

"Yes," I piped up, "but *that* drop is awful."

Both my parents laughed. It was a satisfying moment. But it was not too long before Frank and I were having skirmishes on the border of the imaginary line that divided up the back seat into my side and his side.

"Don't start." My mother gave us the profiled eye. Perhaps Picasso's mother resembled mine.

Frank and I might go for a couple of rounds of Who Can Hold Your Breath the Longest? or Bet I Can Make You Blink, risky activities because of the possibility of inadvertent body contact.

After another five or ten minutes, I might discover that Frank had indeed edged his way onto my side of the car, and I might give his leg a little shove back into his own territory, and he might move my hand back into my territory with his shoe.

You never knew when—*wham!*—my father's hand would cantilever out to strike whomever he could reach.

"Bûma! Kuzzer-kut!"

The prized seating location was directly behind the driver, who, of course, was always my father, because he could not reach directly behind him without first stopping the car and losing time. That was where I always tried to sit, out of harm's way—at least in the car.

As my mother was getting dinner ready, she would turn on the radio to listen to Martin Block's *Make Believe Ballroom*, often singing along with the popular tunes the program broadcast. She had a pretty voice, but she would clown around, too. When it was close to Christmas, my mother would teasingly wag her index finger at Frank and me to be good as she danced around singing "Santa Claus is Coming to Town." I clearly understood Santa as the gift-giver who was all eyes and kept track of everything.

One day I was happily walking on Edgemont Road on my way home from second grade for lunch. An older boy, a fourth grader, was idly riding his bike in circles on the street near me, dragging one of his shoes as a pivot. He pulled up to the curb alongside me.

"I bet you still think there's a Santa Claus, don't you?" he taunted. "Only babies believe in Santa Claus."

Here is an ignorant person, I thought. "That's not true," I asserted. "I heard him myself on the roof."

"That's your parents," he scoffed, walking his bicycle now with one foot still on the pedal, the other giving little pushes off the curb.

"Oh, yeah?" I stopped, and he stopped. "I have *proof!*"

"Yeah, what?"

"A footprint in the fireplace."

"That's your father," he sneered.

"It was much bigger than my father's shoe!" And not knowing what else to do, I socked him, proving right the psychologist Haim

Ginott's assertion that spanking children only teaches that when you are angry, hit!

Losing his balance, the boy fell with his bicycle on top of him. Before he could get himself untangled, Jim, the traffic guard, was already helping me back across Valley Road toward home.

Not too many days later, I was out in our garage hunting around for something I could use to make a fort. I had started building one with some tree branches that my father had stacked up behind the grape arbor. I happened to glance up. There, stored across the rafters, was a brand-new sled, the new sled I had fervently hoped Santa Claus would deliver. Like radio's soap opera Helen Trent, I was "dashed against the rocks of despair." You mean no one keeps his eye on you while you're asleep or running around? No one was watching? No one, as C. S. Lewis put it, "marked" me? I felt stripped of both notice and protection.

How embarrassing to have been fool enough to put out cookies and milk! That I could be so easily tricked, that I could so wholeheartedly throw myself into believing something that was not true, made an irrevocable impression on me. Conflating Santa Claus with God, I slid into disbelief on a Champion sled. Looking back, maybe it was not such a bad step to eliminate God as the Santa Claus who gives you what you want if you're good.

But at the time as a child, I could not go back to believing. I would try to be a good sport and not spoil things for Frank, but how I envied my brother's ignorance! I made the mistake, however, of fixating on the ignorance part of innocence, so that instead of aspiring to be as guileless as a child, I would spend many years wandering around wishing I was not smart. Thinking too much made me a freak. If only I were as simple as the peasant kneeling to light the votive candle. Finding out there was no Santa Claus, I felt cheated out of the profoundly good feeling that life had purpose.

"Americans have trouble with my name," my father explained after he decided to change Nejib, which in Arabic means "noble," to Neal, which he believed was equivalent in meaning. He kept his middle initial, N, which stood for his father's name, Naoum. I don't think my father experienced prejudice at work; at least I never heard him say anything about being discriminated against. In America, like me, I think he wanted to blend in.

I'm not sure Uncle Kamil could see the point of his brother Nejib becoming Neal.

In the culture of the United Nations, everyone was proud to be from his or her original country.

My father's name change did not make a difference in our household, because my parents never called each other by their names anyway, except when referring to each other to a third party. At home they both addressed each other as "Honey."

"How did you and Daddy meet?" I asked my mother one day. My mother was pregnant and busy in the kitchen, and I was just hanging around. I had noticed that our family was not like most of the families of the children my age in my neighborhood and school. My mother was a lot younger than the mothers of my friends, and my father was an Arab.

"At a tea," my mother answered with a dreamy, glazed-over-eyes look. "The ladies in Neosho had a tea for the visiting foreigners, and we met at the tea." She smiled an ironic little smile, as inscrutable as the Sphinx.

"Why didn't you live in Neosho?"

"Oh, Daddy had to get back. He had a good job in Basra, so we eloped."

"What's 'elope'?"

"That's when you secretly get married."

"How come it was secret? Didn't you have a wedding?"

"Oh, sure. A justice of the peace married us here, but we got married in a church when we got to Damascus. Someday I'll write a book: *East Meets West*. It was love at first sight. We were in all the papers."

My mother told me that she and my father had attended a birthday party in Basra for the queen of England, but when I asked my mother if she had met the Queen, she said no. I did not understand why the Queen had not come to her own party. Were my parents famous? Should I be proud? Was my mother telling me the truth?

She dismissed me. "I'll tell you about it someday when you're older."

That is exactly the same thing she said when I stood in front of the full-length mirror on the closet door between the front hall and the kitchen. I was standing sideways, studying my profile, as I stuck out my stomach to imitate my mother's stomach, which was then protruding with the production of my soon-to-be-brother Neal, named after my father.

"Where do babies come from?" I called to my mother in the kitchen.

"I'll tell you when you're older."

That July, when I was still seven, my mother took Frank and me to Neosho to be there for her delivery date. There she would have her mother, Bebe Lorene, and her grandmother, Nanny, to take care of her and us. For the same reason, when I was eleven, my sister, Tootie, also sprang to life in Neosho.

We left for Neosho in July because it was the latest month in her pregnancy that the doctor thought would be safe for my mother to make the trip. We did not return to Montclair until the end of October, after my mother had recovered and the baby was old enough to travel. Four months was a long time for my father to be without his wife, but I did not think about that. Nor did it occur to me that my mother was without her husband. I was happy as a clam.

Our trips to Neosho began with the hurried ride to Newark's Pennsylvania Station in my father's Studebaker, which he would usually park in a taxi loading zone. My father walked so fast to the station that we could only string out behind him, running along in single file as we tried to keep up. Then we would bunch together again while he checked our luggage with a Red Cap, string out behind him again as he speed walked to the ticket booth, and bunch together there until he set out for the track. We had another race behind him on the platform alongside our train as he leaned over, on the run, peering into the windows to survey them for good seats. We rode coach. When he spotted two double seats in a row, we followed him onto the train. Then he heaved my mother's small suitcase up onto the overhead rack and switched the backs on the forward seats over, so that the four seats cozily faced one another. Frank and I could each have a window across from each other, and my mother could put her feet up on the empty seat, because her ankles swelled. I wanted to ride backward. My mother joked my preference was because I liked to see where I'd been. Then my father looked at his watch.

We each kissed him goodbye. "'Bye, Daddy."

"Be a good girl. Be a good boy. Take care of Mommy."

Then he kissed his pregnant wife goodbye. "Take care of yourself."

My father walked up the aisle and back out onto the platform, conferring briefly with the conductor. When he leaned over, smiling, to wave at us through the window, we blew him kisses. He straightened up and looked at his watch again, for our train was scheduled to leave Newark at 5:45 p.m.

"All 'board!" the conductor shouted, looking at his big pocket watch as he leaned out of the train and signaled somebody with a wave. *Clang, clang!* The Pennsylvania Railroad's no. 31, the *Spirit of St. Louis*, lurched to a start and slowly began to roll. My father, walking along beside the train, bent over to wave at us again through the window. I wasn't sad until the train began to go too fast for him to keep up, and he stopped walking and straightened up for the last time, getting smaller as we left him all alone on the platform.

As we rolled alongside another train, it felt like everything outside was moving while we on the train stood still; but soon, we gradually picked up speed, and I felt we were really on our way the almost one thousand miles to St. Louis. We were not scheduled to arrive until the next afternoon; there we had to change trains to Neosho.

On the floor between the seats Frank and I had a little suitcase in which my mother had packed coloring books, pads of paper, pencils and crayons, connect-the-dots and activity books, and some cars and trucks for Frank. We really needed these things more for the long stretch the next morning. There was enough happening on the train itself that night to occupy us.

We went walking through many cars to the dining car for supper. That first trip I remember having to wait between cars in a long line to get seated. With the combination of the jostling movements and the fumes, I was nauseated, and, as my mother called it, I "urped." There was my vomit on the train floor, looking and smelling embarrassingly disgusting. I cried. But I cried when I threw up at home, too, partly in fear of reprisal.

And as the philosopher Ernest Becker might observe, there, too, was the shame of my mortality for everyone to see.

A man came through our car selling sandwiches, and my mother decided that we'd better eat supper in our seats. Frank and I got up and down to go to the toilet and drink water from cone-shaped paper cups out of a dispenser. When it started getting dark, a porter came by, and my mother rented a pillow from him for each of us, so that we would not have to put our faces on the train seat upholstery. When all the lights in our car were turned on for the evening, it was hard to see out the window because of the reflection. When the lights were finally turned off for the night, except for the private pools of light in which some people were reading, you could see out if you got close enough to the glass. Frank went to sleep. My mother went to sleep. But even with the soporific, rhythmic rocking, I was burdensomely alert, and it was a long time before I gave in to sleep. There was something lonesome about passing so many houses, some with lights off, a few on. Were the people inside sleeping? Was someone sitting at the kitchen table? Who were all the people? What was that man thinking, the man who had his chair tipped against the wall of that little gas station? Had anybody else noticed that neon sign flashing "Diner" on and off? Harrisburg, the sign said at the station. Pittsburgh. I realized I must have been sleeping when the train jerked to a stop in Columbus, Ohio, to change locomotives. And there, too, were men on the tracks in overalls, carrying lanterns, calling to each other in the middle of the night, laughing; there were conductors on the platform, chatting—all this life going on without its knowledge of me.

After a bright morning of monotonous cornfields and farmhouses and telephone poles flicking by, it was interesting to approach St. Louis. The conductor came through our car to tell us to change our watches. We had entered Central Standard Time, and my mother turned the hands on her wristwatch back an hour. This seemed mysteriously important to me. How could there be a different time?

Observing one house after another out the window, I wondered why one had cheerful red geraniums on the windowsill and another, broken chairs and car parts all over the yard. I imagined myself living in the different houses and wondered at what point a rusty box spring in the yard would make you give up. Our train crossed the big bridge over the Mississippi River, and I saw along its edge little shanties. (Another year, when we crossed after terrible flooding, the shanties were gone. What had happened to the people who lived in them?) St. Louis was a railroad hub for long freight trains, and freight and passenger cars were parked on sidings everywhere. Frank spotted a roundhouse. It was exciting to be arriving.

In the big St. Louis Union Station, in the six hours from 1 p.m. to 7 p.m., we had to wait for our train to Neosho. We made at least two round trips up and down the long flight of marble stairs to the big, clean, white-tiled ladies' room on the second floor, where giant fans hummed on stands; their whirring sounded cooler than the hot air they moved around felt. Here we went to the toilet, and my mother gave us a once-over with the washrag she had brought for the job in a waterproof oilcloth envelope that snapped closed. Then she combed our hair. Sprucing up would become a lengthier project when we traveled with a baby whose diaper needed changing and formula needed warming.

Then the kind ladies' room attendant, a Negro woman in a white uniform, would help my mother stand the bottle in hot water. But while Negroes worked in the upstairs ladies' room, they were not allowed to use it—on this first trip I spotted a sign that said so, although I didn't know why. My mother taught me the proper way to refer to people whose skin was black was "Negro." She said it was rude to call a Negro "black," as if it would hurt his feelings. But *The Story of Little Black Sambo* was OK because it was just a story. Apparently, referring to Negroes as "colored," as they did in Missouri, was permissible, for the word was softer, in the same way it was softer to say someone had "passed away" rather than "died." My mother explained that it was all right to say in Neosho, "Eeny, meeny, miny, moe /Catch a nigger by the toe," but people in Montclair did not think it was nice to say "nigger," so in New Jersey I should be careful to substitute "tiger."

After my mother checked our bags in a locker, we had our big meal of the day in the Harvey Restaurant on the main floor. Instead of regular milk, I always asked for buttermilk, which I loved. I thought Missouri was the only place that had buttermilk; we never had it in New Jersey. It seemed a heady freedom to have my mother reaching into her purse to pay the bill, for my father usually handled all the money. My mother let Frank and me each buy a comic book and Life Savers or gum, whichever we chose, at the newsstand.

Stiff with sitting, we walked around Union Station, and I looked up at the big stained-glass window of three women, symbolic, I later learned, of the cities of New York, St. Louis, and San Francisco. My mother found a booth where she could write a telegram to my father to tell him we had arrived in St. Louis safely, while Frank and I, in our leather-soled shoes, tried to see how far a running start would allow us to slide across the marble floor standing up. But when we began getting rambunctious, my mother had only to give us the slitted eye and jutted jaw: "Don't start." I remember peering out the entrance of the station at the buildings and wondering what the city was like, but we never even saw what the station looked like from the outside. Mostly, we sat on the long wooden benches in the waiting room, worn smooth by a million rear ends.

We ate sandwiches on the Frisco line as we set off at 7 p.m. from St. Louis for the three-hundred-mile journey to Neosho. Our weariness had subdued us, but still, when it came time to sleep, I preferred looking out the window. A distant light flicked by, but you could not tell if it was sitting on a pole or had a house around it. The light from tiny farmhouse windows cast little patches of inside onto stubbly moonlit expanses. I was asleep on my rented pillow longer than I realized, for I was startled when the conductor came through our darkened car and, bending close to my mother, said: "We'll be pulling into Neosho soon. I thought you'd want to know."

"Thank you." My mother had to wake up Frank. "We're almost in Neosho."

We were bleary-eyed while my mother ran a comb through our hair, but by the time she had taken out her compact and powdered her nose, put on lipstick, and combed her own hair, we were wide-eyed with excitement. Most of the passengers in the darkened car were still asleep. Because it was the time for dreaming—two o'clock in the morning—there was a dream-like quality to our arriving in Neosho.

"Are you all goin' to see your folks?" the conductor asked us as we waited with him at the closed door for the train to pull into the station.

"My grandmother!"

"Yes," said my mother. "I'm from Neosho."

The train lurched to a stop, and the conductor opened the door, helping my pregnant mother down the steep stairs, with Frank and me dropping down drunkenly onto the platform behind her. Our passenger car was longer than the little Frisco station. The only sound in the delicious summer night was the labored breathing of the big train, steaming and hissing, impatient to pull away and disappear down the track. After the train had gone, then all you could hear was the pinging of the big moths colliding against the metal shades of the station lights. And there in a circle of light was my grandmother, fiddling with her car keys, the only person waiting on the platform.

"Bebe Lorene!"

"Well, look at you! I declare you've gotten so big." She leaned over for our kisses, for we had learned to kiss from our Iraqi relatives. "Both of you!" Bebe Lorene almost chuckled, she seemed so pleased to see us. She turned to my mother. "Hello, Doris. Here, let me take that suitcase. You shouldn't be carrying that." She nervously tried to make herself useful.

"Hello, Mother."

I don't think my mother and my grandmother even kissed.

We all piled into Bebe Lorene's Plymouth sedan, which she called "Plymmy," for what would become our ritual entry into Neosho. Frank and I were entertained by my grandmother's talking to her car as if it were a horse. We children sat in the back seat and my mother, up front in the passenger seat. Bebe Lorene always drove because she was the only one in her family who had her license. She settled herself behind the steering wheel, sitting straight and gripping the wheel as if she were going to box with her fists, the underside of her arms facing up and the face of her Bulova watch looking ahead.

Contacting the steering wheel thus from wrist to elbow, she actually steered not only with her hands but also with her forearms and shoulders.

The whole of Neosho was asleep when we pulled away from the Frisco station and drove past the Pet milk plant in the direction of town. Like many small midwestern towns, Neosho is laid out at right angles from the public square. In the center of the square sits the gray Carthage stone county courthouse. When my grandmother got to town, she drove us ceremoniously all around the square so we could see everything: Sterling's dime store, Foster Evans Drug, the Band Box movie theater, the G&L Drug Store, McGinty's Department Store, the First National Bank, Briggs Hardware, the Deluxe Cleaners, Newton County Hardware, J. C. Penney, Lindsay's Department Store, Owsley's Drug Store, the Coffee Cup Café. After we had traced the square without seeing another thing moving besides our car, Bebe Lorene would say, "Well, it looks like they rolled up the sidewalks around here." And then we would head to 303 West Spring Street.

There awaited my great-grandmother Nanny, who could have been a model for Grant Wood's *American Gothic* painting. She was spare with words and undemonstrative, and Frank and I would give her a careful kiss on her papery, translucent cheek. She always seemed pleased to see my mother. Sometimes, though, if Nanny was not feeling well, we would have to come in the house as quietly as possible so as not to wake her. I remember our first arrival, sitting in the kitchen on the cane-bottomed chairs at the round oak table covered in red-and-white checked oilcloth. Before we went to bed, Bebe Lorene poured us cups of steaming cocoa that she had ready, even though by then it was close to three in the morning. The beds were prepared for us, and it felt good to slide between cool, clean sheets and to be able to lie flat for the first time in thirty-three hours. With Bebe Lorene, you felt there was no holding back. She gave us one hundred percent.

Frank and I considered the five or six acres of Big Spring Park part of our backyard. We would run down the grassy slope from my grandmother's house into the valley of the park, where we could use the swings and teeter-totters (we called them "seesaws" in Montclair) whenever we wanted. At the peak of the slope was a white wooden bench. Once, while I was sitting there, I spotted both a thrush and a flicker. On the days that the man who took care of the park came with his big gang mower and cut all the grass, Frank would run in the house to spread the news that the "fark man" had come! This announcement sent Nanny and Bebe Lorene tittering. My mother said Nanny always liked a good off-color joke, and Frank's mispronunciation of *park* put it one letter away from the "Noise." But those were the days when even the boys at Edgemont School would shake with silent laughter when we sang in class, "And all the zephyrs do blow," which today seems rather highbrow bathroom humor.

In the late afternoon, after the mowed grass in the park had dried, Frank and I would lie down at the top of the slope and roll down to the bottom. With our states duly altered, we would try to stand up, groping the air as we dizzily staggered. In this field, Frank and I ran around shooting each other with loaded cap guns. As we got older, we took turns hitting out grounders and pop flies to each other after supper.

But the most important feature of the park to us was right in the center, at the far end of the long sidewalk: the children's wading pool. The dressing rooms were designed like an ancient Greek temple, with fluted white columns concealing them. In front of this backdrop was the round pool itself, its blue floor sloping gradually down, so that the water went from shallow to armpit high at the center. A broad sidewalk circled the pool. If you got cold from swimming, you could drain the blue from your chattering lips by spreading your towel on the baking cement and lying down to absorb the sun not only from above but also from below. Several semicircular cement benches were placed around the pool. Before we were old enough to go on our own, my mother would sit on one of these benches to watch us swim after our naps.

"Look at me, Mom."

"Yes, I see you."

Naps! In the middle of the day! Admittedly, we felt full after midday dinner, and admittedly, it was hot out, but I would go crazy having to lie there while everyone else actually went to sleep. What did my mother do all day that made her tired? She couldn't go anywhere unless Bebe Lorene drove her, and if she drove her, my grandmother did whatever my mother was doing with her or else waited for her in the car. Finally, my mother conceded that since I could not get to sleep, she would let me read in bed, so after dinner I would go to my grandmother's built-in bookcase with the leaded-glass doors in the living room and pull out a book of fairy tales that my mother had read as a child, called *East of the Sun*. When I was finished with that, I would dip into a big book called *Children's Literature*, a collection of writings for children that my grandmother had used in a college course she had to take. I was drawn to read "The Hardy Tin Soldier" by Hans Christian Andersen several times, for it hit a nerve. The brave tin soldier, whose love for the beautiful paper ballerina is not returned, survives a fall from a third-floor window and a terrible journey in a paper boat, down a drain, and into the belly of a fish. He is rescued from that fate only to be thrown into a furnace, where, undaunted by misfortune and unrequited love, he melts into a little tin heart.

Often in the evenings, to cool off after the heat of the day, Bebe Lorene would take us for a mystery ride. As we bounced along back roads, my grandmother would let us roll down the windows and feel the fresh, sometimes rain-cleared air on our faces, like happy dogs. Other times we left trails of billowing dust behind us. Once we saw a rainbow. Sometimes I observed redwing blackbirds, bobolinks, and meadowlarks sitting on the telephone wires, oblivious to all the conversations passing beneath their feet. On the paved highway, if we passed five Burma-Shave signs one after another with one line of a funny poem on each of the signs, my mother entertained us by reading them aloud:

He played a sax

Had no BO

But his whiskers scratched

So she let him go.

The mystery of Bebe Lorene's mystery rides was our destination: Would it be Monett? Carthage? Webb City? Aurora? The first person to identify the town correctly won. Of course, we had to have been there at least once in order to recognize it. But then Frank and I caught on to reading signs. The dead giveaway, we eventually learned, was the town's name emblazoned on its water tower, usually the tallest structure for miles.

Always, when we pulled into town, we would park nose to the sidewalk in front of a drug store and scoot in for Cokes to go from the fountain. Frank would get a lime Coke, and I would get a cherry Coke or sometimes a Dr. Pepper. In an era of fast food on a national scale, it is hard to appreciate how this seemed such a regional treat to us. We would carry our paper cups back to the car and try to make our drinks last as long as possible, sucking on the crushed ice as we headed back home.

I always referred to the house at 303 West Spring Street as Bebe Lorene's house, but it still belonged to her mother, our great-grandmother Nanny, who also owned several rental houses around town, including two behind the big house. I remember going in the car with Bebe Lorene and Nanny to a couple of these houses. We pulled up to the curb, and Bebe Lorene and I waited in the car while Nanny, as if playing a live Monopoly game, knocked on the door to collect the rent. I thought she and Bebe Lorene were rich, and I assumed Bebe Lorene was in charge, because, like my father, she drove the car, had a job, and did the grocery shopping.

The Safeway supermarket stood across the street catty-corner from the big house, and sometimes I got to go shopping with Bebe Lorene—the only times as a child that I was in a supermarket. At home, my mother, who did not have a driver's license, would write down a list of what she wanted, and my father would do all the grocery shopping for the week after he finished work on Friday nights. Perhaps this was a cultural remnant of the men in his family going to the sûq. My father often left my mother his own list on the kitchen counter; it outlined how she should best organize her time to do her chores around the house. My mother didn't get out much except to go to church.

―――

When we visited Bebe Lorene, we entered a foreign culture, an exotic land as different from Montclair as Montclair was from Basra. The food was different—pan gravy, fatback always simmering with the green beans, fruit cobblers for dessert. The language was different—not only the accent, a slow Southern drawl, but the vocabulary as well. The gas station was the "filling station"; the beautician who gave my grandmother a permanent was a "beauty operator." The groceries were not packed in bags but in "sacks." We caught "lightning bugs" instead of fireflies; we saw "red birds," not cardinals. In the spring "jonquils" sprang up, not daffodils. We drank "pop," not soda. Even the coins were different: for a while you paid Missouri State tax with green and red plastic coins called "mils." Instead of a minister, church had a "preacher," whom men referred to as "Brother" instead of Reverend or Mister. The clothes were different, too—farmers wore denim overalls buckled over their shoulders. In the summer in Neosho the men wore short-sleeved, open-collared shirts to church, while in Montclair, they wore long-sleeved white shirts with neckties and jackets, even when it was boiling hot. Culture!

Since my brother Neal was not born until September 19, well after school started, I had almost two months of third grade in Neosho's Central Elementary School on the hill above my grandmother's house. In school, I got to know many children my own age, a few of whom went to the First Baptist Church that we attended every Sunday with my mother and Bebe Lorene. I didn't mind going to Sunday school and church in Neosho. The stories from the Bible, illustrated with cutout characters stuck to a flannel board, were interesting. The songs Mrs. Seevers taught us, such as "Jesus Loves Me," were catchy. But the song that particularly moved me was

> Jesus loves the little children,
>
> All the children of the world.
>
> Black and yellow, red and white,
>
> All are precious in his sight.
>
> Jesus loves the little children of the world.

Even though I did my best to blend in with whatever group I was in, and even though, because I resembled my mother, I believed I passed as American, underneath I felt like an outsider. The feeling that I was one of the "children of the world" motivated my adult fantasy for a world passport, but did nothing to assuage the feeling that I belonged nowhere.

Back in Montclair from Neosho, one afternoon after I had gotten home from school my mother was headed from the kitchen to the front hall to answer the doorbell. I followed her and saw when she opened the door that it was Mr. Sykes, the nice-looking laundry man, who once a week delivered the box of my father's starched white shirts. Mr. Sykes wore a starched white shirt himself with a perky bowtie. He smiled as he tipped his uniform hat to my mother.

"Good afternoon, Mrs. Tooni. It's a beautiful day," Mr. Sykes started, but then interrupted himself: "What in the world happened to you? It looks like somebody socked you."

"Oh," my mother said, "it was so stupid of me. I ran into a door."

"That's too bad." He frowned. "That's quite a shiner."

When did my mother run into a door? I didn't remember seeing her black eye before I went to bed the previous night or notice anything before I left for school in the morning and came home for lunch. There was just something about her explaining she had run into a door that seemed fishy.

After we got back to Montclair, our new baby brother, Neal, suffered for several months with colic. During the night, when my mother could not get the bottle to plug his cries, she would have to pick him up. Sometimes, if Neal was particularly agitated, she would carry him out to the darkened sun porch in between our bedrooms and hold him as she rocked him in the wicker rocker my father had lugged upstairs. "I should rock him to sleep with rocks" was my mother's little joke. But as I lay in my bed, I could hear my mother softly singing through the closed French doors. Neal's cries would soon subside to the sound of the wicker creaking and her plaintive crooning of "The Missouri Waltz," sometimes called "The Missouri Lullaby."

It didn't take long for my mother to forget herself, and her whispery lullaby would branch out into her whole out loud repertoire of "Little Sir Echo," "Daisy Bell," and "Let Me Call You Sweetheart." When I read the lines from T. S. Eliot's "The Love Song of J. Alfred Prufrock," I think of my mother rocking her baby on the upstairs sun porch: "I have heard the mermaids singing, each to each. / I do not think that they will sing to me."

Brother, come and dance with me.

Both my hands I offer thee.

Right foot first, left foot then.

Round about and back again.

This is the invitation Gretel sings to Hansel in Engelbert Humperdinck's operetta *Hansel and Gretel*, based on the Grimm fairy tale about a poor brother and sister whose irritable mother sends them to find strawberries for dinner in a forest where a witch lives. I know this because my third grade class at Edgemont School was going to perform the operetta for the whole school and the parents, too.

Our teacher, Miss Hogan, did not assign the major roles for *Hansel and Gretel*. We had to audition for them in front of the class, which voted by secret ballot—that is, with our heads down on the desks, eyes closed, and raised hands. I wanted to play the Witch, and, throwing myself into the cackling *heh, heh, heh*s, I got the part. But even if you were not one of the lead characters, everyone in the class was involved in the production. There was the Sandman, who puts the exhausted Hansel and Gretel to sleep when night overtakes them as they get lost in the woods. There were the guardian angels, played by the girls, who, keeping watch over the children as they slumbered, sing a haunting lullaby that moves me still. And trying to stand motionless, there was the fence of all the boys the Witch had caught and turned to gingerbread. It stretched across the front of her gingerbread cottage, and Hansel and Gretel discover it when they awake.

Everyone in Miss Hogan's class also worked on some aspect of the scenery. A mother of one of my classmates had cut out of corrugated cardboard a flat outline of the Witch just my size. My job was to draw and paint the Witch on the cardboard, using the same colors as my costume, for a surprise at the end of the show. An appliance store had donated a big box that another mother volunteer had cut a door into to make the Witch's life-size oven.

In the operetta, the Witch immobilizes Hansel with a spell and plans to bake him in her oven to eat. Performing the role, I asked Gretel to open the oven door for me. She pretended that she didn't know how. I opened the oven to demonstrate, and Gretel shoved me in and slammed the door shut. That was the end of the Witch. With her power gone, all the gingerbread boys came alive, including Bill Corderey and Ed Mallon, who, red-faced, had been silently shaking the gingerbread fence with their painfully pent-up laughter. Now they could laugh out loud because they were supposed to be alive, milling around the stage and rejoicing with all the other liberated boys. Hansel and Gretel's parents walked in the door, relieved and grateful to find their children.

During the finale of reconciliation and celebration, Hansel and Gretel suddenly remembered the Witch baking in the oven. They leapt to the oven door, opened it, and extracted the life-sized cardboard cookie I had painted to look like me as the Witch. The audience roared. It was a gratifying moment.

We gave two performances of the operetta during the day for both the lower and the upper grades assemblies, and we repeated the performance at night for all the parents. As an eight-year-old, I found it exciting to be at school when it was black outside our windows and the glass glittered with the reflection of the lights inside our classroom, enchantingly transformed into a makeup and costume room.

I loved the music from the operetta; and because the class rehearsed together, I knew all the other roles almost as well as my own. One afternoon, I was teaching Frank, then six, how to do Hansel's dance. We were in the living room on the rug in front of the radio/phonograph console playing the record album of *Hansel and Gretel*, which my father had bought.

Since we were not allowed to use the phonograph, my mother had to put the records on for us. "Brother, come and dance with me ..." As she watched us dance, she sang and clapped the beat. Frank and I twirled round and round, and I was out of breath and admittedly revved up. My mother's frequent observation of my behavior was that I was "always so ex-ci-ted," which made me feel there was something wrong with enthusiasm. I didn't learn until I was an adult that the root meaning of *enthusiasm* is "having a god within."

After the last round of twirls, I flopped breathlessly down on the couch. I knew the instant the backs of my legs registered the feeling of cool, smooth cardboard that I had landed on top of the album. The records in the sleeves inside were hard and brittle 78s, and they cracked down the middle.

They were the last records to come into our house while we were children. Why waste money to replace them, my father reasoned, when we had obviously demonstrated that we were not responsible enough to take care of them?

It was during assembly in the third grade that I fell in love for the first time.

Miss Roe's third grade presented a program about Switzerland, a subject her class had been studying. I do not remember anything else about the presentation except for the moment a boy stepped to the front of the stage like our Hummel figurine come to life.

Dressed in a pair of real lederhosen, with a feather in his cap, he had long, dark eyelashes, rosy cheeks, and big, white front teeth. He sang:

> From Lake Lucerne
>
> To the highest hill,
>
> A ho-dee-ree-dee,
>
> A ho-dee-ee-o.

The refrain had a doubly haunting effect: it sounded as if it were not only being echoed in the valleys between the Alps but also yodeled by my favorite movie star, Roy Rogers, and the Sons of the Pioneers out on the lonely range under the stars.

The audience cheered and applauded and brought beaming Ricky Crane back to the stage for several bows. I don't remember having seen Ricky before, but the following year we found ourselves together in Miss Leibold's fourth-grade class, and we became known as what would later be called an "item."

Ricky began giving me a steady stream of little gifts, which did not look all that new and which I stored in a pink shoebox. The ultimate offering was a stubby gold ballpoint pen, coiled with gold vines and studded with different colored jewels. When I received this latter present, my mother suggested I return all his gifts in case some of them might belong to his mother.

Ricky also addressed notes to me in class. But the note I remember as particularly inventive was one I composed and passed to him. At the top of a slip of paper, I wrote, "If you kiss this spot"—there I left a big space on which I had touched my lips—"you will have kissed me." I watched the note being furtively passed from desk to desk until it reached Ricky. I watched Ricky unfold the note and consider its contents. He looked up to catch my eye and grinned as he lifted the note to his lips and kissed it. Then—making sure I was still watching—he wadded up the note into a little ball, and in what to me is still an unforgettably erotic act, he popped it in his mouth and swallowed it.

There were times when our family was piled in the car, tooling along Route 46 toward the Lincoln Tunnel on our way to Bebe and Jiddu's for Sunday dinner, when my father would take his eyes off the road to glance at my mother. She was all dressed up and, I thought, looking pretty. But my father would remark, "Don't you have any other dresses?"

"What's the matter with this one?" My mother's eyes glazed over. "I thought it looked perfectly nice."

"You should go look in the stores and see what they're wearing."

"Well, if you would ever let me have some money to go shopping …"

And they were off and running. Even though it was my father who had just hurt my mother's feelings, he was the one who acted like the offended party, getting all worked up, shouting and gesticulating. As the air in the car thickened, my mother's chin would jut out and her face would toughen up. Sometimes I couldn't figure out what the fight was about, but I felt ashamed when the drivers in passing cars turned their heads to look at my father shouting and my mother crying.

Depending on the traffic, sometimes my father drove to Bebe and Jiddu's over the George Washington Bridge, and sometimes we went through the neon-bright Lincoln Tunnel. I asked my father one time how they could hold back all the water to build a tunnel through the river. He said they built the tunnel under the water, but I didn't understand how they could do that, either.

In the middle of the Lincoln Tunnel, Frank and I always looked for the big line painted down the wall with New Jersey on one side and New York on the other. It amazed me how, crossing the line, you could actually feel the difference of being in another state—the peculiar personality of place.

If my father went through the Lincoln Tunnel, crossed through Manhattan, and took the Queens Midtown Tunnel to get to the Long Island Expressway, we would pass the East River and the site of the future headquarters of the United Nations. We would look for progress on the construction of the buildings, because it was where Uncle Kamil was going to have his office; it was finally completed when I was thirteen. I could never understand why my mother seemed to have an attitude towards Uncle Kamil. I was proud of him.

Bebe and Jiddu's two-family brick house in Jamaica was clean and neat and carpeted throughout with Persian rugs. Curtained French doors separated the living room, dining room, and kitchen from a little hall onto which opened the guest room, bathroom, and Bebe and Jiddu's bedroom. I liked going in my grandparents' bedroom because there was something peaceful about it. Over the big double bed hung a picture in an ornate tin frame of Mary, Our Lady of Perpetual Health, holding the baby Jesus. A rosary always lay on top of one of the bedside tables—it must have been on Bebe's side of the bed.

There were a dressing table and bench and two bureaus, over one of which hung a crucifix, similar to the one hanging over my parents' bed, and behind which were propped several folded fronds that had been distributed in Bebe's church on Palm Sunday to commemorate the entry of Jesus into Jerusalem. The bedroom had a pleasant smell of rose water and Brilliantine, the perfumed pomade Bebe touched into her naturally wavy salt-and-pepper hair. Because I liked the smell so much, I tried using my father's Brilliantine at home once, but it only looked like I hadn't washed my hair in about two years. In the summer, with their shades pulled down to keep out the hot sun, my grandparents' bedroom was soothingly dark. On the radiator cover perpetually shone a small electric icon of the Virgin Mary. I liked to stand in the otherworldliness of the room, smell the rosewater smell, and wonder what the mysterious electric Mary meant to Bebe.

But the scents of rose water and Brilliantine were peripheral to the wafting odors of the main event of our Sunday visits—food! Covered in a white linen tablecloth and heaped with steaming bowls and a huge platter of rice, my grandparents' big table and chairs filled the dining room to its edges.

There is something about the smell of Iraqi cooking that sucks at your taste buds. While most Iraqi dishes have a tomato-sauce base, they are different from Italian cuisine because of the spices—cardamom instead of oregano—and the frequently called for addition of freshly squeezed lemon juice at the end. With his own heavy brass mortar and pestle, Jiddu ground all his spices, even producing his own curry powder, a blend of four different spices.

On those Sundays in Jamaica, a huge roast turkey might be a side dish. Depending on the season, there might also be *kousa mashi*, squash stuffed with spicy ground meat and rice; or *bedhinjan*, baked disks of eggplant; or *kibbi*, a meatloaf-type dish made with cracked wheat and layered with pine nuts and raisins; or *hamuth hulu*, a lamb stew in tomato sauce with apricots and almonds; or *bamia*, another lamb stew in tomatoes but with okra and garlic; or lamb or chicken or shrimp curry. The list was endless. But my favorite of all was dolma, ground beef and rice mixed with an ineffable seasoning comprised of seven different spices and wrapped in a grape leaf or stuffed in an onion. Auntie May always steeped seven threads of saffron with a tablespoon of rose water and added a small amount of this liquid to the meat mixture, which, together with a seven-ingredient spice, gave the dolma their elusively exotic flavor. Packed in a big pot, the dolma was steamed in a tomato sauce with the juice of a freshly squeezed lemon.

Dessert would follow later, at teatime, around four or five o'clock. Auntie May and Uncle Kamil always supplied a cake from a bakery. My mother often brought an applesauce cake she had made from scratch or a cake-mix vanilla sheet cake with chocolate icing. Sometimes there was *baklawa*, the filo pastry layered with ground nuts, sugar, and cardamom, or rosewater-scented cookies with cardamom, sometimes filled with dates, called *klaicha*. On rare occasions there was the Turkish taffy-like confection called *mannesima*. My mother told me it was the manna mentioned in the Bible that miraculously kept the Israelites fed when they were wandering around in the wilderness. I loved the inexpressible taste of it.

Usually, after the big meal, the men would stagger back into the living room, collapse in armchairs, smoke cigarettes, and doze off in the blue haze, resting up for their arguments. In the meantime, the women, dressed in their best, cleared the table with countless trips to and from the kitchen, where their high heels clicked on the linoleum floor, rinsed and stacked the dishes, and washed and dried them with tea towels. Then the women would return to the living room to sit down for a minute.

Sometimes my father would look at my mother and frown. "Go put on some lipstick. Comb your hair." And, looking wounded, she would take her purse and slink off to the bathroom to make the necessary repairs. She would have powdered her nose eventually, but he wanted her perfect at all times, just as he wanted his children perfect, too.

It felt to me that Jiddu quietly presided from his wing chair in the living room. Firmly rotund, he was considered fair by Iraqi standards: his eyes were hazel and his smooth skin looked lightly tanned. He often sucked on a cigarette through an unusual handmade silver holder. It was constructed like a skinny pipe, with a long stem that elbowed into a tiny bowl only wide enough to grip a cigarette, so that when he inserted the cigarette into the holder, it did not stick out horizontally, but up vertically. Above him, the smoke circled the air just as his own fringe of white hair circled his shining, bald head.

Once Frank and I were sitting on the rug at Jiddu's feet, seeing who could build the biggest card house before it collapsed. Our grandfather thrust at us a wooden box, beautifully decorated with inlaid mother-of-pearl. Unlatching its little hook, we found inside a board game with checkers and dice, but no squares marked out on the board.

Jiddu nodded encouragement for us to play, but unfortunately we didn't know what to do. It was frustrating not to be able to speak each other's languages.

Another time, when my mother was in the kitchen with the other women, Uncle Joe let Frank and me go upstairs to explore his half of the house. My mother was pretty mad when she found out, because she knew Uncle Joe kept a hubba-hubba calendar hanging on the back of his bathroom door, which you can be sure Frank and I discovered—Miss December wearing a Santa hat and not much else. "Hubba-hubba" is what my father said, giving Frank a wink, as he leered out the car window at a pretty blond he spotted strutting along the sidewalk. It made me feel like one of the boys because I understood what they were appreciating. It made me feel inadequate. How did this make my mother feel?

After a long day at Bebe and Jiddu's, we would leave in the dark, our car becoming a bead on the glittering necklace of headlights strung along the highway. My mother would lean her head back on the front seat and fall asleep. Frank sometimes curled up in his corner of the back seat and conked out, too. No matter how many people were around, I noticed, when people slept, they were alone. And because they were asleep and I was not, even with my father awake at the wheel, I felt alone.

I enjoyed copying the pictures of birds from a big book Bebe Lorene had bought for me when we were in Missouri. For the operetta *Hansel and Gretel,* I had copied an illustration from a picture book of the Witch in front of her gingerbread house, and Miss Hogan used my drawing for the cover of the program. By fourth grade I was copying cartoon characters, like Little Lulu and Tubby, Bugs Bunny, Mickey Mouse, and Donald Duck. I became expert at drawing Shmoos, those endearing armless creations by the cartoonist Al Capp that made faithful pets and would fall down dead out of love for their human friends, offering themselves as sacrificial steaks. A career in art or cartooning was for me.

In fifth grade I was at the house of my friend Connie, who also liked to draw. She told me about the art classes she was going to take on Saturday mornings at the Montclair Art Museum. Why didn't I sign up for them too, Connie suggested, and we could go together? Her mother was already going to drive her, so I could ride with them. I got excited. Just think: real art lessons at a real museum where they really knew about art!

Ducking through a few hedges and cutting across a couple of driveways and several backyards, I ran home with the news about art classes with Connie. I asked my father if I could go too. The answer was simply no.

"But *why,* Daddy?"

"I have more important things to spend money on than art lessons. Besides," my father added, "you don't need art lessons. You already know how to draw."

That was true. I was good at drawing. It made sense that only the people who weren't good at drawing needed lessons. But why was I so disappointed? And why did asking my father for something make me feel vaguely bewildered?

As a teenager, I saw a card trick that held me in thrall. Whoever showed me the trick taught me to do it; and the reason I'm passing the instructions on is that the trick helped me recognize a truth about my father.

The object of the trick is for the magician to withdraw from the deck of cards in his or her pocket any card an audience member chooses. The trick is that the audience believes it has chosen the card, but the magician has actually talked the audience into picking the card *he or she* has already chosen. You can skip this part if you don't want to know how to do it, but as an analogy, the trick has far-reaching implications.

HOW TO DO THE TRICK: Hand someone—let's call him John—a deck of cards, which you ask him to shuffle and return to you facedown. As John hands you the deck, you sneak a peek at the card on the bottom—let's say the seven of diamonds—before you slip the deck into your pocket. So far it appears you have only accepted from John a shuffled deck of cards, which you have put in your pocket. But since you now know the exact location of the seven of diamonds, you proceed to talk John into wanting you to withdraw that particular card from your pocket.

You might say, "Out of the four suits—hearts, clubs, diamonds, spades—pick two."

"Hearts and spades," John might answer.

Don't forget you are trying to talk him into picking diamonds. So you respond: "That leaves clubs and diamonds. Now out of clubs and diamonds, pick one."

"Clubs."

"Right," you answer. "Now you have diamonds left."

Now, looking as if you are randomly pulling some figures out of the air, you say, "Out of these four numbers, pick two: six, seven, eight, nine." You proceed as above to get John to pick the seven.

Once you have established that John wants you to find the seven of diamonds out of the deck in your pocket, you reach into your pocket, pull out the bottom card, hold it up facing John, and say, "Is this your card?"

"Yes! Wow! How'd you do that?"

Now, if I said to my father that my patent leather shoes were too tight, he would point out that they were still good. If I said that my bathrobe was worn out, he would say it still fit. If I wanted art lessons, he would say, "But you know how to draw."

It's a pretty good trick.

───⌒───

My father was the kind of person who, upon reading in the newspaper of the Hula-Hoop craze that swept the nation in the late fifties, would strike his palm to his forehead, as if beating his brain for having let the idea get past him. Thirty million people shelling out two dollars apiece!

"A simple plastic ring! *Ai-yi-yi!* Why didn't *I* think of it? A simple plastic ring."

My immigrant father loved America for its grounding in equality, but it took me a long time to figure out what was at the heart of it. His love was not so much for the equality that speaks of all men and women, regardless of their obvious differences in race, creed, and abilities, being of equal worth in the eyes of their fellow humans and of God. Rather, it was for the equality that could be summed up thus: in America all men have an equal shot at a million bucks.

A cartoonist's bubble of the American Dream followed my father around like a cloud creating his own personal climate. It carried one large mark—a dollar sign.

This cartoonist's bubble, however, was not a daydream, for my father was not a commonplace and unadventurous man trying to escape reality. His cartoonist's bubble was, rather, a preoccupation. An uncommon and risk-taking man, my father was all too ready to wrest reality of its million. Not by crook either, as he was honest, but by hook, if only he could find the right angle, the right gimmick. My father passed down to us children the attitude that we could do anything once we set our minds to it. The only value he gave us to determine what was worth striving for, however, was "How much?" In the pot at the end of my father's rainbow beckoned a mink coat for my mother and a Cadillac for him.

But in post–World War II America, I don't know what made my father think that bubblegum was the wave of the future. My mother claimed Fowler's Grocery, her grandparents' store, was among the first in Neosho to carry Fleer's new Dubble Bubble gum, which was introduced in the late 1920s. As an eight- or nine-year-old, she was in the first wave of those who mastered the art of bubblegum blowing. I was rather proud of myself for winning the bubblegum-blowing contest at my seventh-grade homeroom Halloween party; but by then, I had had plenty of practice.

One night, my father arrived home with a delicate instrument, which he set down on the metal-top table in the kitchen. It was a set of scales with a tray hanging from either side, like the ones held high by the blindfolded statue dispensing justice. In a wooden box that came with the scales, a row of graduated brass weights sat in little holes. You could lift the weights out by the their knobs on top, but my brother Frank and I were instructed not to touch anything. My father put a big chunk of paraffin in one tray and then tried out several weights in the other tray until he got the right number to balance the two trays.

When he added up the weights, he knew how much the paraffin weighed. Several cases of paraffin, which my father said was an ingredient of bubble gum, were stacked on the basement landing by the side door. But since my parents experimented on the bubblegum in the kitchen after we were put to bed, we did not get to see how they cooked it.

Somehow they figured out a recipe for bubblegum.

My father called his bubblegum Chico, after the Spanish word for "little boy," he explained, but never told us why Spanish? He himself designed the box the bubblegum came in. It was about six inches long and looked like the kind of box a tube of toothpaste would come in. On the front was a drawing of a boy in a sombrero (Chico himself) with his cheeks puffed out, blowing a huge bubble, and my father's slogan: "Chico Bubblegum—Five Flavors, Five Colors, and a Prize in Every Box."

My mother always told me I inherited whatever artistic abilities I had from my father. My father said a drawing he had done of Abraham Lincoln was still hanging in his high school in Basra. My mother modestly claimed she could "not draw a straight line," but I always enjoyed a couple of standards she would draw for us if we begged her. One was a profile of a thug with a broken nose and an X for an eye, and the other was the rear view of a cat or a rabbit with whiskers, images that differed only in ears and tails. When Frank and I were small, I also liked the several times she penciled a girl's face and "Suzy" and a boy's face and "Frank" on the shells of our soft-boiled eggs.

My father was definitely the best artist in the house. When I saw the design on his finished bubblegum box, I thought it was good, but it bothered me that, while it was technically correct, it was not cute. Of course, I did not say anything. As an adult, I can only wonder why he did not take his design to a professional artist for finishing, whether he did not have the money to spend or whether he thought his design was professional enough. Now perhaps I would think his drawing charming.

One Sunday, my father piled the family in his Studebaker for a drive to nearby Passaic, New Jersey, to see a factory that was for sale. Out the back window of the factory, you could see the muddy Passaic River flow by. The building had been cleaned out, so that there were no artifacts lying around that might have tipped prospective buyers off about what had previously been produced in it. But no matter how many times you scrub wood, the effect is never one of shining cleanliness. Standing in the middle of that dark factory, I had the feeling of wet wood.

The factory consisted of one large room whose most memorable feature, seen as you came in the front door, was a conveyor belt that ran the length of the right wall. At the back to the left was a small office with a door and an observation window that looked out on the conveyor belt. It was on this conveyor belt that Chico bubblegum went into production.

I don't think my father had five different vats with their own extruding machines, one for each flavor of Chico bubblegum. I think he made up a big batch of one flavor, and when he had run that batch through the extruder, he cleaned it out for the next flavor. The extruding machine squeezed out the bubblegum in three-quarter-inch-thick ropes that were cut at one-inch intervals. I don't know who packed the five different pieces and prize in each colorfully printed box or who assembled every twenty-four boxes in a display carton, whose lid stood up to show Chico in his sombrero blowing his big bubble and saying, "Chico Bubblegum—Five Flavors, Five Colors, and a Prize in Every Box." Maybe my father packed the boxes himself.

Accompanying my father in the Studebaker one afternoon, I sat up front where my mother usually sat. Just the two of us drove into Manhattan. Immediately after we exited the Lincoln Tunnel, he turned into a neighborhood of gray, cheerless buildings and warehouses. We parked in front of one of these buildings with its dingy window displaying dusty plastic toys in sun-faded boxes. We went inside, and I watched my father haggle over prices and learned you can buy things cheaper by the gross wholesale. But if this were true, my nine-year-old brain could not understand why anybody would ever buy retail. It was to this section of the city, too, that my father took me years later, when I was going to my first formal dance and needed some jewelry. In one of these buildings, he let me pick out a matched rhinestone necklace, bracelet, and earrings. And to one of these buildings we returned on the occasion of my high school graduation to select a Bulova wristwatch and green Lady Baltimore luggage. He also bought me, in a regular store in Montclair and at top-dollar retail price, an Olympia portable typewriter that I had my heart set on to take to college. He was irked that Olympia did not sell wholesale.

My father seemed pleased with the gross of things he loaded into the trunk of his Studebaker that day, along with a much smaller box that was also a gross. When I questioned him why different sized boxes were called the same name, he explained that a gross was twelve dozen. The big gross contained the miniature toys that would be packed into Chico bubblegum as prizes, little puzzles and booklets and plastic animals and people, the same kind of prizes you might find in a box of Cracker Jack, the popular caramelized popcorn. I was disillusioned to suspect that Cracker Jack prizes might have come from as dismal a source. The small gross contained more prizes destined for the Chico bubblegum box: miniature sets of plastic dice, each smaller than a cubic quarter of an inch.

In the days before we got our Studebaker, if you walked left at the top of Brunswick Road onto Valley Road, past the front of the

Montclair Athletic Club and tennis courts, along smooth slate sidewalks that would not tickle your feet in roller skates, and past several tree-lined blocks of houses, you would come upon a short strip of stores on the left. The first store in the group was Greenberg's stationery, which mostly sold newspapers and dusty magazines and from where Frank and I collected our penny black-and-white and sepia-colored movie star cards, a little bigger than postcards. The store was a gloomy hole-in-the-wall presided over by burly, unkempt, sullen, and eponymous Saul, who stood behind his counter chewing on a cigar that looked as if it had exploded. Greenberg's was the first store to carry Chico bubblegum.

The second retail outlet for Chico bubblegum was Poll's Stationery in Upper Montclair, a clean, up-to-date, well-run family business. My father developed such an amiable relationship with Mr. and Mrs. Poll that Frank ended up getting his first job at Poll's Stationery as soon as he turned fourteen, an after-school job that he would keep all through high school instead of playing baseball, which he was good at. The proprietors of both stores were Jewish, but my father thought it was perfectly fine to do business with Jews as long as you did not marry them.

Before the development of synthetic gum bases after World War II, the basic ingredient in most chewing gum was chicle, a sap tapped from the sapodilla tree in the jungles of Mexico, Central and South America, and the Amazon River valley. Even before they developed Dubble Bubble gum, the Fleer brothers were the ones who experimented with those candy-coated chicle pellets that became Chiclets, the recipe for which they would eventually sell to the American Chicle Company. It was from the American Chicle Company that one day my father received an unpleasant letter.

While there were no patents on bubblegum, the American Chicle Company thought the name Chico was too close for comfort to Chiclets and was meant to intentionally capitalize on their product's worldwide fame. If my father did not voluntarily desist from distributing his bubblegum under the name Chico, the American Chicle Company would be forced to sue.

On the way to Bebe and Jiddu's for Sunday dinners, we regularly passed the American Chicle Company building in Queens. From the car window, as we solemnly rode by it, I regarded its palatial proportions anew. The factory was a block long and looked as if it should be flying a coat of arms from its tower. This Kingdom of Chewing Gum in America, this juggernaut, had threatened to crush my father.

My father instructed Frank to take the leftover miniature dice to school to sell on the playground for twenty-five cents a pair, quite a profit and an assignment Frank seemed to enjoy until his teacher, Mrs. McDermott, told him he was not allowed to sell on school property. Whether the leftover cases of Chico bubblegum in our basement were stored in a spot that was damp or whether the recipe had behaved unpredictably from batch to batch, the consistency of the gum was randomly startling. When you popped a piece in your mouth and began going at it, you wouldn't know if it would turn into a workable wad or if it would suddenly disintegrate in your mouth, crumbling rapidly into an overwhelming volume of blue (or red or yellow or green or purple) juice that you did not know whether to swallow or spit out.

Most of my friends were not allowed to chew bubblegum because it was, their parents warned them, "bad for your teeth." When I was invited to a birthday party, however, regardless of how many hints to the contrary my hostess might drop, my father made me take as a birthday present a leftover display carton of twenty-four boxes of Chico bubblegum. To the dubious looks of my friends' mothers, I would hopefully counter, "My father invented it." But for me, giving the gift of Chico bubblegum was torture, for I never knew which batch I was bearing.

My father decided to move from our house on Brunswick Road because of two developments he worried might devalue his property. The first was a newly installed bright light in the entrance to the A.C. parking lot across from our house, a light that was kept on all night. And the second was that a Negro family had just bought a house not too many blocks away from us. "What's so bad about Negroes?" I asked my father, but I did not understand his answer about not wanting to lose money on the value of our house.

There were no Negroes in Upper Montclair, my father said, and that is where he began looking for a house for us.

"Our house is too big," my mother said about my beloved dwelling on Brunswick Road. "I can't keep up with it." But with our numbers increased to include my little brother Neal, I did not understand either why we were moving to a smaller house. Even though the new house would have four bedrooms upstairs, the rooms were tiny. The kitchen was much smaller than our old one, and there were no big halls, no back staircase to the second floor, and no third floor. Because the new house was more modern as well as being located in the public school district that included Mount Hebron Junior High School in Upper Montclair, my father thought it had greater resale value. I felt he looked at a house less as a home than as an investment.

One government and one high school served Montclair and Upper Montclair combined, but there were three neighborhood junior high schools. While all my friends from Edgemont School would be going to George Inness Junior High, because we moved into Upper Montclair, I would be going to Mount Hebron Junior High (now Buzz Aldrin Middle School). We might as well have moved to Texas. My consolation was that at least the new house on Brookfield Road was still in the Edgemont School district, and before I left all my friends for a new junior high, I could graduate with them from elementary school.

After we moved, I walked to school for basically the same short number of blocks, but I approached Edgemont School from the opposite side as before. By coincidence, Jim, the traffic guard, had been transferred to see us safely across busy Watchuung Avenue, where it intersected Edgemont Road.

Had we fallen on hard times? The houses on the upper half of Brookfield Road were older, single-family dwellings with yards around them, like those on our former street, but the houses below ours, on the bottom half of Brookfield Road, were blue-collar, sometimes two-family structures, crowded in one right after another, with only driveways between them. So were those across the street. Where did we belong?

On either side of our compact new house was one identical to our own. Facing the house, to our right lived a policeman and his wife and teenage son. And to our left lived the DeFrance family, famous in Montclair, I would soon learn, for having twelve children—thirteen, if you counted the cousin who often stayed with them. The wooden sills of their doorframes were worn down by the ceaseless traffic of fourteen pairs of feet. Mr. DeFrance, who was not often home, was handsomely rugged and sunburned from operating a backhoe all day. Mrs. DeFrance was short and square, and she waddled—sometimes painfully because of the varicose veins in her squat legs—as she lugged out countless baskets of laundry to hang on the line. The DeFrances's front yard was beaten-down dirt, pounded as smooth as the sills. The pot on their stove was a huge cauldron. The family would have been a fitting subject for a portrait by the Depression-era photographer Dorothea Lange.

Our front yard was equally worn-out from the activities of the previous owners—a chef, his wife, and their four children. The first thing my father did was to install, all around the property, a chain link fence, spiky at the top where the wires ended in the air. Did my father mean to keep all the neighborhood children out of our yard, or us in?

Either way, it did not take him long to get lush grass growing. We were not allowed to play in the front yard because soon the garden bordering the inside of the fence was full of dahlias, snapdragons, salvia, marigolds, pansies, zinnias, asters, bachelor's buttons, and phlox.

In the backyard, a bounteous peach tree sagged in season with huge fruit, which my mother shared with Mrs. DeFrance. Exchanging words as they worked at their clotheslines, my mother became Mrs. DeFrance's sympathetic neighbor.

Before we moved in, my father had the new house wallpapered and painted inside and out. The upper half of the exterior was white, and the bottom half was barn red, a popular new color then for modern houses. Those were the days when picture windows and pine-paneled dens were coveted features. Although our new house lacked a picture window, the windows on the little enclosed sunroom the front door opened into had Jalousie windows with opaque glass louvres. And it did have a pine-paneled playroom with a ceramic tile floor in the basement that included a bathroom with a stall shower.

The last thing I did before I closed the door on my room on Brunswick Road forever was a secret ceremony I promised myself I would never forget: I stood on tiptoe, and under the sconce to the right of the door, two printed garlands of white flowers down on the green wallpaper, I solemnly kissed my wall.

Our black-and-white tomcat, Peeshu, ran away from our new house. I cried inconsolably every night that he was missing. Who would feed him? Who was there to care about him? Was he lying under a bush somewhere, injured? Was he dead? My mother tried to comfort me with the report that one of our former neighbors had seen Peeshu alive and well around her house in our old neighborhood.

We managed to find and retrieve Peeshu, but he ran away again from the new house on Brookfield Road. "Don't worry about Peeshu," my mother tried to assure me. "He's a tough old cat and can take care of himself."

But I was not reassured. Wouldn't Peeshu think we had abandoned him? How could he understand we had moved and that he couldn't go back into our old house, where he thought his food dish was waiting for him, where he had staked out his favorite spots to curl up in the sun? My sorrow would have for me a familiar and recurrent feel— if only we could speak cat language! For I believed that if we could lay out the developments logically, make plain all the reasons—in short, *explain* the situation—then surely whomever we addressed, animal or human, would understand and, by understanding, not suffer or cause suffering. For years, I short-circuited experiencing my own pain by explaining to myself *why* things happened. Focusing on the cat, I forgot about my own feelings.

Because I didn't want to move, my mother pointed out two things in the new backyard that she felt would appeal to Frank and me. Beyond the lilacs at the very back of the property stood both a swing frame, rusted but with one of the two swings still serviceable, and a prefabricated log-cabin playhouse that my father said he would allow us to fix up.

We looked at our father. "You mean we could use your tools?"

"Yes."

We looked at our mother. "You mean you would make curtains for it?"

"Yes."

"Oh, boy!"

The renovation of the cabin turned out to be an even better project than I had anticipated, for when the company my father hired came to put a new roof on the house, the workmen let me have enough shingles to put a new roof on the cabin. Not only that, they also threw in a supply of nails and showed me how to lay the shingles. At ten, I thought laying shingles had to be the most satisfying work imaginable. As I straddled the cabin's peaked roof, I felt like the child in the Robert Louis Stevenson poem my mother had read to us, who "looked abroad on foreign lands," master of all I surveyed.

The swing frame was only a leg's length from the cabin roof, so I could maneuver onto it without touching the ground. Dangling hand over hand like a chimpanzee, one afternoon I made my way over to sit on another high perch I had constructed. I tied one end of a rope to the top of the frame and the other end around a short piece of board. I could hang onto the rope and lower myself to sit with one buttock on each side of the board, the rope between my legs. I was suspended thus, gazing around a good five feet from the ground, when the rope snapped, and I dropped on my tailbone with a stunning thud. The wind was knocked out of me, and my vertebrae felt fused into a rod. I thought I might have to sit there for the rest of my life.

It is a wonder so many of us make it out of childhood, but as Davy Crockett said, "If a fellow is born to be hung, he will never be drowned."

On my way home from our Halloween party in school, I was walking along the sidewalk with my ghost sheet wadded up under my arm. A boy named Bill caught up with me just before the corner of Brookfield Road. He was new in school and had recently moved into a big house at the top of Brookfield, on the corner of North Mountain Avenue. He was a year older and certainly bigger than I was. He was still dressed in his costume for the Halloween party in his class, a real top hat and tails.

He did not get off on the right foot. Looking me over, he said, "My father has more money than your father."

"He does *not*."

"My father has a hundred dollars."

"Oh, yeah? So does mine. My father has a hundred dollars." I felt pretty safe about saying this. When we had banking on Wednesday mornings in Mrs. Leibold's fourth-grade class, my father without a fuss actually parted with a quarter every week for me to bring to school to bank. A man from a real bank in town came to our classroom to teach us how to write out deposit slips, and we lined up in front of the table where he sat to bank our money and see it accrue in a real savings book. The man never mentioned withdrawal slips. My father said I was saving for the future. Yes, I was sure he had a hundred dollars.

"Yeah, well, I bet your father doesn't have a thousand dollars," Bill taunted. "My father has a *thousand* dollars!"

A *thousand*? Even though my father was always talking about the importance of saving money, if he did have a thousand, why were we living on the block among the two-family houses and Bill, in the big house at the top of the hill?

Bill freely interpreted my silence. "I knew your father didn't have a thousand dollars."

I felt I was lying when I retorted, "He does, too!"

Trained that hitting solves problems, I socked him, and he grabbed my arm. We grappled standing on the sidewalk before we fell onto the grass of Squeaky Adams's front yard, where, keeping an anxious eye on a pile of dog do, we rolled over trying to pin each other down. As I sat on Bill's stomach and dug my knees into the insides of his upper arms, I felt that all my winning did was embarrass me for being strong and able.

It was just the way I felt when I rang the doorbell of a house on the upper half of Brookfield to earn some money by offering my services shoveling snow. The woman who answered the door looked at me, horrified. "*Girls* shouldn't shovel snow!" She shook her head as though wondering what the world was coming to. Rather than stand undaunted because of confidence in my own abilities, however, I allowed her statement to cast doubt on my femininity: Would I want to shovel snow if I were a real girl? If I were a real girl, would I always be borrowing Frank's basketball to go over to Squeaky Adams's house to shoot baskets into the hoop on his garage? Maybe there was something wrong with me.

Why didn't I stop while I was ahead? After I got off of Bill and watched him hightail it up the hill to his big house, I easily rounded up a posse of reliable younger DeFrance boys—Joey, who had buckteeth, and Donnie, who had lost the vision in one of his eyes, I later learned, from cancer. We ran up the hill to Bill's house and, standing in his yard, called his name to come out. But why would he want to come out after we shouted, "You think you're so great!"? Bill stood in an upstairs window. He opened it and called down that we were on private property and if we didn't get off, he would call the police. "Go ahead, chicken!" we yelled back. Bill closed the window, turned, and disappeared inside his house. It didn't seem many more minutes before a police car pulled up to the curb, and a policeman got out and walked over to us.

"What seems to be the problem?" he asked.

Nobody was quite able to explain.

After the policeman told us that we had to learn to respect private property, he pulled out a pencil and notebook. "Before you go home," he said, "I want to take down your names." Take down our *names*? You mean we were going to have criminal records? After scribbling our names in his book, the policeman got back in his car and drove off.

Joey, Donnie, and I called not a word up to Bill, who was standing in the upstairs window again, looking smug. Where was his mother? We ran down the hill, and Joey and Donnie peeled off through the front door of their house while I ran around to the back door of our house, where I found my mother in the kitchen preparing dinner. Catching my breath, I told her, through my snivels, how everything had gotten out of hand. The policeman had scared me, and I was nervous about having my name in the police files. I *begged* her not to tell Daddy, and I know she did not tell him because nothing else happened.

I had felt that same kind of relief before. One night, when I was supposed to be asleep, I called downstairs for my mother to come up to my room. I confessed to her that when I went to play at my friend Nancy's house after school, we had smoked some of her mother's cigarettes. I made my mother promise then that she would not tell my father, and she had kept her promise. This is why I felt my mother was there for me.

It never occurred to me that she might not have told because she didn't want to be blamed for not keeping me in line.

The DeFrance cousin was a nice-looking blond boy, seventeen or eighteen years old to my ten or eleven. Even though the gap in our ages was socially unbridgeable, one afternoon, when he visited next door, I could contain myself no more. I marched out our chain link gate and over to the DeFrances' driveway, where he was standing around whistling.

"How do you do that?" I boldly asked him, enthralled with his talent.

"What?"

"Whistle like that?'

"You mean like this?" He trilled another whistle.

"Wow! That's great! Do it again."

More whistle warbling.

"Could you show me how to do that?"

"Sure." He grinned generously. "Like this." His whistling in slow motion was no small feat. And even after I learned how to break the sound down, duplicating it took hours of practice. The DeFrance cousin taught me that my tongue must move as if it were saying *lu-lu-lu-lu-lu-lu* at about six times per second while I blew air through my puckered lips. By the end of that summer, combined with the *tuck, tuck* robin call and the dove coo I had already mastered on my own, I sounded like a walking aviary. The bonus of the warble-whistling technique was that I could throw it into interludes of songs like "Blue Skies," the way the singer Bing Crosby did. Whistling was one of my best things.

As I was whistling around the house one day, my exasperated mother cut me short.

"Suzy, stop that whistling."

"Why?" I was puzzled.

"Because it is not ladylike."

The negative "not ladylike" translated immediately in my mind to the confusing affirmative "you are man-like." Why is it that words directed to one person ricochet off bricked-over ears while the very same words directed to another can penetrate and wound? "The tongue is a small member," Saint James wrote, "but it can make huge claims."

I had forgotten myself in Neosho one morning and unselfconsciously whistled through Bebe Lorene's dining room on the way to the back porch door.

"Stop that whistling, Suzy," my grandmother had also demanded, at her nerves' end. "Don't you know it's not nice for girls to whistle?"

I felt like the minor bird in the poem by Robert Frost, who admitted "I have wished a bird would fly away /And not sing by my house all day." But at least the poet, self-aware, had added: "And of course there must be something wrong /In wanting to silence any song."

My father did not believe in the free ride of an allowance, although I could earn a quarter from him doing such jobs as weeding the garden or cutting the grass, tasks I preferred to dusting. I learned the cost of doing business one summer afternoon when I opened up a Kool-Aid stand in front of the fence on Brookfield Road. By the time I repaid him for the packets of Kool-Aid, the sugar, and the paper cups he'd staked me for, the gratifying pile of change I had raked in by quaffing the thirst of neighborhood passersby dwindled to a dime.

Twice in my life I licked soap so I would not have to lie. I could not bring myself to eat soap, but I licked it so that I could say I had a stomachache, which my mother honored without questions. I felt fine, but I believed if I licked soap, I wasn't lying because I *should* have a stomachache. Both times were occasions of humiliation. The first began during fifth-grade lunchtime, when my mother put her foot down: she knew I hated to be late to class, but she would not let me go back to school until I had cleaned my fishbowl. I had a pet goldfish, Goldie, that I had bought at the dime store. I loved peering into his bowl and watching him swim around his universe, marveling that he could breathe water and wondering if he had thoughts or feelings. But I had never cleaned his bowl, and I kept putting it off. First, I did not know how to clean the bowl, and second, I was chicken: a moss-like green slime had developed on the inside of the glass, and I was afraid to touch something so disgusting.

"I don't care if you're late for school," my mother called up from downstairs. "You're not going back until you clean that fishbowl!"

Facing the ultimatum, I carried the bowl into the bathroom and set it down in the tub, while I figured out how to approach the job. I decided simply to pour out the old water and, putting the bowl under the faucet, pour in fresh water. As I tipped the bowl slightly in the bathtub, the dirty water trickled a long path to the drain. But suddenly my goldfish was carried in the cascade over the side of the bowl. If I had been able to move, I might have scooped the fish up in my hand. But I was afraid of touching him, so I only knelt at the tub, paralyzed and appalled as I watched Goldie slide toward the drain and disappear with a flip over its edge.

"Oh, no!" I burst into tears. All I could imagine was his lonely passage, like that of the Hardy Tin Soldier, with no one to comfort him through an endless labyrinth of pipes, ending up who knew where? Maybe like the dead fish left white-belly-up in the mud when they dredged Edgemont Pond. If only I had had the courage to grab him. If only I could have spoken fish language. If only I could explain I didn't mean it.

My mother ascended the stairs to see what was the matter. "Why didn't you put the plug in?" she asked.

I hadn't thought of it. I cried some more.

"You'd better get your face washed, or you're going to be late for school. Honestly, Suzy, you're so dramatic. It's just a goldfish. You can get another one."

I ran all the way to school. Back at my desk, all I could see in my mind were the big, surprised eyes of my innocent, helpless, frightened little fish. Down the big drain. And I was the murderer. I started to cry, jumped up, and ran into the cloakroom.

"What's the matter, dear?" Mrs. Gildner, our teacher, hurried in after me. "Are you all right?" I explained to her through my tears what had happened to Goldie, and she said I could stay in the cloakroom as long as I wanted, until I felt better about joining the class. But after a long time, when I did not come out, she came in to check on me.

Understanding that I was upset, she asked me kindly if I would like to go home, and I said, "Yes."

That was the first time I licked soap so I could be sick and not go to school the next day.

The second occasion occurred in sewing, a class that for me ran a close second to Sunday school. Sewing was a mandatory once-a-week practical course for sixth-grade girls in which we spent a whole year sewing, by hand, first a half slip and then a half apron. We did not sit at desks in tidy rows, as in regular class, but in a circle of chairs, using the big tables only for cutting out patterns and pinning them to the fabric. With our hands busy, there was the temptation of mental freedom. For some reason, the slightest eye contact with my friend Kay over our needles and threads sent one or both of us into convulsions of laughter. We were finally made to sit in corners of the room with our chairs facing the wall, where peeks at each other only made us laugh more. While this was the first time I had ever been in trouble in school and I was somewhat ashamed of my rude behavior, I did not feel humiliated by the punishment.

But one afternoon, the sewing room was occupied, and our class had to convene at a table set up for us at one end of the long, dark upstairs hall. We might as well have met in an echo chamber. As I bent my knees to sit in my folding chair, Kay chose that moment to thrust a needle between the chair and me. My yelp ricocheted off the marble floors, and our sewing teacher immediately ordered me to the principal's office. I cried. I did not want to be in the category of people sent to the principal's office; they were not the good students, the nice students from nice families, but the rare boys who started fights, the occasional mischief-maker or sluggard who did not do well in school. But mainly I cried for fear of the unknown punishments waiting for me from both the principal and my father, who would surely find out.

When I reported to the principal's office, Miss Day, the school secretary, raised her eyebrows in surprise and gave me a sympathetic nod. She had me take a seat on the bench against the wall in front of her desk, while I waited ten years for Mr. Hartman's door to open.

Finally he stepped out, but he kept his back to me as he and Miss Day exchanged a few words. At last he turned to face me. With his coat draped over his arm and his hat in hand, he was on his way out. He said that he trusted this kind of thing would not happen again, and I assured him it would not.

At home that night, I could not bring myself to eat soap, but again I licked it, so that the next day I could say I had a stomachache, which my mother again honored.

Although my feelings were inarticulate at the time, what humiliated me in both instances was that everyone—my teacher and my friends—had seen me cry. No one said anything to me about my crying, but I was ashamed and embarrassed for having publicly exposed my cowardice, fear, and sorrow, as if they were emotions I should not have.

───

Miss Boyd's social ballroom dancing class was egalitarian. Any student in the fifth or sixth grades of Edgemont School who paid the modest fee was welcome to learn to dance. Edgemont itself, however, was not egalitarian. In those days only children who lived in the mostly middle- to upper-middle-class neighborhood of the school were eligible to attend.

A new girl had entered our class the year before, and even though some boys with whom I got along made fun of her, I instantly identified with her. I was surprised she did not wear pierced earrings as I did. Her name was Gabriela Arciniegas, and her sister, who was a year ahead of us, was named Aurora. They were from Argentina, and they did not "pass." Their skin color matched my father's, but they did not speak English. I looked more like my American mother than like my Iraqi father and spoke like an American, but I understood the sisters' foreignness in my bones. They were well-to-do, for they moved into a big brick colonial on North Mountain Avenue. The boys might have made fun of Gabriella even if she had spoken English, which she was learning by the plunge-in method. The fact is, Gabriella was unusually big and tall for her age, more hirsute than her lighter-skinned peers, awkward as a newborn fawn, and so painfully shy that when Mrs. Gildner addressed her, Gabriella would blush and try to comfort herself by looking at the floor and chewing on the ends of her long, straight black hair. She and her older sister, however, were both very smart: each played a stringed instrument—Gabriella, a violin, and Aurora, a cello—which nobody else our age could do. An adult could have readily assessed the likelihood of the Arciniegas sisters' eventual transformation into cosmopolitan beauties, but it must have been painful going for them in Edgemont School in Montclair, New Jersey, in 1950.

When Mrs. Gildner passed out the notice and application forms for Miss Boyd's dancing class, which met once a week after school, everyone signed up, and by some miracle of persuasion ("But,

Daddy, I do want to know how to dance when I grow up ... But, Daddy, even Gabriella is going ... ") I got to sign up, too.

On dancing class days, everybody went straight home after school to get cleaned up and change into his or her best clothes. The boys wore white shirts and neckties, blue suits or slacks, and sports jackets. The girls wore white socks and black patent leather shoes and a dress of fancy material, like taffeta or velvet. My dress was brown taffeta with a brown plaid bodice and puffed brown sleeves, and it tied in the back with a bow, as many girls' dresses did in those days. Why brown I don't know. It is not my best color. Probably it was the last taffeta dress in my size at the store, but I was happy with it.

Because my classmates were wearing their good clothes, the mothers of some of them drove them back to school, where Miss Boyd conducted the dancing class in the auditorium. The heavy velvet curtains, ordinarily open, were pulled closed, giving the room a dressy look. Since my mother did not have her driver's license, I walked back to school—or, rather, ran.

Miss Boyd greeted us individually as we came in the door. She taught the boys to bow and the girls to curtsy to her.

The girls sat in folding chairs along one wall, and the boys sat in folding chairs along the opposite wall. Miss Boyd stood in the middle in her high heels and svelte V-necked and V-backed black cocktail dress with shoulder pads, so sophisticated in my fifth-grade eyes. Then we rose, standing in the same lines, as we watched Miss Boyd demonstrate the various steps, signaling with a nod to her accompanist at the piano near the stage to play the music.

In spite of the subtle swaying of her hips, which would have made my father whistle when she demonstrated the rumba, there was something about Miss Boyd that made me sad, the way the tired people behind the booths at carnivals did, trying to look like they were having a good time.

After watching Miss Boyd demonstrate a new dance, such as the fox-trot—first facing one way to show the boys and then the other to show the girls—we tried to imitate her, staying in our long lines, girls facing boys. "Step together, step together, one and two and one and two and step, slide, step, slide, that's it, step, slide ...."

Or for the big box: "One and two and three and four and ... "

In this manner we learned the waltz, the samba, the rumba (the small box), the bunny hop, and the jitterbug step we couldn't wait to perform—the Lindy—for "doing the Lindy," as ten- and eleven-year-olds, we felt like real teenagers. The Lindy was always danced to the song "In the Mood": "Ball-heel, ball-heel, step-step, ball-heel, ball-heel, step-step ... " Ricky, the boy I liked since fourth grade, was a good dancer, but with his cheeks aflame and a grin that stretched from ear to ear, he was especially deft at the Lindy.

After the demonstration and practice, we finished class with the boys choosing girls for several dances and sometimes the girls choosing boys. If it was the boys' turn, the girls sat in their chairs waiting to be asked. At a signal from Miss Boyd, the boys charged across the room, each sliding to a stop on his leather-soled shoes in front of the girl of his choice. Sometimes, if there had been too much of a stampede, Miss Boyd made the boys go back and do this part over. As each boy stood in front of the seated girl, he was supposed to bow, say, "May I please have this dance?" and then escort his partner to the dance floor.

It never occurred to me to be anxious about nobody asking me to dance. So many of the boys were my friends that sometimes two or three of them at once slid to a stop in front of my chair. So secure was I socially that, seeing Gabriella forlornly excluded, I could say to Ricky on the dance floor, "I'll sit the next one out. You get Gabriella dancing." And Ricky was such a nice guy and so secure himself, he would. When he bowed before Gabriella's chair, what pleasure it gave me to see her startled smile as she rose to dance like a wobbly Bambi.

The last class of the year was our first real dance, boy ask girl, with no instruction, just dancing and refreshments. I had a wonderful time at my first dance with my first love, Ricky Crane. His smiling mother picked me up in her car to take us and bring us home. Ricky presented me with my first flower, a pink carnation, which his mother, who seemed to be enjoying chaperoning us, helped pin to my taffeta dress.

Unlike the commercial flowers bred today for sturdiness in shipping, Ricky's carnation retained its richly romantic aroma even months after I had pressed it under the big Shakespeare books we inherited from the previous owners of our Brunswick Road house. My mother told me girls in Neosho pressed their corsages in order to preserve them in their scrapbooks.

When did the tiny cracks appear in my confidence, and when did they become fissures? Even though I missed my old neighborhood, at least our new house was still walking distance from Edgemont. I was frankly sentimental about "Edgemont, Our Dear School." In the words of the school song we learned in kindergarten and sang at all important functions for the next seven years, "You're the one which we hold so dear. / We will always cheer / Hu-ur-rah for Edgemont School!" While our new location became increasingly unsettling toward the end of sixth grade, when everyone began speculating on grownup life at George Inness Junior High School and I knew I would be going to Mount Hebron Junior High, at least I could finish out my grade-school years with my old friends.

What happened in sixth grade is analogous to a hairline fracture: too small to treat except with time, too inconspicuous for sympathy, but nonetheless painful.

One Sunday night, after a day of Arabic food and the usual Arabic arguing among the relatives at Bebe and Jiddu's house in Jamaica, the traffic was particularly thick as we crossed Manhattan in order to get to the Lincoln Tunnel. I enjoyed being stuck in traffic in Manhattan, especially on 42nd Street, because I could look out the window and study all the amazingly different flavors of people jostling down the sidewalks. We could watch the man on the "I'd Walk a Mile for a Camel" billboard blow huge smoke rings over Broadway. It was while chugging through this start-and-stop traffic that my mother, whom I had noticed was getting fatter, but not, I had already guessed, from eating, turned to us in the back seat and told us forthrightly that she was going to have a baby. (I was eleven, Frank, nine, and Neal, three.) My father, whom traffic usually put in a tense mood, seemed as pleased as my mother, who always said she liked babies best. I do not remember my brothers' reactions to the news. I only remember that by the time we got to the Lincoln Tunnel, I had determined that a girl would be the best thing to wish for, as she would balance out our numbers, and that if the baby indeed were a girl, we should name her Sally Kay.

"The bells are ringing for every Suzy and Sal," my mother sang to the tune of "For Me and My Gal" in teasing response to my suggestion; and although the lyrics were mixed up, they sounded right. My parents liked the name Kay because of their own friends Kay and Herb; and I pushed Kay because of my friend Kay, though she was really a Katherine. "My great-grandmother was named Catharine," my mother said, "only spelled with a C." I had no idea who she was talking about.

I couldn't wait to tell my friends Kay and Connie that my mother was having a baby. This was not just a doll to play with but the real thing!

"Wow!" my friends exclaimed on the stairs to the playground Monday morning. "You're so lucky!"

That was the good news. The bad news was that we were leaving for Missouri in April and that I would not be in the graduation ceremony with my class at Edgemont in June but would, instead, finish sixth grade at Central Elementary School in Neosho.

"Why?" I asked my mother. "Why can't we stay for graduation and go after school finishes?"

"Because the doctor says I shouldn't wait too long before I travel."

"Why can't you have the baby here?"

"Because Bebe Lorene and Nanny are there to help me."

"Why can't Bebe Lorene come here to help you?"

"Because she's teaching school, and besides, she would not want to leave Nanny alone."

The explanation made sense, of course. And I liked the kids in Neosho, many of whom I had gotten to know when I started third grade there the year Neal was born. But I felt sad to be missing out on goodbye parties, getting a graduation dress for the closing day exercises, and being in the processional. Connie and Kay promised to write me lots of letters, telling me such things as who got paired up with whom in the processional, which they faithfully did. Connie was thoughtful enough to send me the program. She made certain that my name appeared in the list of "Boys and Girls to Leave Edgemont," but I felt left out to learn I had missed a class trip to Hayden Planetarium and the American Museum of Natural History in New York, where I had never been.

Miss Boyd's dancing class had started up again, and with a year's instruction under our belts, sixth-grade dancing was more fun than ever. Maybe I had broached the subject of a new dress. I don't remember what it was that got my father thinking, but the next thing I knew, he was telling me why he was having my mother go to school the next day to get his money back for the dancing class.

"But, Dad, I *love* dancing."

"You're going to Missouri in another five weeks, and I am not going to pay for dancing lessons you will be missing."

"But, Dad, I've already gone to the first two classes!"

"I don't care. Your mommy can just explain she is going to have a baby and that you have to leave in April to go to Missouri."

"Dad, please," I begged in tears.

"I don't have money to waste."

As our voices rose, "*Lat-say-ya,*" interjected my mother, using her Arabic, I thought, on my behalf to *take it easy*.

"That's it! *Bess!*" Enough! My father closed the case.

The next day I lived in dread of bumping into my mother in the hall at Edgemont with my little brother Neal in tow, mortified at the prospect of her approaching Miss Day, the principal's secretary, to ask for her money back after I had already taken two of the lessons. And I felt sad to have to miss dancing when I was still present.

Then, of course, came the questions from my friends.

"Hey, Suzy, how come you weren't in dancing?"

"I can't."

"How come? You mean you're not taking?"

"I have to go to Missouri," I answered, as if that were a perfectly good reason.

I finished sixth grade at Central Elementary School in Neosho. Unlike Edgemont School, it had a cafeteria, and school buses brought children in from the other side of town and from out in the country. In Montclair, since children lived within walking distance of their neighborhood schools, we did not need school buses and could walk home for lunch. In Central, there were loudspeakers above the big clocks in every room for announcements, a feature Edgemont did not have. One afternoon in Central, we all folded our hands on our desks and listened to General Douglas MacArthur's voice crackle out of the speaker: "Old soldiers never die; they just fade away." I didn't really understand what was happening. I thought the war was over, but something was going on in a country called Korea.

There was a huge dictionary in our classroom in Central, the size of the one in Edgemont's library. Once, when our teacher, Miss Kenney, was not looking, several of us furtively looked up the word *breast* because it was the only forbidden word anybody could think of.

Central had competitive spelling bees, which seemed a Southern activity. I thought the spelling bees were fun, and I didn't know why we did not have them in Edgemont.

Our class participated in Neosho's May Day festival, held in Big Spring Park, where a dozen tall maypoles had been erected flanking the long sidewalk, with ribbons attached to their tops. Holding the ribbons as we danced in great circles, schoolchildren from all over Neosho wound and unwound the maypoles, just as they had done in my mother's day.

At least three boys let it be known that they liked me. Several new friends invited me over to their houses to play after school. I wasn't used to the directness of my peers in Neosho, who would walk right up to me and say, "You're so cute!" But I liked it.

I told my mother at supper, "Everybody at school says I'm cute."

My mother straightened me out pretty fast. "It's just an expression. That's the way they talk in the South. It doesn't mean what you think."

The grandmother of Judy Haas (pronounced Hayes) knew my grandmother, and one day she brought Judy down to my grandmother's house, for the grandmothers thought the two granddaughters should meet. Forced family introductions don't always work, but Judy and I became instant friends. Judy lived just up the hill overlooking Big Spring Park in the most modern house I had ever seen. It had a spiral staircase to an inside balcony overlooking her two-story-high living room with Danish furniture, a kidney-shaped coffee table, and butterfly chairs. Judy's mother, who had a good sense of humor and tolerated our many rounds of "Chopsticks" and "Heart and Soul" on the piano, was the kind of mother who didn't mind driving all the way to Kansas City to buy special orthopedic shoes for Judy or to take her to the dentist.

There was somebody in my sixth-grade class I will never forget. She wore dusty leather shoes with the shoelaces missing and no socks. Her dress was a shift made of sacking, and her thin blond hair was greasy. She was slow and thick bodied. When I mentioned my classmate at supper, I figured out from my grandmother and mother's askance, wordless signals that she was thick from being pregnant and that she didn't have a husband. When I said, "Hi" to the girl in school, she looked away with a surprised smile that seemed more ashamed than shy. Every now and then I'd catch her looking at me, and I'd smile, but she would look away as if she couldn't believe I would smile at her.

One evening after supper, while it was still bright, Bebe Lorene took us for one of her famous rides, for she wanted to try out her brand-new Plymouth sedan. In the back seat, I always sat forward to look out the window, and as we tooled along a dirt country road, I observed a tarpaper shack on cinder blocks. Two bare-bottomed children were playing in the dirt out front, and framed in the doorway, leaning against the jamb, was the girl from my class. I know she saw me because she straightened up and waved. Waving back, I felt a peculiar emotion that I can only now express as "out-of-jointness." Why was I in my grandmother's brand-new Plymouth and she, in that tarpaper shack that fast disappeared in our dust?

In the summer, while the rest of the family took naps during the hottest part of the day after dinner, my mother allowed me to walk through the tree-shaded alley behind my grandmother's house to the Neosho Library, its interior coolly dark with its shades drawn against the baking sun and its electric floor fans humming. Miss Sally Stewart, my mother told me, was the same woman who had been librarian when she was a girl. Miss Stewart introduced me to a series of biographies with orange covers and a black silhouette of the subject's head on the front.

Back at home, if I promised not to make noise and wake everybody up, I was allowed to pull from the refrigerator a cold root beer or Dr. Pepper. Sometimes I would help myself to whatever current confection Bebe Lorene had on hand in the hobnail blue glass bowl on the buffet—sugarcoated gumdrops or jellied spearmint leaves or orange slices. With the cool stone porch all to myself, I sat on the glider, sipping a soda or sucking on an orange slice, and read inspiring stories of Abraham Lincoln, Stephen Foster, Clara Barton, Luther Burbank, and John Audubon. (It didn't sink in that Audubon shot all the birds he painted; I think now his friends were lucky he had not gone in for portraiture.) But the story that indelibly moved me was the life of George Washington Carver, my childhood hero, not so much for his discovery of a million valuable uses of the peanut, but for never letting himself be overcome by the many obstacles and discouragements he faced. I was proud George Washington Carver and I had Neosho in common, the town where he first went to school. The only reason he left Neosho was that he had learned all he could at the colored school, which went to the equivalent of only the second or third grade. But he never gave up.

In the car with my grandmother, when we happened to pass the obscure marker commemorating where George Washington Carver had attended school, I asked her why the colored children in Neosho didn't go to school with us. "They have their *own* school," she huffed and promptly closed the subject.

That summer I slept on the big double daybed in my grandmother's dining room. Lying in bed, I discovered two hard disks growing unevenly under the skin on my chest, and because of an article about cancer I had read in *Reader's Digest*, I worried that maybe I was developing the disease. I was relieved when I found out the disks were budding breasts.

At the beginning of June, I woke up to see the lights on through the curtained French doors leading to the big bedroom my mother, Neal, and Frank shared. My mother walked past my bed in the dining room to get to the bathroom, but I pretended to be asleep. After she returned to her room, I got up to go to the bathroom, too, and stepped on something wet and sticky. In the light of the bathroom, I discovered it was red and seemed like blood, which made me worry that something was wrong. I washed the spot off and slipped back to bed. Now I could hear my mother and grandmother scrambling around in a hurry as they passed my bed and went into Nanny's room to tell her they were off to the hospital.

The next morning, Frank and Neal and I learned that we had a new sister. She was named Sally Kay, but when my mother called her "a little sweet patootie," the name stuck. We all called her Tootie. Tootie had thick black hair and long black eyelashes and a dimple. I wrote Connie and Kay all about her.

Not a week after Tootie was born, I was awakened a second time in the middle of the night, this time by an argument in Nanny's bedroom. I heard a strange man's voice saying, "Now, Mrs. Fowler, just you take it easy."

And my grandmother saying, "Mother, you can go when you get there. It's more important that we get you to the hospital right away."

And Nanny loudly protesting, "But I want to go in my *own* bathroom! If a body can't go in her own bathroom if she wants to, then I might as well die!" Those were the last words I ever heard my great-grandmother say. My mother had just come home from Sale Memorial Hospital, where only the week before Bebe Lorene had taken us to visit her and see the baby. We were all smiles when we had brought my mother a big chocolate shake. Now my grandmother's face was serious. In a tiptoe atmosphere, she ushered us into a different room at Sale Memorial Hospital, where Nanny lay in the bed with her head on a pillow and her eyes closed. She had had a heart attack, and although she looked peaceful, she was not expected to live. My grandmother had brought us in to tell her goodbye.

The next afternoon I walked home from a matinee at the Orpheum Theatre with my first movie date, Larry. He waited in the park for me while I went inside to tell my mother I was home. When I came back out, I stood on the hill overlooking the park and yelled to Larry across the field, "I can't come out. My great-grandmother died!"

"What?" he shouted back, "I can't hear you!"

"I said I can't come out. My great-grandmother died!"

"What?" he shouted back. "I can't hear you!"

I looked around to see if anybody from the family was around and then ran down the hill to tell him. Since Nanny had died, I was not allowed to be outside playing; it wasn't nice. But when I trudged back up the hill to return to the house, I didn't know what to do with myself. Everybody who came to pay their respects after Nanny died peered into Tootie's bassinet and made some remark or other about how wonderful it was to have replaced a death with a birth, as if people are interchangeable. My mother, of course, was busy with the new baby, but she was also stoic. "Death is natural," she instructed us. She had often remarked that Nanny was like a mother to her, but now my mother's lips were pressed together in her defiant you-can't-hurt-me look, her tears stoppered but leaking. "I don't think children should be kept from death," she said matter-of-factly.

At the First Baptist Church, I attended my first funeral, and when we filed past the open coffin, I saw my first dead body. I remembered Nanny alive, sitting on the porch, swinging her foot to some soundless melody as her platform rocker creaked back and forth like a metronome. What a difference being dead made! The corners of my mouth pulled down, struggling as if they had been caught in a magnetic field, but following my mother's example, I resisted my genuine emotions and fended off sobbing, because I thought that was what I was supposed to do.

When it was time to go back home to New Jersey, Larry and I arranged to meet at the wading pool in the park to say goodbye. I ran down the hill from my grandmother's house, already in my bathing suit, and waited while Larry changed into his suit in the boys' dressing room. Larry and I were both too big for the pool, but we teasingly splashed water on each other and waded out to the center of the pool, where, stretching out, we each held our breath and tried to sink to the bottom. With no one else around, we kissed for the first time underwater.

One Sunday afternoon not long after we had returned home to Montclair, my father invited his secretary, Helen Stuart, and her husband and two sons to our house for Sunday dinner. Helen and her husband were not a matched set. He was a baker, slightly shorter than his wife but twice as wide, and he hardly said two words, not out of perversity, but from displacement. He looked as if he would have been more comfortable in an undershirt, sitting around the boiler room of a ship. He perked up for a few minutes, though, when everybody talked about the bakery goods he had heaped on us—a gigantic box of assorted cookies and a huge cake that had whipped cream spread all over it and real strawberries arranged on top. Oh, yes, he had made them himself. But after Bebe Lorene's strawberry shortcake, his cake tasted like a window display. To their two sons, we said, "Boy, it must be great having a father who brings home all those free desserts."

"Ha ha," we all laughed, and Mr. Stuart shyly patted his potbelly to indicate who did all the eating. Their pale sons, alongside whom I felt robust, were thin as rails and looked like they never touched the stuff. They all had Brooklyn accents except for Helen, who was definitely trying not to. Why had my father brought them all here?

The way Helen addressed my father as "Mr. Tooni" with her eyes cast down, you could tell she thought she had been allowed in the presence of the Shah of Iran, whom, as my father aged, he physically resembled. And when my father spoke, she treasured his every word as if each were a pearl rolled out of his crown. It was enough to make me sick.

My father lapped it up, raving about what a wonderful secretary she was, the best he'd ever had, and how nicely she took care of herself, and will you look at her clothes? Beaming all the while at Helen, he suggested to my mother, "Why don't you get some clothes like Helen's?" My mother had just vacuumed the house, cleaned the bathrooms, mopped the kitchen floor, ironed our clothes, cooked the company dinner, and put on makeup and a good dress. Couldn't he see my mother was much prettier than Helen Stuart? And smarter!

Helen was brunette and big-boned. She looked older than my mother, but she did take care of herself. She rouged the smooth skin over her prominent cheekbones. Her mouth was wide. Did she have extra teeth? I am sure she took her job as my father's secretary seriously. She was friendly to us all: "Your father is a wonderful man. Your husband is one of the nicest bosses I've ever had. It's such a pleasure to work for a real gentleman." Yes, enough to make me sick.

"Now you must come to our house," said Helen, who said she'd had "such a good time" at our "lovely home." When she and the baker and their pallid sons said goodbye, she made my parents promise to visit, and it was not long before she invited us to their apartment. It was Sunday afternoon, and attendance, as at all family functions, was compulsory. None of this "I have homework" stuff.

It was a day that felt all wrong to begin with. In an eerily empty section of Brooklyn that seemed as if it had been evacuated because of some disaster, the Stuarts lived in a tenement with no elevators and the smell of cabbage caught in the dingy stairwells. It was the kind of place my father would have refused to let me go if I'd asked. But here was my father, as if he hadn't noticed the depressing surroundings, all smiles and courtly manners as he herded our entire family up the stairs and crowded us into the Stuarts' clean but cheerless apartment.

Mr. Stuart had ready for us a gigantic box of cookies and a huge cake with whipped cream and strawberries on top. "Boy, isn't it great having a father who brings home all these free desserts?" We all laughed as Mr. Stuart patted his potbelly. Then there was nothing left for me to do but sit in a chair. Now Mr. Stuart looked bewildered to see us so out of place. All the boys and Tootie piled into a narrow bedroom alongside the tiny kitchen to play with little cars, although Frank was really too old.

"Maybe while we're here," my father suggested to Helen "you can show Doris where you shop for your clothes. Maybe you could help her pick out something."

"Now, Neal, come on, stop it. Doris dresses very nice." She smiled at my mother.

It was Sunday. The stores were closed. We lived in New Jersey, and they were talking about my mother shopping in Brooklyn with Helen, who worked in my father's office. My mother was smoldering in an armchair. She had on her pseudo-haughty, I'm-fine-and-I-don't-care look.

The galling finale was that Helen, the secretary from the tenement in Brooklyn, sent my father, her boss, home to Upper Montclair with a carefully folded stack of hand-me-down clothes that her younger son had outgrown. The most memorable items were earmarked for my brother Neal: a blue suit for Sunday with coordinating plaid panels at the side of each lapel and a matching clip-on necktie. The plaid reminded me of the trim on the pedal-pusher outfit my father made me buy to wear to a big office picnic when I had wanted to wear a pair of plain dungarees.

Even though I was almost twelve, I didn't know what was going on. But my body suspected something was wrong.

At an early age, perhaps at birth, I had been fitted with a pair of invisible glasses, the kind of glasses used in experiments of perception, which turn everything upside down. If the wearer keeps the glasses on long enough, the mind eventually adjusts and rights everything in its field of perception. The person can even learn to walk around in them. Because the glasses were invisible, nobody else noticed I was wearing them. I got so used to them, I forgot I had them on.

My new junior high had a Friday-night dance in the gymnasium, which I attended, the first big social activity at my new school. Because I had to start from scratch getting to know people, I jumped at the chance to be on the only dance committee the seventh graders were privileged to comprise—the cleanup committee. Here is an example of an instance when I did not understand whether my father's response was because of his Arab culture or something else.

"Where are you going?" my father caught me on my way out the door early the Saturday morning after the dance, the morning usually devoted to cleaning my room.

"To school," I said.

"To school on Saturday?"

"I'm on a committee for the dance."

"What committee is this?"

"The cleanup committee."

Laughter. "The 'cleanup committee,'" he repeated flatly. "You're not going."

"But why?"

"No daughter of mine is going to be a garbage collector."

"Lat-say-ya," my mother said, acting as a buffer as she came to my defense. "It's just to take the decorations down from the dance."

"Dad, please, it's an honor. All the good kids are going."

"Have you cleaned your room?"

"I will just as soon as I get home." My father was such a martinet that he ran his fingers around the baseboard to be sure we did a good job.

"And don't forget, there's work to be done in the yard."

"I know." I was already out the door.

Yet it never occurred to me that my father went to college in the United States. Didn't he know that the students organized the dances and decorated for them? Was this culture or control or what?

Church services bored me stiff. If only people talked about something important like the meaning of life. The biggest event for the Montclair Heights Dutch Reformed Church was the Country Store held each fall as a fundraiser. The Country Store offered games and rides for the kids, used books for sale, sit-down turkey dinners, hot dog stands, candy, and sodas. My mother would cleverly copy items we would see in gift shops in the Ozarks, such as stick horses with work-sock heads. (When Neal was four, he had a bad fall riding one such stick horse that my mother had made and bawled that the horse had thrown him.) For countless years, my mother made work-sock horse heads and whole monkeys and various stuffed animals and, because she could crochet without looking, baby sweaters, blankets, and booties, all to sell in a booth at the Country Store.

At the age of thirteen one Sunday morning, I was dragging my heels to have to get dressed up for Sunday school and church yet again. I ventured, "Do I have to?"

"Yes!" said my father, but my blasphemous question had started our conversation badly.

"Why?" I asked. Then to his silence I risked declaring, "I don't even believe in God!"

My father promptly grabbed me by the arm and flung me in my closet, slamming the door shut. "If you will not have the light," he roared, "you will stay in the dark where you belong!" It is easy to see why the analogy of God as father did not work for me.

From that time on, there was never any question that weekly Sunday school and church attendance was compulsory. Even though I enjoyed singing the hymns, I sat through every class and church service with ears closed, arms unreceptively folded, and eyes critically scanning. I smugly noticed only the details that supported my cynicism: Didn't the blood of our Lord and Savior, Jesus Christ, come straight from the A&P supermarket in Welch's grape juice bottles? And when Reverend Schenck in his robes tossed back the contents of his communion cup like a shot at a bar during our solemn confirmation ceremony, my friend Joyce and I silently imploded with laughter and could not stop our shoulders from shaking. A few years later, I would attend evening young people's meetings with her older sister, Gail, so we could smoke cigarettes in her car on the way. But Sundays are mainly one big blur.

I had enough money to surprise my father with a present for his birthday. It was money I had saved from the dollar bills Bebe Lorene always tucked in her letters and from the occasional babysitting job I had with the couple across the street. In the dime store, I spotted a red-and-white plastic doughnut maker for $2.98. It looked like a gigantic hypodermic needle into which you loaded dough. The picture on the box showed a hand pressing down on the plunger to squeeze out a ring of dough that dropped down into the hot fat in which the doughnut would fry. I was certain my father, who was always thinking of things to invent, would appreciate how clever the gadget was, and didn't the whole family love doughnuts?

My father did not say much the morning he unwrapped his birthday present. He removed the plastic components from the box and turned them over, pursing his lips and scrutinizing them the way I would imagine an assessor in a patent office might review an application. He read the directions and recipe on the box and handed the box to my mother, who also read the recipe.

"We'll see." He shrugged his shoulders, giving my mother the high sign to try out the doughnut maker.

After lunch, my mother got the kitchen all spick-and-span, then she mixed up some doughnut dough from the recipe on the box. We all stood around watching the Alp of white Crisco in the frying pan melt down to a clear liquid. Meanwhile, she spooned some dough into the plastic syringe and inserted the plunger. It worked! Out plopped a skinny O of dough that took a shallow dive into the grease and then surfaced to float on the top, where it began to sizzle and slowly turn a golden brown. I kept hoping the skinny O's would fatten up a bit, but they did not. My mother fished them out of the grease to cool, and we each sampled one. I thought the doughnut tasted pretty good.

But my father's eyebrows were arched and his eyelids stretched tautly down to half-mast. He wolfed down his doughnut, shaking his head as he swept the crumbs off his teeth with his tongue.

"You see?" he asked rhetorically, as if the doughnut had taught me an obvious lesson. "You call *that* a doughnut?"

"Well, not exactly," I admitted, although I thought as a bakery item, the skinny O wasn't bad sui generis.

"So your mommy can get this thing cleaned up for you, and you can get your money back."

I was appalled. "But Daddy, we *used* it already."

"Look, you can see it doesn't make doughnuts, so why waste your money? Your mommy will wash everything, and you put it back in the box. It will look like new."

"I can't *lie* to the lady in the store."

"Don't be silly, Suzy. You don't tell her you used it. You just say you want to return it because it wasn't what you wanted or something like that."

Well, I guessed that wasn't a lie, exactly. It was certainly true my father did not want the doughnut maker.

The plastic parts were still warm from my mother's washing them as I packed them back into the box, making sure the instruction sheet was replaced just the way I had found it. The doughnut maker did not look used, at least not so that you would notice right away. Had that little curl on the edge of the instruction sheet been there before? I put the box in the wire basket on my bicycle and pushed off. I dreaded the task so much I just wanted to get it over with, the sooner the better.

Leaning my bike on its kickstand in front of the dime store, I wrapped my arms around the box, took a deep breath, shoved through the door, and headed down the aisle to the housewares section.

"May I help you?" It was a different salesman, not the nice lady who had sold me the doughnut maker.

"Yes, I got this for my father's birthday," I said, handing the salesman the box, "and I'd like to return it because it is not what he wanted."

"That's too bad," the salesman said, opening the box to inspect the contents. It had passed the test, for he looked down on me and said, "I suppose we can give you a refund." But then he asked, "You didn't use it, did you?"

You didn't use it, did you? You didn't use it, did you? I had to choose between telling a lie or having my father think I was a jerk.

I finally answered, "Yes."

"You *used* it?"

"Yes."

The salesman closed the lid and handed the box back to me. "I'm sorry," he said. "We can't take this back if you've used it."

"I know," I said. "I'm sorry." I took the box back from him and walked out of the store. It was my money down the drain, and my father hadn't even thought the doughnut maker was clever.

The first time I heard my grandfather Lloyd's name mentioned was the day I discovered a spot of blood in my underpants. Even though I had seen the movie about menstruation in school and I felt fine, I was greatly perturbed and took to my bed. I figured with blood and all, I shouldn't feel fine. But the morning wore on, and when my mother asked me if I was feeling any better, I told her about the blood.

My mother smiled and allayed my fears by telling me that "getting your period" happened to all females my age. She went to my parents' bedroom and returned with a sanitary napkin and belt, and as I sat up in bed, she matter-of-factly demonstrated how to use them. Then she told me that her mother had never explained anything to her when she was a kid and that she could remember, to my amazement, the days before sanitary napkins, when women wore flannel rags and washed them out to use again. I loved hearing about the way life used to be, and suddenly I was asking if she could remember her father.

"Oh, sure," she answered. "He used to come get me in a horse and buggy to take me for rides."

"He did? How old were you?" I was surprised. My mother, a normal little girl. My grandfather, a normal American who took his little daughter for horse-and-buggy rides.

"Seven or eight."

"Wow! I didn't know that! But didn't he live with you?"

"No. Now, you don't need to go telling anybody this"—she gave me the slitted eye ...

"I won't."

"... but my parents were divorced when I was a baby." Divorce in my mother's time was scandalous, a stigma full of shame, disgrace, and embarrassment. I knew only two classmates myself whose parents were divorced. It was not something you talked about.

So Bebe Lorene had had a husband! "Did you like being with your father?"

"Oh, I loved it. I couldn't wait till he came. We had a lot of fun. I loved going to the farm with him in the horse and buggy. He'd take me down to the creek, and we'd go catch crawdads. There was a boy named Billy, with red hair and freckles, who was just my age. He was great."

"Who was Billy?"

Her eyes glazed over. "Oh, a friend of mine. He was like a brother. Mother didn't like me playing like that, though, because she said I'd always come home all dirty and with chigger bites all over me." She paused. "You know, my father was so blond they called him 'Cotton.'"

"Where is he now?"

"Oh ... he died," she said with her that's-all-right-it-doesn't-hurt-me-one-bit look, but I could tell she really loved her father. She let slip one more thing about him. "He quit coming to get me, though. When he came to pick me up, Mother told me to run away." I felt a great, tender sadness for my mother.

In August 1953, Uncle Kamil telephoned my father to tell him how Bebe had found Jiddu alongside her in bed that morning: he had died in his sleep of a heart attack, aged seventy-three. Auntie Jeanette said he died in America of boredom. I was sad to think Jiddu was no longer alive. We had become a passel of kids: Tootie was two; Neal, six; Frank, eleven; and I, thirteen. Were our numbers the reason my father said that funerals were not for children and left me home to babysit? I don't know. While I didn't get to go to Jiddu's funeral, we went as a family to visit Bebe the following weekend.

The first time I ever saw my father cry was when I accidentally came upon him wiping his eyes with his handkerchief in the little guestroom where we put our coats on the bed at Bebe and Jiddu's house. I was moved by my father's tears for his father. It was strange not having Jiddu there.

Home on leave for Jiddu's funeral, Uncle Joe was at Bebe's, too, and he brought presents: a big box of chocolates for our family and, for me, a red satin bed jacket with *Okinawa* embroidered on the back. By now a major in the US Army and on his zillionth wife—Auntie Aileen was long gone—he stood around in his khaki shirt with his uniform jacket off and tie loosened, clinking the ice in his tall Scotch and soda as he looked me over. Asking my father if I had a boyfriend yet, he offered to take me to his officers' club to meet some men. My mother was appalled. I was thirteen, the same year I learned that Bebe Therouza was praying to Saint Jude, the patron saint of lost causes, for me to find a husband.

———

While I was still at Edgemont School, I had bought a small metal box and three-by-five-inch index cards that fit into it for my joke file. On each card I pasted an individual joke I had cut out of old *Reader's Digests*, and I filed them in different categories, such as "seasons." Then in the spring, for instance, I would try to work into the conversations in the bike shed with my eleven-year-old peers such witticisms as, "Spring is when a young girl's fancy turns to what a young man has been thinking about all winter." My efforts were met with odd looks. I was much more successful raising a laugh walking around on the inside of my ankles, as did my comedic exemplar Milton Berle, saying, "Duh!"

After we moved to Brookfield Road, my joke file would come in handy for my unpaid job as joke editor of *Hebron Highlights*, my junior high's newspaper. The desperate poem I submitted to the *Sentinel*, its literary magazine, was rejected. Reading it now, I can easily interpret it as an unconscious message in a bottle washed back up on the marooned's own shore:

Plink, plunk,

I'm a ukulele.

Plunk, plink,

My master's cruel to me.

He plunks my strings so hard they pop.

If I could talk, I'd holler, "Stop!"

But since I can't, Oh, day of woe,

I guess I'll have to let it go.

But the *Sentinel* did publish a couple of my cartoon-like woodcuts. My art teacher counseled me to concentrate my studies on art; but all my friends were on the academic track, and I did not want to get off track from them. The road not taken.

Although I don't know the circumstances, in New York my father happened to meet the professional cartoonist Stanley Stamaty and told him of his young daughter's love of cartooning. The kindly cartoonist gave my father his name and address and invited me to write him with questions I might have about how to get my cartoons published in a magazine. He said he would be interested to see any cartoons I might care to send him. When I sent Mr. Stamaty my cartoons, he wrote me back to suggest what size paper to use and to explain the procedure for submitting cartoons for publication. He liked one of my ideas so much, he asked if I wouldn't mind if he drew it up himself?

Excited, I wrote back that I would be honored, and with dreams of glory, I set to work to mail my other cartoons to the *Saturday Evening Post*. My father, who must have thought he had finally launched me into gainful employment, was as disappointed as I was by the printed rejection slips I received. I was fourteen.

Out of the blue one day, I received a letter in which was enclosed a check for $8.75 from Mr. Stamaty himself, the first check I ever earned. He said that *Esquire* had bought his cartoon of the sign in the cafeteria window saying, "Courteous and efficient self-service," and he was enclosing a third of his payment for my idea. I did not understand at the time that the funny *Reader's Digest* punch lines in my joke file, which inspired my cartoons, had already been published in cartoons. More important than my first check, though, was the fact that Mr. Stamaty treated me respectfully as a budding cartoonist. That I will never forget.

Not only the "good kids" in my new junior high went to Sawyer's dancing class, but kids from all over town, including my old friends from Edgemont. Everybody in school was talking about Sawyer's, the name everyone called it instead of the official name, Suzanne Sawyer Dancing Classes or something like that. Sawyer's lessons and formal dances were held at the Woman's Club of Upper Montclair at night. Wilson's dancing classes were also held at night but could not be called the competition: the tiny stage at the nearby Commonwealth Club, where its lessons and dances were held, was just big enough for a piano, bass, and saxophone, and anyway Wilson's was on its last legs. I begged my father to let me go to Sawyer's, but Wilson's was half the price. Because Miss Wilson was often short on boys, both Frank and Neal at junior high age got paid to dance at her events. For me, my father had to pay.

Since the Commonwealth Club was less than a mile from our house, my father, who had worked hard all day and did not want to go back out with the car, felt there was no reason I could not walk. But because classes were held at night, as soon as I got ready in my strapless organdy formal and satin pumps, my mother had to walk me there and walk home and then walk back later to walk me home. It was not the kind of walk to take in satin heels. When we moved to yet our third house in Montclair, the walk would have been twice as long, so my father was forced to drive me.

I remember two things about Wilson's: first, the poignant throatiness of the alto saxophone, which stirred up my longing when it played "Good Night, Sweetheart" for the last dance each session, and second, dancing with David Cox the night he pulled out of his jacket pocket a live white mouse.

"Here! You can hold it if you want," David said, dangling the mouse by its tail. "Really. Go ahead."

The mouse fit right in the palm of my hand.

"He's cute, isn't he?" David asked.

"Yes," I answered, amazed at its living substance.

"If you want it, you can keep it."

I looked at David. "Really?"

"Sure," he said. "He's nothing to take care of. All you have to feed him is water and Rice Krispies."

"Really?"

He pulled another white mouse out of his other pocket. "This is his pal. You wouldn't want him to get lonesome now, would you?"

"Are they male and female?"

"I'm not sure." He flipped the mouse on its back. "See? It's hard to tell. Anyway, they're yours if you want them."

"Sure! Thanks!"

"I'll keep them for you in my pockets until it's time to go home, and then you can put them in your coat pockets."

"Great! Thanks."

The mice ate through the cardboard box I put them in that night. I found them in the morning hiding under my bureau. My father, who surprisingly did not object to my new pets, dug up a sturdy wooden box for them and made a screen cover for it. I kept the mice in the spare room across from mine on the third floor of our new house. Three school nights in a row, I tiptoed out of bed, flicked on the light, sprawled on the floor on my stomach with my chin propped up in my hand, and peered into the box, studying them, waiting to see them do it. But the only thing that happened was that I got bleary-eyed and worn out for school, and my interest in them waned.

So that Tootie and Neal could have their own rooms, I was happy we had moved to a white clapboard colonial in a nice neighborhood on Highland Avenue. Because it was in the same junior high school district as our house on Brookfield Road, I didn't have to change schools, but I lived anxiously under my father's restless explorations of different places to live. He was constantly looking to improve his investment. On our compulsory Sunday drives, the whole family traipsed through untold numbers of model homes in northern New Jersey; two chicken farms, one in nearby Clifton and one on Long Island; and a Cape Cod house in Caldwell, just over the mountain, which my father actually bought and had painted, going so far as to have me choose wallpaper for the room that would be mine and then changing his mind. Somewhere he read that Daytona, Florida, was the place to live; and one weekend he made the long drive down by himself to look around. He came back with tales of driving right on the beach and brought home two coconuts, one for us all to taste and the other, in which a face had been carved and painted, to hang on the new playroom wall in the basement, where we had a Ping-Pong table and Frank kept his record player. But we didn't hear much about Florida after that.

The painters had just finished refurbishing the downstairs of the new house on Highland Avenue and taken up their drop cloths, unrolled the rugs, and moved all the furniture back in place. My parents had agreed that we needed new curtains for the sun porch, living room, and dining room. But when my father bought the new curtains without consulting my mother or inviting her to go with him to pick them out, they had a fight that I thought might end in divorce.

There was an almost predictable rhythm to their battles. Although I could not articulate it then, it fell into a kind of "spanking cycle," as the psychologist Haim G. Ginott might have recognized it, in which the tension mounted and mounted, with my mother as victim asking for it until my father finally let her have it with verbal criticism until the air was cleared. But then with the slate wiped clean, she often said, "Oh, but making up is so much fun."

Lying in bed in my new room, I had been anxiously listening to the rumble of battle from the living room, but up on the third floor I could not make out their words. When my parents started shouting, I crept out of bed, tiptoed downstairs, and sat on the top step of the second-floor landing. The living room was dark. Suddenly—*crash!*— something porcelain broke on the floor. From what my mother was shouting, I gathered that it was my father's teacup, and it had not smashed on the floor but against the wall when he had hurled it at her.

"If you think I am going to continue letting you treat me like dirt," my mother said, "you have another think a-comin'." When I heard my mother threaten to take us children home to her mother in Missouri, I brightened up. What a great idea! My grandmother had plenty of room. We didn't argue at my grandmother's. She loved us.

My father laughed sardonically. "Oh, yeah, and what are you planning to use for train fare?"

We could write my grandmother, I thought. Bebe Lorene would send us the money in a flash. My gut told me that all we had to do was say the word, and my grandmother would do everything she could to help us. I was even getting excited. I would miss my friends in Montclair, sure, but at Neosho High School, where I already knew a lot of kids, I could be a normal person.

My father seemed to be enjoying his power as he pointed out that not only did my mother not have any money, but did she think he was going to let her take his kids to Missouri? Was my father implying that he wanted us? I didn't think he wanted me any more than a hill o' beans, as my mother would put it. The worrisome thought crossed my mind that I would have to stay with my father and take care of the house and my brothers and sister. Or maybe he would want Neal and Frank to stay with him and split us kids up. But even if we all went to Missouri, it still would be sad to see him left all alone.

When I came downstairs the next morning, I inspected the small scar on the wall where the fresh paint was chipped and the plaster gouged. My father would have killed us if any one of us had inflicted similar damage. I entered the kitchen expecting my parents to say, "Sit down, because we have something to tell you," and they would lay out their plans for divorce. What happened instead was nothing. Although both their mouths were similarly pursed, my father was oddly smug. My mother's eyes were puffed, but they did not express hurt and vulnerability. The cold warriors were exhausted, moving silently around the kitchen, pouring themselves a cup of tea for my father and a cup of coffee for my mother—the quiet *after* the storm. There was security at least in the absence of fighting. But my mother's powerlessness raised for me the questions: Why didn't my mother ask her mother to help her? Why didn't my mother want to go live with my grandmother?

―

Our house on Highland Avenue faced up the mountain. My mother sarcastically called my bedroom my "Ivory Tower" and me, "the Great I Am." But from the window of the third-floor landing, every day I could see the New York skyline twelve miles away. Our steep blacktopped driveway, bordered by a tall hemlock hedge, ran from the top of the street down past the side of the house to a detached two-car garage and turnaround area in the backyard. My father's two-tiered garden was terraced into the back slope. Chipmunks often darted in and out of the rocks in the garden wall. My father had a green thumb, and his beautiful garden was full of zinnias and gladiolus, marigolds and salvia, asters, phlox, and dahlias.

A huge plum tree spread its old arms over the level part of the grassy backyard.

The tree had a platform built into the forks of its branches by the previous owners, which my father reinforced. Busy with high school, I was too old for the plum tree. Frank, at thirteen, tauntingly showed Neal that he was also too old to play in the plum tree by demonstrating a feat that Neal, at nine, was too young to mimic: Frank jumped off the platform and landed in a roll on the ground.

I took a kind of parental pleasure in Neal and Tootie. Tootie at five had befriended a society of ants who had established a highway out of the crack between concrete slabs in the front sidewalk. She spent several mornings stretched out on her stomach on the grass alongside the sidewalk to watch them go in and out of their underground city. Naming her favorite ants, Tootie averred that she could recognize them when they emerged above ground. Now she was assisting Neal, my father's future engineer, who had rigged an Erector set pulley system from the platform in the plum tree down to Tootie waiting in the grass below to load the empty bucket he lowered to her.

Filling the bucket with leaves, Tootie signaled Neal to hoist it to the platform. When I asked her what they were hauling, she replied, "Messages from God."

Alongside the plum tree, against the side of the garage, my father built a hutch for Neal's pet rabbit, George. Neal made regular trips to the hutch with cupfuls of brown pellets of rabbit food, which George transformed into black pellets that dropped through the wire floor and accrued in a stalagmite underneath. Often Neal would lift George out of the hutch to let him hop around in the yard, where he and Tootie would play with him.

One night Neal forgot to latch George's cage. In the morning my mother, looking out the kitchen window, discovered that his hutch was empty. With boundless freedom before him, George had hopped on top of his cage, where Neal found him, trembling.

On summer Saturday evenings, my father would occasionally roll his grill out of the garage for family cookouts. Sometimes he barbecued shish kebab, the marinated lamb or beef cubes and vegetables on a skewer familiar to Americans. But when he grilled the perhaps not-so-familiar *kufta* kebab, Frank and I were in danger of losing self-control and being sent to our rooms. The kufta is seasoned ground lamb, which is patted around the length of the skewer before it is grilled. It is delicious wrapped in bread with parsley and a scallion. But right after it is grilled, when the kufta is pushed off the skewer onto a platter, it is shaped like something a dog might leave in the grass. Catching each other's eye, Frank and I exaggeratedly chomped into the kufta, trying not to choke on our silent laughter.

One afternoon I was putting away the lawnmower after I had cut the grass, a chore I was good at and liked because it took me outside. As I leaned it against the garage wall, I suddenly remembered I had not fed my white mice—for over a week! As fast as I could, I bounded up the driveway. In the house I took the steps to the third floor two at a time and burst through the door of the spare room. Panting and panicked, I scanned the newspaper shreds in their wire-covered box and was relieved to spot one of the white mice scampering around—until I discovered that to survive, it had made a meal of his companion. I almost lost consciousness at the sight of its red, raw head.

"He's your cousin, you know," my mother commented, taking a seat on the sun porch, where we kept our television. My siblings and I were lounging on the couch to watch the new Walt Disney series based on the life of Davy Crockett. I wanted to believe my mother, but she had a defiant look on her face that said, "You think you're so smart"—which she actually often did say to me—"but I know something you don't know." She laughed as if it were some kind of family joke when coonskin caps and fringed jackets became all the rage because of the popularity of the show. I would have been proud as punch to tell my friends I was related to Davy Crockett, who, to me at the time, was America personified, but I had trouble believing my mother's claim of kinship to him. Years later, researching family genealogy, I found out that she was right: I *am* a first cousin six times removed from Davy.

It was in the darkened sun porch where, a year after Jiddu died, I saw my father cry a second time. Our family had gathered one weekend night to watch television. When Eddie Fisher sang his number one hit song at the time, "Oh! My Papa!," the blue light of the screen was reflected on my father's cheeks in the shine of his tears.

"Sheep!" my father declared disgustedly. "You are all sheep! One gets Bermuda shorts; the whole flock must have Bermuda shorts. Now slickers. Have you ever seen a flock of sheep? You can't tell one sheep from another."

"I know, Dad, but slickers are in. I need a raincoat anyway, and it'll keep me dry when I walk to school. Everybody's got one." Rain or shine, I walked the mile to Mount Hebron Junior High School every morning and the mile back home in the afternoon, a walk I enjoyed. But a determined look developed on his face, and I could tell he was locking into something. Finally, my father said, "You need a raincoat? *I* will take you for a raincoat."

"But Dad, you don't have to. I know just what I want and how much it costs. If you'll give me the money, I can just walk down and get it at the Olympic Shop. I already know they have them in my size because I stopped in after school yesterday and tried one on just to be sure and everything."

"Get ready. Tell your mommy to get in the car. I'll get you a raincoat. Someday you'll thank me. You'll see."

"But, Dad ... " I could not help it; I started to cry. "I already *know* the raincoat I want. I wasn't going to get a yellow slicker. I don't look good in yellow."

"Go get your mother. Get in the car."

"They have them in red too. I was going to get the red one."

"Yella! Hurry!" My father barked.

"Dad, I could save you all this trouble."

"Yella, yella."

We piled into the car, my mother up front with my little sister, and me slouched in a sulk in the back seat. The weather in the car smelled of thunderstorms. We passed the Olympic Shop in Upper Montclair. I expected that. But then we were downtown on Bloomfield Avenue, driving past Louis Harris and past where we could have turned for Hahne & Company, department stores where my friends shopped, my last chance.

Salesladies there would have said, "Why, yes, it is what all the girls are wearing." I would have tried one on and shown him, and he would have seen right away that it was fine. The slicker would certainly keep me dry. And he would have to admit it looked cute, didn't it? But where was he going? What town was this? Why had he come all the way here? We had slipped out of the Technicolor world into a dreary black-and-white one, and I could not believe my eyes: we were pulling into the parking lot of Robert Hall. Robert Hall! The sleazy, low-overhead, pipe-rack place in the jingles on the radio. I slid further down into the seat. If I ever saw anybody I knew here, I would be mortified, I thought, so panicked that I forgot this would be the last place on earth I would run into my friends. When I got out of the car, I feigned interest in the wall as I slouched behind my family and walked toward the entrance.

A pleasant enough saleswoman, bleached blond, heavily made up and buxom in her gray Robert Hall suit, approached us with clasped hands.

"May I help you?"

"Yes." My father indicated me with a nod in my direction. "Girls' raincoats, please," he said in his most ingratiatingly courtly voice.

Appraising my size, the saleswoman smiled kindly at me. "We don't have a girls' department. But I think I have something that might fit. Right this way."

I did not fault *her*. Robert Hall was the best she could do. But I had one last hope. As we followed single file down the narrow aisles between the racks of clothes, I asked her, "By any chance do your carry slickers?"

She turned, continuing to walk backward as she looked at me. "No, I'm sorry, dear," she tilted her head sympathetically, "but we do have a nice selection."

My father threw me a haughty look, as if to say: "Slickers are so in, huh, they don't even carry them?"

Our party came to a halt behind the saleswoman, who had stopped and was now waving her hand across the rack of raincoats that might fit me. My mother let go of Tootie's hand, and my sister disappeared under the coats, all but her little shoes, as she tried to sit on the frame of the rack.

"Don't wipe yourself all over the floor." My mother glowered a warning at her.

"Well, go ahead," my father gesticulated impatiently, his hand palm up, swinging from me to the rack. "Look." Not an invitation but definitely a command.

My heart sank. I could tell just from the lineup of limp sleeves there was no raincoat at Robert Hall I would be caught dead in.

"Is that how you look?" My father began picking through the coats himself.

The saleswoman hitched uncomfortably.

"Here!" he announced triumphantly, extracting a coat from the pack. "Try it on." He began undoing the buttons as if he were the salesman.

I put the coat on and stood there.

"Go. Look in the mirror." My father was nodding as he looked me up and down, obviously pleased with himself.

"It's a very nice coat," the woman smiled at him and discreetly backed away as I looked in the full-length mirror. The raincoat was awful. It was made of red corduroy with a round collar and red-corduroy-covered buttons. I felt like the center pole in a two-man tent.

"With a fabric coat like this," the saleswoman pointed out to my father, "you can wear it in good weather, too."

My father clicked his approval at this bonus feature, rocking with satisfaction on his heels.

"It's too big," I whimpered.

"You'll grow into it."

"Well, you could adjust the size with the optional belt," the saleswoman said, trying to be helpful. Reaching both of her arms around me, she pulled each end of a floppy red corduroy belt around to my front, where she tied them. I remembered my Brownie uniform in second grade. My mother actually took me to Louis Harris department store for it. It was the only place that sold them. I was wiry and thin, and the only size left was "chubby." I didn't even mind that it wrapped around me twice because it was the official Brownie uniform, and it came from Louis Harris. I belonged. I could always laugh, "It was the last size left."

This was different.

Glancing down at the price tag dangling from the sleeve, I was astonished and broke into a big smile. "Dad, this is six dollars *more* expensive than the slicker at the Olympic Shop. The slicker is *cheaper*!"

"But where can you wear a slicker besides in the rain?" he asked rhetorically. "You can wear this coat to church."

"Dad"—the tears started—"I *don't want* this coat."

"It's red, isn't it?" my father said, as if my insatiable wants would never be satisfied.

"*Lat-say-ya,*" my mother attempted, I thought, to intercede.

"So!" My father turned to the saleswoman, who was awkwardly waiting. "We'll take it," he said as he reached into his back pocket for his wallet. The saleswoman looked questioningly at me and back at my father. But my father indicated with a tilt of his cheekbone for me to take the coat off, and then he pointed with his cheekbone toward the cash register at the front of the store. "Yella."

I fumbled with the buttons and handed the coat to the saleswoman, who pressed her lips into a feeble smile, but I could hardly look at her.

This is what was so confusing: the red corduroy raincoat could be worn in both foul and fair weather and was therefore twice as useful as a slicker. It was red, my favorite color, and my father was willing to pay even more for a coat for me than the one I had asked for. Plus he was teaching me not to be just one of the flock, but to stand out as an individual. What was wrong with me that I was so ungrateful? Why did I hate him?

ITT Federal Labs in Newark, where my father worked, encouraged its employees to take graduate courses in their fields of interest and offered to pay for them. When my father took a graduate course at night at the Stevens Institute of Technology in Hoboken, I don't know if it was in electrical engineering or in quality control. He did the work for his class, not at his desk in my parents' bedroom, but downstairs in the dining room, with his papers spread out all over the dining table. The dining room was open to the front hall. It was not the ideal study environment with five other family members moving around the house. Perhaps a graduate degree would have assured my father of the kind of engineering job he would have enjoyed, but he had to do the course work on top of a full-time job and the worry of supporting a family of four kids, and he must have been beat when he came home at night. He did not go for the graduate degree in electrical engineering, but he somehow reinvented himself as a quality control engineer.

"At each meal a quarrel, with each bite a worry," goes an Arab proverb. There was an annual meal I mostly enjoyed, during which my father acted very Arab. It was in the spring, when the shad began to run. They run up the Hudson River in New York to spawn just the way they run up the Shatt al Arab in Basra. To me, shad tastes not only like spring but also, more specifically, like Saturday afternoon in spring. Once each year in season, my father purchased from a fish stall in New York the biggest shad he could find for our invented annual family shad feast, which we called *sabûr*. *Sabûr* is simply the Arabic word for "shad."

The meal was noteworthy in our household for several reasons: first, we all relished the food; second, we spread newspapers like a tablecloth on the Formica kitchen tabletop, on which it was my job to set the plates and silverware; and third, my father was involved in the preparation of the meal.

The sabûr was split in half along its spine so that it opened into two symmetrical halves. Before broiling it, my mother spread a paste of chopped onion, curry, and lemon juice on each half of the fish, dotting it with butter. She had prepared a two-quart pot of rice mixed with yellow split peas beforehand. After scrubbing his hands, my father made the salad, chopping its contents—lettuce, cucumbers, tomatoes, parsley, bell peppers—so finely that it was almost pre-chewed. The dressing was lemon juice, which gave the salad a fresh-air taste. But maybe my memory of fresh air is of the literal drafts of spring air wafting through the back door, purposely left ajar. My parents made a big deal about how indigestible sabûr was if eaten in the evening and how important it was to have all day to digest it; consequently, we ate this dinner in the middle of a regular Saturday, when the fare was ordinarily baloney or cheese-spread sandwiches. I never understood the reasoning, but eating sabûr anytime was all right with me.

We children readied ourselves in our places at the table, watching our parents' moves like a nest of baby robins with their beaks expectantly open. As soon as my mother pulled the sabûr out of the broiler and spooned a portion of the topping over the mounds of rice and split peas on each of our plates, she attended my father at the kitchen counter like an operating room nurse. When the sabûr was cool enough to handle, he picked through the flesh of the fish with his fingers. Its many tiny bones make eating sabûr such a slow procedure that when a child in Basra was late in returning to school in the afternoon, the teacher's standard question was, "Did you have sabûr for lunch?"

"Be careful of the bones," my mother cautioned us as my father tossed the fish tidbits onto our plates, for as carefully as he combed the sabûr, several bones were bound to turn up poking into your tongue. This is what the newspaper tablecloth was for: anything you discovered in your mouth that you didn't want was deposited directly onto it.

As a fourteen-year-old, I had worked my way up to mixing the bite-sized pieces of fish into my rice and split peas, but I preferred my salad separate. Neal, at seven, was still in the phase of not wanting any of the different categories of food on his plate to touch. On the other hand, when my father finally sat down, he mixed every item on his plate into one single mountain. And then, as we did every year, Frank and I begged our father for the annual featured attraction—to demonstrate how a real Arab eats. With a little grin, he set aside his knife and fork and complied, scooping off the top of his mountain of food with the tips of his fingers as deftly as if he were playing jacks. To negotiate a handful of rice from his plate to his mouth without getting rice all over the place seemed to us an amazing feat.

"Please, Dad, do it again."

Before my father got down to serious eating with the handy tools of modern occidental civilization, he obliged us with several more neat, bare-handed swipes at his plate and deposits into his mouth.

Little Neal remarked wittily, "You are a slob!"

Wham! My father's hot temper flared as he struck Neal. "You insult your father!"

Wham! Wham!

"*Lat-say-ya,*" said my mother; but Frank and I did not jump to Neal's defense with "He was only joking!," for if we had, we would have been next.

Aside from this incident, sabûr was usually a happy occasion: by combing the fish for bones to protect us from choking, my father displayed a mindfulness of us, and he demonstrated playfulness by eating with his fingers.

———

The family was in the car for one of our compulsory Sunday drives, and my father wanted to show us where he was working. I don't know whether he had left ITT Federal Labs or ITT Federal Labs had left him, but he had found a new job as a quality control engineer. He pulled the car up to a building on a street corner that looked on the outside more like a store than a factory. After he unlocked the door, he waved us all in. Massive machinery affronted us as we stepped inside. It dominated the floor space and seemed stacked to the top of the high ceiling. I didn't know what town we were in, what the name of the company was, or what the machinery manufactured; but when my father threw the switch, the noise the machinery's moving parts made was deafening.

"That's what I have to listen to all day long," my father said, and I could understand why when he came home from work he needed peace and quiet.

―

Three of the greatest girls in my class asked me to be part of an exciting plan the summer after eighth grade. The families of two of them had neighboring summerhouses in Cape Cod. Sonja was invited to stay with Gina, and I, to stay with Marcia. Sonja and I could travel together on the train and be met by our respective hostesses, and the four of us would have a week together on the beach. Our only expense would be the round-trip train ticket.

I broached the proposal to my parents. My father listened half-heartedly, but he smiled at my enthusiasm and said, "We'll see." I was overjoyed. He had not responded with his usual "No." "We'll see" was a big opening, a probable "Yes," because what possible objection could he come up with? I had pointed out that the families of my friends were such good families that we would be properly supervised. The girls were all nice girls, good students, popular and upstanding; and I'd been to their homes in Montclair millions of times. And think of it! A whole week's vacation in Cape Cod for just the price of the train ticket! All that had to be done was for one parent to put us on the train in one place, and we would be met by another parent on the other end. It was also our last chance to spend time with Marcia, because in the fall her father, who worked for an oil company, was moving their family to South Africa.

The four of us girls began making all kinds of plans, discussing the best beaches, which beach had the cutest lifeguard. It was nearing the time to buy the train tickets, but when I reminded my father, he answered simply, "You're not going."

"What?" I couldn't believe my ears.

"You heard me. You're not going."

"Why?" The dam leaked; tears trickled down my cheeks. "I don't understand. Why can't I go? Everything's all set. What could you possibly have against it? It's such a wonderful invitation."

"You're not going, and that's final."

Waters spilled over the top. Crying, I threw my own Arab fit, stomping up the stairs to my room. I hated him. I hated him. This can't be possible, I thought to myself, trying to calm down. Maybe I had not explained everything clearly enough to him: how well we would be supervised, what nice families our hosts were, what nice girls my friends were. Washing my face and gathering my wits about me, I stacked a few sandbags against the stressed dam and descended the stairs.

"Dad," I began presenting my case, calm and collected. "For the last three weeks you let me think I could go to Cape Cod. It's all I've been talking about. Now you suddenly say I can't go. You know what nice families the Tuppers and Whipples are. They are very responsible people."

"You're not going."

"Dad!" I burst, the dam collapsing. "I don't get it. Give me a reason." I could tell he did not have one. Casting about, he finally blurted, "You don't know what kind of people travel on the train."

"What do you mean? Sonja and I will be traveling together, and we'll be met at the station."

"Bûma! You don't know what kind of people ride the train. Some crazy soldier or sailor."

"What do you mean?" I shouted, not respectfully deferring as a subservient Arab female to my father. "What do you think could happen on the train?"

"You're not going, and that's that."

"You can't do this!" I shrieked, not responding as a disinterested anthropologist. I went crazy crying and ran up to my room again, slamming the door in bewildered rage and slamming myself around the room as well. I had to go to Cape Cod! He couldn't do this to me! But, of course, he could.

What Sonja did next I consider one of the bravest and most faithful acts of friendship ever done for my sake. "That's terrible!" she exclaimed when I told my three friends that my father was not going to let me go. "Why?" They could not understand. "It just isn't fair," Sonja said. "I'm going to call him up myself," she declared, determined to see justice done.

"You are?" I was astonished. "You'd do that? But listen," I said, having immediate second thoughts, "he's not going to like it. He might get very mad." But maybe she could convince him. I reconsidered. She was, after all, so beautiful, and I knew my father was a sucker for blonds.

I heard my father's side of the conversation the afternoon Sonja telephoned: "Yes ... No ... You could have saved yourself the trouble ... I said she's not going. Goodbye."

Sonja recounted at school that she had told my father how much we'd all been looking forward to going to the Cape and how many plans we'd made to do things together. She said she emphasized how her own parents would never let her go unless everything was safe. She told me she started crying when she said, "I am on my knees *begging* you to let Suzy come to the Cape with us."

"You said *that*?"

"Yes, I really was on my knees saying a prayer that you could come."

I loved Sonja. I hated my father. I was brokenhearted and powerless. And this time I had a witness.

But then my father put a little twist on the events.

One evening, after my friends had already departed for the Cape, I was passing through the front hall. He called me, nodding to the wing chair opposite his. "Sit down," he said quietly, and I sat.

"I just didn't have the money for the train ticket."

"What?"

"The reason I couldn't let you go to Cape Cod is because I don't have the money." My father looked tired and tense.

"Why didn't you say so in the first place?"

"You know it costs a lot of money to live in a nice house like ours. We live on one of the nicest streets in Upper Montclair." Wasn't a shiny Buick Special parked in our driveway? Didn't we always have good food on the table and nice clothes on our backs? He went on in this vein, adding how hard he was working and doing it all for us. By the time he had finished, he had accomplished two things: first, completely changing the subject, he succeeded in having me pick the card he was holding; and second, like a comic-book strong man, he swooped down on all the hate and rage beaming out of me and bent it back to aim at myself.

My last trip to Neosho as a kid was the summer between ninth grade, my last year of junior high school, and tenth grade, my first year at Montclair High School. It was the summer I shot up to almost five foot six inches, attaining my adult height. It was the summer I got my first pimples. I didn't know then how the body can speak symbolically, or I would have recognized that something deep inside me wanted to "break out." It was the summer when, bucking down dirt roads and around a country pasture between the cows, John, a boy I met the year I finished sixth grade at Central, tried to teach me how to drive in his antique floor-shift Model A Ford, which he had painted red. Bebe Lorene was amused to tell me that John's car was the very same model as her first car. John was nice looking, with strawberry blond hair and freckles. He was a member of DeMolay, an international organization for young men in Neosho modeled after the Masons, something I'd never heard of in Montclair, but I went with him to the organization's tractor-pulled hay ride and wiener roast, which was fun. I felt John was a friend.

My friend Judy told me that the boy I had been especially attracted to, Larry, had a girlfriend but that it was an on-again, off-again thing. After Judy told Larry that I was back in Neosho visiting my grandmother, he telephoned to ask me for a date to play miniature golf. I was going on fourteen. When Larry picked me up in his father's '51 Chevrolet, I learned he was not the requisite fifteen years old one needed to be to get a permit to drive in Missouri. He told me that not only did his father have enough confidence in his driving abilities to let him drive the family car, but his father was also a friend of the sheriff. There's a good chance that if my mother had known Larry did not have a driver's permit, I would not have been allowed to go out with him in his car. But I had a good time with him. I had never played miniature golf before, and we laughed and teased each other the whole time before we went for cones at the new Dairy Queen.

Judy and I cooked up another date with Larry, a double date with my brother Frank and Judy in the back seat. Larry drove us to see a movie at the Edgewood Drive-In. From the front seat, we heard Frank ask Judy for her "meat hook," so that they could hold hands. We all laughed. Up front we quietly held hands, too, but it was the next time, when Larry and I drove to the Edgewood alone, that was a watershed. We briefly held hands, and then we steamed up the windows with what seemed like one long, delicious kiss that lasted for the entire movie, which we never watched. His starched short-sleeve shirt smelled so clean, and our breath together was as sweet as a spring breeze. I don't think we came up for air until we started hearing people in the cars around us clunking the car speakers back onto their stands and scrunching gravel as they got into the line of cars inching out the exits. Larry drove me back to my grandmother's house and walked me to the door. When I came inside, everyone was already asleep. I changed into my pajamas in the dark and then sat cross-legged on the bed on top of the sheets to look out the window onto West Spring Street, where I saw Larry's car go slowly past our house— three times.

In the 1950s Uncle Kamil was working at the United Nations. He had to go on "home leave" every two or three years to maintain his Iraqi citizenship. The only caveat in going to Iraq, under the still-British-influenced monarchy of Faisal II, was that he was not to talk about politics or prominent people in the government; he was just to visit. Auntie May, his wife, and my cousin June, their daughter, always went with him.

One Sunday our family was having dinner at my aunt and uncle's house in Larchmont, and they were talking about their upcoming trip to Iraq. I commented how wonderful it would be to get to see Basra.

My uncle said, "Why don't you come along?"

"Really?" I asked. "I would love to go."

"Sure. Why not?" he said.

Wow, I thought, getting to see where I was born and going with Uncle Kamil and Auntie May. That would be great! How could my father refuse chaperones like them?

But he did, and I was disappointed. If he didn't have the money to send me to Iraq, I would have understood, but he never gave me a reason. If he didn't have the money, though, maybe he was too proud to let his older brother know he could not afford the trip, but he could have told me. Why didn't I ask him? I don't know. Maybe I didn't want him to think I was starting an argument.

Like the man in Auntie May's joke who hoped his flatulence would be forgotten, maybe my father was afraid that when people learned that I was the daughter of Nejib Tooni, someone would be reminded, "Oh, yes, the lieutenant who went AWOL." Maybe it was fear, but probably it was money.

⁓

On the crowded public bus for which students could buy discounted tickets to ride to Montclair High School, a classmate introduced me to her new stepsister, coincidentally, another Marcia, who was going to be living with her. We were all in the same grade. In 1955, having a stepsister was unusual. Until now, Marcia had been living with her mother on a sheep farm outside a little town in Georgia, an environment I understood in my bones because of Neosho. She spoke Southern, too, which I also understood, but there was more in the music than in the words that created an instant bond in us.

Marcia had big blue eyes with long brown lashes, long, shiny, straight blond hair that she had to keep pushing out of her eyes, perfect teeth in an engagingly crooked smile, and a dimple in her chin. She thought I was funny, but I can't think of a single funny thing I said. Although she was athletically muscular, she carried herself awkwardly in a vulnerable way. She was pretty, she was smart, and she jumped right into life at Montclair High School, where she would be voted Most Likely to Succeed, but they didn't say at what. After we got to be best friends, she told me she had been a star forward on the championship girls' basketball team at her high school in Georgia. Her athletic prowess did not have currency in Montclair, however, as it was gauche for a girl to be too good in sports after ninth grade. But Marcia didn't have to worry; the boys knocked themselves out to meet her.

Marcia and I found ourselves in two classes together. She invited me over after school and soon thereafter to stay for dinner, so I got to know her father and stepmother, too. One afternoon after school, we took our Cokes into her living room. As I sat on the floor in front of the couch, she put her Coke down on the coffee table and pulled out the piano bench. Taking a seat at the keyboard, with her back to me and her hands poised in the air, she collected herself like a concert pianist. When she brought her fingers down tenderly to touch the keys, the notes pierced me with their beauty. It was the first time I had ever heard the music that she played. I was as intoxicated by her ability to play such moving music, from memory and with such great feeling, as I was stirred by the music itself. I felt her knowledge knew no end when she explained the composer was French, Claude Debussy, and his composition was called "Clair de Lune."

Marcia was visiting my house once when I started to steer her toward our playroom in the basement, where my father wanted us children to entertain our friends. "Let's go upstairs," she said, as any typical American teenager would. "I want to see your room." My mother shot me the slitted eye, and I gulped. My father would not like this. He was like the owner of a bed-and-breakfast who roped off the private part of the house.

"Come on." Marcia boldly bounded up the hall stairs. What could I do but follow her through the opening she had brazenly punched into an impenetrable barrier?

"We won't be long," I called to my mother, feigning nonchalant cheeriness. There was nothing to do in my immaculate room. I did not have a stereo like Marcia, who, while our peers spun

Fats Domino records, introduced me to Beethoven, Brahms, and Rachmaninoff. I made sure Marcia was out of my room before my father got home from work, so there were no repercussions.

It took several such afternoons before I felt daring enough for us to sneak a cigarette (as we did at her house), blowing the smoke out my third-floor window while we talked. Then, sitting on my Arab rug with her back against my bed, Marcia began relating the story of her complicated and, I believed, important life. I listened intently, jotting down notes on a yellow pad as she spoke, for she had consented to let me base my first novel on her life, the book I planned one day to write. Marcia believed in me as a writer.

As the only girl my age I knew who went on an overnight date at a college, Marcia brought me news of the larger world. Returning from a weekend at Yale, she reported on a foreign film she had seen with her date, a movie full of symbols, called *The Seventh Seal*, which she said everybody on campus was talking about. She also recommended that I read Albert Camus's *The Stranger*. With no equipment to deal with existentialism, a new word I could hardly pronounce, I read the book while ignorantly wondering: If life was as absurd as Camus claimed, why did he bother to write a book?

In those first months, introducing me to the language of psychology, my new friend diagnosed my case. Assessing my lack of confidence, Marcia observed, "You have an inferiority complex" and took me on as her willing project. Despairing of my wardrobe, she sewed as a gift a classic wool boat-necked jumper whose pattern and fabric she invited me to select. This must have been hard to take for my mother, whose handmade garments I rejected. As a candidate herself for secretary of Student-Faculty, our high school's student council, Marcia convinced me I had what it took to run for the office, too. My friend Gina was also running, as well as another friend, Sue.

Miraculously, I won the election. But since I did not have a typewriter and didn't know how to type, Marcia typed the minutes for me and showed me how to make copies on the mimeograph machine in the school office. There seemed no limit to her knowledge and generosity.

Marcia's Southern friendliness won my mother over, too. "Mmm, what are you cooking, Mrs. Tooni? Your dinners always smell so good," Marcia called into our kitchen. Sniffing the *bamia*, an Iraqi lamb stew with okra and garlic, she stopped to discuss with my mother their mutual appreciation of that viscous Southern vegetable rarely enjoyed in the North. But my mother never invited Marcia to have dinner at our house, and I never asked if I could invite her. Less than three months after our meeting, Marcia gave me a copy of Kahlil Gibran's *The Prophet* for my sixteenth birthday, introducing me to poetry, not as a school assignment, but for the pleasure of reading.

I had never before told anyone about anything that happened in our house, but I confided in Marcia about an argument my parents had after my mother lit the candles on the cake she had made for that very birthday. My mother and father had angrily risen from the table in our darkened kitchen and, taking their shouting into the living room, left me alone with my siblings with the cake ablaze. When I told Marcia the abandoned birthday cake made me especially sad because it was lopsided, she immediately understood. Henceforth, the phrase "a lopsided birthday cake" entered our private vocabulary to describe any instance of innocent joy shining in the midst of no one paying attention. We also coined a new word, *resire*, for the poignant oceanic feeling brought on by music like "Clair de Lune," the beauty of the color of sunsets, the expectant hush of snow, as well as our feelings of friendship for each other. The most we could articulate was to agree that our experience felt like desire but with restraint, hence, resire. Many years later, reading C. S. Lewis, I was startled to discover *Sehnsucht*, an equivalent German word that describes the longing that beauty arouses. But as in Aesop's "Androcles and the Lion," who wouldn't feel love for the person who removed the big thorn of family secrecy from your paw?

What caused the row between my father and me one Saturday afternoon, I do not remember exactly. I had planned to go over to Marcia's, and it most likely started over my never wanting to be home. Both parents accused me of treating my friends preferentially.

That day my father's words rang in my ears as a disturbing accusation: "What? You're going to Marcia's again? Are you going to *marry* her?"

Marry her? Was there something wrong with me for wanting to spend so much time with my friend?

"Don't you have a home? Huh?" My father pushed his face into mine.

"I do, Dad, but … "

If I didn't give the answer he was looking for, my father would rough me up the way a bully threatens smaller children on the playground: "You want to fight, huh?"

The smaller child retreats backward, stumbling with an arm in front of her face to ward off the bully's cuffs. That afternoon, my father inched me back with pokes and jabs, and we worked ourselves all the way down to the basement, right to the cellar door under the stairs.

"You'll see 'strict.'" He continued to prod me backward. "I'll send you away to a Catholic boarding school for girls. How'd you like that, huh?"

My unguarded face lit up, and the subject of boarding school was never broached again. My father and I worked our way back up the cellar stairs to the front hall. "You want to leave, huh? So go!"

"Lat-say-ya," said my mother.

Like a bouncer, my father grabbed me by the back of my collar and the waist of my jeans and heaved me out the front door, where I sprawled down the short brick steps.

"So you don't have a home!" he yelled after me as I ran away as fast as I could down to Marcia's. There, for the first time, I daringly stayed the whole day without letting my parents know where I'd gone and with no plan of returning. I felt guilty and crazy the whole time because I preferred being at my friend's house. Had I provoked my father, hoping for a bruise? With a good bruise, I would have proof that he was cruel, but I had left the scene of the crime clean of evidence.

When it started to get dark, my father telephoned me at Marcia's and calmly told me to come home for dinner. I did not know what else to do. I could not stay at Marcia's forever. I arrived home in time to sit at the table before my mother said grace. I was emotionally drained as we bowed our heads and my mother prayed: "God is great. God is good. Let us thank Him for our food."

But I did not look up to catch Frank's eye and whisper "fud" to rhyme with "good." The only sounds breaking the silence were the clinks and scrapes of our forks against our plates. The storm was over and was not mentioned again—the strange calm *after* the storm. I was as exhausted by the times the blow didn't fall on me as by the times it did. Either way, there was no rest because there was no knowing.

Marcia had her own family experience to contend with, her own story, which is not mine to tell. Considering my family experience, as unarticulated as it was, I empathized with her mounting depression. But in light of all the life she had brought into my life, I could not understand why she would want to kill herself that first time she tried in high school by swallowing a bottle of aspirin.

What she later reported her psychiatrist thought of our "resire" made me nauseated with confusion. Maybe something *was* wrong with me, and my father was right. With all his authority, the psychiatrist affixed the label on our friendship as "latent homosexuality." I didn't know anything about homosexuality except what I then found in the dictionary, but I knew how I felt. Never even expressing it, I knew I loved Marcia.

The one breath of fresh air in my life had been declared polluted. It was only years later when I learned to trust myself that I also learned that it was OK to let love be love.

Society was acting like my father.

As the date of the junior prom got closer, I was worried that no one was going to ask me to go, which would have been conspicuously embarrassing, especially since I was chairman of the event. Consequently, when the president of our student council, Danny Klein, one of the smartest and funniest boys in school, asked *me* to be his date, I was thrilled.

"Here she comes!" my mother proudly announced, eager to watch my father's reaction as I came down the stairs in my new strapless pink organdy formal. As I turned the corner on the second-floor landing, he put down his newspaper, got up from his chair in the living room, and stood in the hall to watch me descend.

Beaming, my father spontaneously tipped an imaginary microphone to the side and crooned into it, "There she is, Miss A-merrr-i-caaah."

"Oh, Daddy." I laughed, giving my reflection an anxious glance as I rustled past the hall mirror. "Do you *really* think I look all right?"

"All right? Honey," he said, taking both of my hands and standing back to appraise me, "your date is a lucky man."

"Thank you," I said, believing him, as he gave me a giant hug.

"But what would you expect," he asked, grabbing my mother—who was wiping her eyes—and swinging her around, "with such a pretty mother?" He planted a big kiss on her cheek. My parents stood side by side with their arms around each other, taking me in. They said, "You look beautiful" and laughed because it came out in unison.

This fantasy scene would have happened if I were the teenage daughter in an episode of *Father Knows Best*. Our parents are mirrors, and that was not the affirmation I found reflected in them.

What really happened was that my father thought a date was tantamount to sexual intercourse, for what male and female left alone would be able to resist doing it? The anthropologist Patai had something to say about this Arab attitude, too. Observing the child-rearing practices of my father's Arab culture—and, of course, there is no way for me to know how my Iraqi grandmother, Bebe Therouza, raised her four boy babies—Patai said that to comfort a crying male baby, the "mother, grandmother, other female relatives and visitors will play with the penis of the boy, not only to soothe him, but also simply to make him smile." He believes that receiving erotic pleasure from his mother and other female caretakers in babyhood may predispose the Arab male "to accept the stereotype of the woman as primarily a sexual object and a creature who cannot resist sexual temptation." And what greater dishonor could befall an Arab man than the sexual misconduct of his daughter? But to me, an American-indoctrinated sixteen-year-old female struggling to be popular, my father's attitude was totally perplexing.

When I told my father that Danny had asked me to the junior prom, he fumed; at first he was not going to let me go. I had to beg. I was chairman of the event, I argued; it would be embarrassing if I didn't get to go. I *had* to go. Considering my dearth of dates, I heatedly pointed out, I was lucky I had any date at all, but especially lucky to have such a good one. But to compound Danny's being male, he was also a Jew; and to my father, the Jews stole Palestine. I didn't understand what my father had against Jews. Danny was a school leader, and yes, I liked him very much, but we were just friends. We were just going to a dance. I wasn't going to *marry* him.

"Lat-say-ya," added my mother, as powerless as I, but at least giving me some sympathy. Under the extenuating circumstances of the junior prom, my father sullenly conceded. Just this once, he said, but he didn't want me to think that he was going to let this become a habit.

To my mother, brought up a Southern Baptist, the Jews were the Israelites who gave us Moses. When Danny stepped in the front door to pick me up for the prom, my mother smiled pleasantly, for she had already met him. One previous afternoon Danny had suggested we get together at my house to try to write a funny television play. He was full of script ideas. But before I had a chance to lead Danny to our playroom in the basement, he suggested we sit at our kitchen table to brainstorm. I could hardly breathe, even though we had plenty of time before my father got home from work. My mother, I guessed, could probably hear us talking. I was so self-conscious sitting casually, yes, just sitting casually, at our kitchen table—a piece of furniture used for meals—that I felt like an audience member watching myself pretending to be a teenager in a play but not knowing the lines. And, although I laughed a lot, I could not think of anything funny for the TV script.

"Good evening, Mr. and Mrs. Tooni," Danny smiled, spiffy in his tuxedo, as he stood in our hall on the night of the prom. My father got up from his chair. He was resentfully reserved, but he condescended to say, "How do you do?" to Danny when I introduced them. My mother said, "Have a good time" as we closed the door behind us.

I did have a good time with Danny at the prom, for we really were good friends, although in my nervousness, I'm sure I cracked more jokes than I needed to. When he drove me home and ran around to open the car door and walk me to the porch, I was happy. I thanked him, we said, "Good night," I went in the house, and he drove away.

I was glad the house was quiet and that everyone had already gone to bed. I turned off the porch light, made sure the front door was locked, switched off the little light in the front window of the dining room, and tiptoed upstairs to my room. My door was closed, but when I opened it and switched on the lamp, I was stunned. It looked as if my room had been ransacked by robbers. The mattress and sheets had been ripped off the bed and dragged to the middle of the rug. All my clothes had been pulled out of my closet and thrown on the mattress. Every drawer in my bureau and desk had been emptied on top of my clothes. The contents of my wastebasket were sprinkled on top of the heap.

Pinned to the peak of the debris was a note in my father's handwriting: "If you are going to act like a pig," it read, "than really live like one."

As violated and angry as I felt, I did not mention the incident the next day, nor did my father. My parents and I both acted as if everything was back to normal. But normal by what standard? Why in the world had my father torn apart my room and left such a note? Was this more than culture or gender? Was he crazy?

On a crisp, fall Sunday, as perfect as the autumn scene printed on the cover of the morning's program of services, I was in the crowd of parishioners exiting the Montclair Heights Dutch Reformed Church. After lining up to shake the minister's hand at the door, we fanned down the stone stairs and clumped into friendly bunches around the lawn. My father turned to me and out of the blue asked, "Would you like to drive home?"

"Sure," I answered, but I was not amused. I wasn't even eligible for my driver's permit until my birthday in December.

"You go home with Mommy." He pointed with a sweep of his forehead to Neal and Frank and indicated my mother's two-door navy blue Hillman sedan with his chin. My father had bought the little floor-shift British car for her secondhand so that she could get her driver's license and take Tootie to school when it rained. Her teacher had notified my parents that on rainy days my sister would dawdle on her long walk to school and arrive late in the classroom soaking wet. My mother was still inside the church, changing out of her choir robe, and Tootie was with her.

"Here, take them." My father dangled the car keys at me.

As Frank and Neal headed toward my mother's car, Frank looked back and exaggeratedly dropped his jaw open and rubbed his eyes in disbelief. "Woo-ooo."

Power flowed into me when I took the car keys from my father's hand. "You mean it? Really?" Slowly walking toward the Buick, I tried not to swagger, but I know I was beaming.

"Yella."

Sliding behind the wheel, with my father oddly in the passenger seat, I began to get nervous. The only thing I knew about driving was what I remembered from John Carver's demonstration of how to use a choke, clutch, and stick shift in his Model A jalopy in Neosho. The transmission on my father's Buick Special was automatic. We were parked in front of the church on the right-hand side of the street, aimed in just the direction for home. While we waited for the cars parked around us to clear out, my father showed me how to turn the car on, put the car in Drive, and put it back in Park. He pointed out which pedal was for the gas and which, for the brakes.

"OK," he ordered like a tank commander, "look behind you, and if nothing's coming, pull out."

Nothing was coming, so as if we were rolling on endless metal tank tracks, I advanced the Buick four car lengths to the red light on the corner of Valley Road, where I stopped. The red light could last ten minutes as far as I cared. I was enjoying the pose of resting my left elbow in the open window while my right hand absently toyed with the wheel. I gazed around as if I had infinitely more important things to think about than driving.

The light turned green, and I proceeded across the intersection and up the hill the half mile or so to Highland Avenue. Extending my left arm out the window to indicate my intentions, I made the left-hand turn onto our street, smooth as could be. Highland Avenue runs straight across the side of the Watchuung Mountains for almost the length of the town. From the corner where I turned, it was only a mile to our house. As we tooled through the open space of Mountainside Park, my father said, "Now pull over to the side of the road and park."

I crooked my left arm out the window, pulled over, and came to a stop. To my left, beyond the band of red, yellow, and orange treetops, past the brown and purple hues of the undeveloped spaces, the New York skyline sparkled along the curve of the earth.

"OK, now try Reverse."

I shifted the car into "R" and depressed the gas pedal. We lurched backward and skidded out onto the road.

"Stop!" My father's whole body radiated impatience. "Put it in Drive and pull up where you were parked." Since we were now facing where we had been, I could see the damp tracks where the tires had swerved onto the grass.

"Pull out. Stop!" he barked, and I braked too fast. "Bûma! Don't turn the wheel while the car is stopped; it wears out the tires. Always turn the wheels when you are moving. OK, drive home. Don't go in the driveway. Turn around at Mountain Terrace and park in front of the house."

I pulled out slowly and carefully drove the remaining three blocks to the corner just beyond our house, where I slowed to a stop.

"Now turn down Mountain Terrace a little. Back up onto Highland and pull up in front of the house."

I turned down Mountain Terrace and braked.

"You forgot to give your left-hand signal."

"Oh, right. Sorry."

Backing the car up, I aimed the rear end of the car onto Highland with the front end pointed at our house on the right.

My father was shaking his head. "You forgot to look to see if any cars were coming."

"Oh, right. Sorry."

Inching the car along, I pulled up in front of the house, bringing the car to a tidy stop alongside the curb. Whew! I did it! My first time driving. Not bad, if I did say so myself. He had never even let my mother drive his Buick Special.

"Thanks, Dad," I said as we both opened our doors and fell out. Heading for the front door, I was surprised at how wobbly I was on my feet.

"Hmm," my father grunted, for he was already absorbed in walking around the car to check for scratches.

In America, learning to drive and getting a driver's license was a national rite of passage. The countdown to a teenager's turning seventeen, the age for getting a learner's permit in New Jersey, began months before the birthday. The highlight of the actual anniversary was the after-school trip to the Department of Motor Vehicles. At least that was the way it was for me and my friends at Montclair High School that fall of 1956.

I didn't understand why my father had been so nice to me, willing to teach me how to drive before I had my learner's permit. He even appeared to be making a big effort to control his temper. I was so elated that out on the church lawn the following Sunday, a day as beautiful as the last, before he had a chance to raise the subject, I asked him if I could drive again.

He didn't say yes right away, but pursed his lips as if to think over my request. Finally he consented and tossed me the keys. I couldn't believe my streak of good luck.

This time the car was parked in front of the church on the opposite side of the street facing down the hill. I thought maybe I'd take the car down to the bottom of the hill, turn it around (but I wasn't sure where), come back up the hill, and go home the same way we did last Sunday. I got in the driver's seat, rocking back and forth on my buttocks as I gripped the steering wheel a few times to get settled. My father sat alongside of me, as stiff as his starched white collar. He never sank in where he sat; at any moment he might spring back up. You just didn't know when. I turned the key in the ignition.

"Look in back of you to make sure no cars are coming."

I swiveled as if in a tank turret, and with the coast clear, I pulled out. The hill made us roll faster than I had planned. "Easy! You're going too fast!" I touched the brakes a couple of times.

"Turn here!" my father suddenly bellowed at a corner before the bottom of the hill. "Turn *here*!"

Responding with blind obedience, I swung into a turn, only I did so too soon. We were short of the corner, and as if in slow motion, I helplessly anticipated the end of our trajectory of travel. The right front fender thudded into a telephone pole, where we jolted to a stop. And worse, ahead I could see the ditch into which we would have careened if the pole had not stopped us.

Without a "bûma" or "kuzzer-kut" escaping his lips, my father got out of the car to look at the damage. I got out and looked too. It was bad, but not as bad as I thought it would be. The glass of the headlight was smashed and the chrome rim around it bent, but the fender, though scratched in one or two places, was not dented.

"I'll drive home," my father said as we crunched through the leaves and got back in the car. Of course, I would not have dreamed otherwise.

"I'm really sorry, Daddy," I said miserably, shrunken like a child again in the passenger seat, waiting for the blow. I expected he would flail like a maniac. But on the way home, he did not say one word. As we drove through the park, the New York skyline glittered like broken glass in the afternoon sun. I could not understand why my father was being so nice to me. Now look at what I'd done. How hard it must be to be the parent of me. I brooded that it was all my fault.

My father turned left into our driveway and parked at the top. We both got out. "I'm really sorry, Dad," I said again. But he only grunted, again pursing his lips as he hunkered down to finger the scratches on the fender.

My mother had already gotten home from church, changed out of her high heels into her slippers, and put on an apron to fix Sunday dinner. I told her what had happened and started to cry. "He didn't even get mad!" I said, but she just set her lips together and raised her eyebrows. I could hear my father come in the front door, and he walked into the kitchen.

"She ran into a telephone pole," he said to my mother, as if I weren't in the room, too, shaking his head as if he did not know what to do. "You should see the car. I can't get insurance to fix it because she was driving illegally. This has to come out of my pocket. So"—he turned to me, speaking in a tone that said he had no alternative—"you can understand why you can't get your license."

"But Dad, I said I was sorry. I'm already signed up for the driver's education class in school."

"When you can pay for things like this, for your own gas and insurance, then you can drive."

"But I can't pay for insurance babysitting for fifty cents an hour."

"Exactly. You can drive when you have a full-time job, not before."

"Dad, it's not fair. Everybody's getting their license." But picking the card he was holding, I knew I didn't have a leg to stand on. I *was* driving illegally. He took such good care of his car, and look what I'd done to it. He wasn't making me pay for the damage, and he didn't even get mad.

―

When Denny Eichler asked me to go to the movies, butterflies fluttered in my stomach. Denny was on the football team and had a sexy smile. Broaching the date with my father, he put his foot down.

"*Yehudi!*" No one needed a United Nations headset to understand the word he spit out like an epithet.

My mother often disparagingly reminded me, "You're just like your father," for I lost my temper, too. His prejudice made me furious. "What have you got against Jews?" I shouted.

"Lat-say-ya," my mother interjected as our voices rose and my father started taking swipes at me. Many years later, I asked a friend who spoke Arabic the meaning of the phrase *lat-say-ya* and learned that it meant "don't shout." It was probably a blessing that all those times in my childhood when I thought my mother was coming to my defense by telling my father to "take it easy" on me, I didn't know she was actually telling him to keep his voice down, as in "What will the neighbors think?" To have known that then might have been too hard to bear.

"We're just going to the movies. I'm not going to marry him." It was the same argument I'd used to plead my case for going to the prom with Danny. What my father had done to my room that night never crossed my mind; I had pushed it far down in my memory. But the more I argued, the crazier my father got. The fight moved from room to room, with his face in my face as I stumbled backward like a boxer with tied hands and no prospect of winning. By the time we worked our way down to the basement, we were both pretty drained.

"Sit down," my father said finally, dropping himself into one of the old wicker chairs. He was at his wit's end. "Look," he began, subdued. "I could go out to bars." His tone of voice was surprisingly confessional. "But I don't go to bars; I come home. I have a wife and family, responsibilities."

Was duty, not love, the only thing that constrained him? Did he mean that, of course, a man would prefer going out? I didn't know what my father was driving at, but I was touched by the unexpected intimacy in his words. He was going to tell me this for my own good, he said, because I was his daughter. I believed it was out of his desire to protect me that he revealed to me the following truth, which I guessed at the time most women were not privy to. I felt he was being honest when he spelled out his reasoning for me. "Men only want one thing," he said. That was why he didn't want me going out with Denny Eichler. "Men only want one thing." I understood that one thing to be sex.

I deceived my father by having Denny pick me up for our date, not at our house, but at a house down the street where I often babysat. I telephoned Mrs. Clinton beforehand to explain my predicament, and she generously agreed to let me pretend I had a babysitting job at her house that night and wait for my date inside.

Denny thought the whole arrangement strange. He couldn't understand why my father would not let me go out with him when he had never even met him. But he picked me up at the Clintons' and took me back there so I could walk home as if I had been babysitting.

Denny and I went to the movies at the Wellmont Theater on Bloomfield Avenue and afterward drove around in his big white convertible with the top down. The night was balmy, but I did not feel like myself. I was scared of the only thing I now knew Denny wanted. And I was scared of myself, because I knew I wanted it, too. And I was scared of my father finding out. But I didn't have to worry about how I was going to handle future dates with Denny. I was such a nervous wreck that I cracked a zillion jokes. I was not surprised that he never asked me out again.

Questions about my mother's Hisaw side of the family were taboo—not that it occurred to me to ask them anyway. My grandfather Lloyd Hisaw had a brother, Frederick Lee, whom I never even heard of until my senior year of high school. I was seventeen and lying on my stomach on the prickly Persian rug in the living room, flipping through a newly arrived *Saturday Evening Post*.

My mother walked in and, standing over my shoulder, looked down at the magazine. "He's my uncle, you know."

"Who?" I asked. Hunting for cartoons, I had not been paying attention to the article on the page my mother was looking at about preventing premature births.

"The doctor in the photograph, Frederick Lee Hisaw," she said with a touch of pride. "He's a professor at Harvard."

I scanned the article. Hisaw had discovered a hormone he named relaxin, which arrests the contractions of premature labor and relaxes the pelvic ligaments during childbirth.

"Wow!" I exclaimed with a touch of pride myself. "Why don't you ever see him?" Uncles in my experience were people you visited.

"Because ... " She fumbled around, unprepared for my question, and finally said, "That side of the family got too ... too 'uppity.'" Wheeling out of the room, she closed the subject as abruptly as she had opened it.

My parents were members of the local Cosmopolitan Club, an organization that devoted itself to the appreciation of different cultures. One Saturday night a month during its short annual season, in the Woman's Club of Upper Montclair building, the Cosmopolitan Club sponsored a program featuring a particular country followed by a formal dance for its several hundred members.

My junior year my parents chaired the Arabian Nights Costume Ball, and my father arranged for some Iraqi musicians to come from New York to play Arab music as part of the program. As my father shaved that night, he practiced chanting the *adhan*, the Muslim call to prayer. He sounded hauntingly authentic. My mother later said he sang it out from offstage, over the painted scenery of minaret tops.

I wolf whistled at my parents when they were all dressed to go. My mother wore strappy silver heels, a light blue strapless organdy gown that matched her eyes, and, over her shoulders, a deep blue velvet cape made for her in Iraq for special evenings. With her fingernails enameled in red, a dab of Chanel No. 5 behind each ear, she was all rouged, lipsticked, and coiffed.

"You look pretty!"

"Thank you." My mother smiled, pleased.

"And you look handsome!" Trim in his black tuxedo with the black satin lapels, starched white pleated shirt, black satin bowtie and cummerbund, and shiny black shoes, my father had pizazz.

I thought his touch of gray at the temples made him look distinguished. He was all aglow and grinning.

"Have a good time!" Frank and I waved to them as they went out the front door, the downstairs people waving to the upstairs people. These were the good times, when I enjoyed seeing my parents happy.

My last year of high school, I joined the junior division of the Cosmopolitan Club, which also met in formal attire for buffet suppers but at the houses of various members.

After supper the parents carpooled us to the Woman's Club, where all the juniors sat in the balcony to watch the adult program and, once all the chairs had been cleared away, attend the dance downstairs, too. My father liked the idea of my socializing with the children of other Cosmopolitan Club members. I resented going at first because none of my friends belonged, and the people my age who did attend were not exactly your football players and cheerleaders but more nerdy. But then, I was no Carrie Co-ed either, so before long I more than tolerated going. I actually began to enjoy it.

As it turned out, I got a fairly big part in a play the adult Cosmopolitan Club sponsored for one of its programs. In trying to escape from the Nazis, my character had to climb a tall ladder and drop over a wall, then shots were fired; and the audience knew I did not make it. Afterward, my mother said the play was good. My father, who enjoyed performing in amateur productions himself, was a member of the Glen Ridge Players, where he had had a small role in *The Man Who Came to Dinner*. He could have said, "Well, a chip off the old block" or something like that; but I don't recall his saying anything at all.

One night, after one program or another about some foreign country, I was fox-trotting around the dance floor with a boy from my class who loved physics, Roger Hook, when Phil Bennett, the locally famous blind orchestra leader, stopped the music and announced a John Paul Jones. In a John Paul Jones, all the men form a huge circle on the dance floor facing one way, while the women form their own huge circle inside the men's circle, facing the other way. When the orchestra starts back up, the females, alternating clasped hands, braid their way through the circle of males (or vice versa, depending on your perspective). When the music stops, you dance with the new partner whose hand you happen to be holding.

Of all the possible combinations of people on the dance floor, when the music stopped there we were, my father and I, shaking hands. And when the music commenced, there we were dancing. My mother always said my father was a good dancer. He looked so debonair two-stepping around the dance floor, but it was a step that predated the ones we'd learned in Miss Boyd's dancing class.

"You'll have to teach me to dance like you," I said to my father, suddenly feeling as if I had two left feet. "I don't know this step."

"Just follow me," he said. A *good* dancer would know how to follow, wouldn't she?

I did my best to follow him, nervously chattering away about the program or whatever, but when I could see that the public urbane smile pasted on his face was not going to change shape, I soon stopped and concentrated on the dancing.

"You're a good dancer," I said when the music stopped, feeling like King Kong stuffed into a pair of Minnie Mouse satin pumps. He did not return the compliment.

One weekend, I came home in the late afternoon and was heading to the sun porch to watch TV when I accidentally came upon my mother and father sitting on the couch there with my father's hand up my mother's dress.

"Sorry!" I blurted, wheeling around to head the other way, but not without catching sight, in the corner on my eye, of a little glass of whiskey on the rug by my mother's foot. The only time I saw my parents drink was on special occasions, like Sunday dinner at Uncle Kamil's and Auntie May's, or when my parents had several couples over on a Saturday night for a party. I intuited that my father had probably offered my mother a drink to help her relax.

The dry dust mop had a metal handle with a little metal ring at its tip so that it could be hung on a nail in the broom closet. The broom closet was at the back of the downstairs hall in between the kitchen and the stairs to the back door and basement.

When my father walked in the front door from work, as Neal would later put it, we children "scattered like cats." You knew that while he was hanging up his coat in the hall closet and mounting the stairs to put away his suit jacket and tie in his bedroom, he was making his appraisal. Down the stairs he returned in his shirtsleeves and headed back to the broom closet. Out came the dust mop. Going back up the stairs to start at the second-floor landing, he dusted down the stairs. The only sounds were the soft plopping down of the mop and the jingle of the ring against the metal handle. The warden's keys jangling as he inspected the cellblock.

Perhaps from his point of view, my father perceived himself as tired from work but still willing to pitch in. But whether he actually said anything or not, how could my mother, who had knocked herself out polishing everything in the house and preparing a fine dinner, not feel inadequate? How could any of us feel otherwise?

Our downstairs telephone sat on a little table with a built-in seat in the corner of the dining room. I hung up the phone after arranging to go over to my friend Betsy's house and was about to go back upstairs to my room.

We were seniors in high school, and it was Saturday night. Betsy already had her own car, a secondhand 1950 navy blue Ford convertible. Because I didn't have a driver's license, she was going to pick me up around eight to hang around her old Victorian house and bring me home by eleven. What we usually did at her house was sit around and talk. I would bum several cigarettes from her, and as we slouched in the deep couch and armchairs in the dusky light of her living room, our conversation would swirl hazily around us like our blue lassos of smoke. The way we held our cigarettes, squinting knowingly through our exhalations, conveyed profundity without words. We confirmed our belief in each other's depth and greatness as the writer and artist we kept assuring each other we would become.

In Betsy's living room, I first heard of an author named Henry Miller, whose books were so lewd, she confided in me, they had been banned. But Betsy's older brother knew someone who had smuggled copies of Miller's *Tropic of Cancer* into the United States from Europe under a false bottom in his suitcase. Maybe her brother could help her get hold of a copy! Or we would spend hours determining what color and number fit our various friends. Kay, we agreed, was definitely a Beige Three. Or we might review Betsy's latest revised love-and-hate list of members of our senior class. Or I might show Betsy a poem I had just written, and Betsy would nod her head approvingly: "Yes. Oh, God, yes, that's great." Or we might fall to harmonizing the new Everly Brothers song "Bye Bye Love." Or we would end up laughing convulsively if, to get a calliope effect, we simultaneously sang the words "Come to the circus, the greatest show on earth" with Betsy starting at the top note and going down while I started at the bottom note going up. Or with the sincerity of scientific ignorance, I might wonder out loud if rust wasn't contagious.

"What do you mean?"

"I mean … what if the air doesn't rust iron. What if iron somehow catches rust like a cold?"

Who knows what profound conversations we would have on this Saturday night, I thought, as I saw my father sitting in his wing chair in the living room in the pool of light from the floor lamp, clipping his fingernails over a wastebasket. He had handsome hands, which he kept well manicured. If I had tried clipping my fingernails in the living room, he would have killed me, but a king can do what he wants.

My father looked up from his task as I crossed the hall to go upstairs. "Where do you think you're going?"

"To Betsy's."

He snorted disdainfully. "You are always going out. You never stay home. Why don't you ever stay home, huh? Don't you like your family?"

"Of course I do. But stay home for what? Nobody ever talks to me."

"Well, you are not going out tonight. Call Betsy and tell her you won't be going out tonight."

"Why?"

"Because I said so. You can spend an evening at home with your family for a change."

"But I've already made arrangements for Betsy to pick me up."

"Call her and tell her you can't go out tonight."

Fuming, I turned and went back to the dining room to telephone my friend. "Bets, hi, it's me. I can't come over tonight after all … I really don't know. My father just says I have to stay home … Yeah, me too. I'll talk to you later. Bye."

"Now come in here," my father summoned me into his presence. He put his nail clipper down on the radiator cover. He had folded his newspaper and put it on the floor alongside his chair.

"Sit down." He motioned for me to sit in the wing chair next to the fireplace across from him. I sat on the edge of the chair.

Crossing one leg over the other, my father folded his arms and gave me his full attention. After an eternity had gone by, he intoned on a high note, "Well?"

"Well, what?" I was bewildered.

"You're the one who wanted to talk."

"About what?"

"So *talk*."

It was as if white paint spilled over my brain, completely wiping out my mind. "That's not what I meant," I sputtered.

After what seemed like another eternity elapsed while I fought back the tears, my father finally picked up his newspaper. Unfolding it with a snap, he threw me a smirk that said, "Case closed." He turned his attention to the page with an air of benevolent tolerance. I had been given the opportunity to talk, and I had not been able to think of a thing to say. Whose fault was that?

There were 320 of us seniors graduating from Montclair High School in 1957. At the annual awards assembly, the last week of school before graduation night, I had as many butterflies in my stomach as a nominated actor at the Academy Awards. The top school honor, the MHS Awards, always went to the greatest boy and greatest girl in the class. For the girls, my friend Marcia won it. Next in importance were the Owl Pin Awards, which that year went to seventeen seniors "whose scholastic, athletic achievement is noteworthy," explained the school newspaper, *The Mountaineer*, on its front page, "whose cooperation and enthusiasm for school projects is outstanding and whose particular abilities in executive or artistic fields are conspicuous in devotion to the school and its betterment." When my name was announced, I rose, elated, from my seat and ascended the stage to the thunderous pounding of palms and whistling and cheering. I had worked very hard to be a great kid. I don't know what the other recipients felt as they were each called to the stage for his or her Owl Pin. Certainly, they must have felt good. They must have been excited. But for me, the sound of applause was like sonar bouncing back to me a reading of who I was. It affirmed I was visible, I was real, I was liked. And there was even more. I had applied for a Girls' Club scholarship. As dance chairman that year, I had been responsible for three big formal dances at the Woman's Club. The dances were always popular because they were the only girl-ask-boy events of the year. The only financial question the application for the scholarship had asked was, *How much do you need?* My father had told me to fill in $350. I was called back up on the stage to accept a scholarship for just the amount he wanted.

As we spilled out of the auditorium, I was surprised to see my mother standing in the crowd in the foyer. She said the school sent letters to the parents of the award recipients telling them to keep the secret and inviting them to attend the awards assembly. I felt awkward that she had witnessed me in the world my father criticized me for preferring, but I said it was nice she got to be there. When she didn't turn to leave, I wondered if she thought I was going home with her, but I told her that I'd be home later because everyone was staying at school to sign yearbooks. She didn't say anything, but I felt bad because I think she took my not going home with her personally.

~

I had enjoyed my fifteen Warholian minutes of fame. But the sooner we get fame over with, the better, for we quickly learn that it flares as prettily as a Fourth of July sparkler and is as swiftly spent. Eventually, I trudged up the hill toward home alone.

My father hadn't attended the awards assembly because he was still on bed rest.

His doctor had prescribed for him the first Miltown, a new tranquilizer for what he diagnosed as my father's hypertension. "But you don't need to go telling anybody," my mother warned me when she saw me pick up the bottle of capsules on the kitchen counter and idly read the label. Because of my father's persistent complaints of indigestion, however, the doctor determined that he had probably suffered a mild heart attack and ordered him to bed for four weeks.

During my father's recuperation, he stopped smoking his two packs of Pall Malls a day. Between his nicotine deprivation and his forced confinement to bed when he felt fine, his short fuse only got shorter.

"Hi, Dad. How are you feeling?" On the way up to my room, I stuck my head in the wide-open door of my parents' bedroom. The foot of my parents' double bed faced the door, so that propped on his pillows, my father could see all the hall traffic.

"Where have you been?" he asked.

"At school. Today was awards assembly."

"Do you know what time it is?"

"It's five fifteen."

"You're late."

"No, I'm not. It's not even time for dinner."

"You had only a half day today. You should have been home hours ago to help your mother."

Yes, my poor mother, having to take care of my father all day and still clean the house, do the laundry, get dinner. I answered guiltily, "I'm in time to set the table."

Surely my mother had told him about my awards. "Dad, didn't Mom tell you I got the $350 scholarship from the Girls' Club? And I got an Owl Pin!"

"Owl Pin? Bûma!" he yelled, perversely relishing the irony: I had been awarded the Arab symbol of stupidity. Reaching down alongside his bed for his slipper, he hurled it at me. One more Arab insult, for if a shoe is considered dirty, I was even as low as the dirt itself.

"You're *killing* me!" he shrieked as I ran up the stairs to my room.

The University of Delaware was conveniently only a two-hour drive from our house in Montclair, and with my Girls' Club scholarship, my father could afford the tuition. When I attended the year of 1957–58, the student body numbered only two thousand, bigger than high school but not overwhelming. Chance assigned me a single room. My first night in it, sitting alone at my bare desk, I looked out the window at the lights in the neighboring dorms and thought of my mother and father and little brother and sister, Neal, ten, and Tootie, six, who that morning had driven me down. Even my parents looked small and vulnerable against the campus of my new world. Frank, going into his junior year in high school, couldn't come because of his job at Poll's Stationery Store.

Tears rolled down my cheeks as I imagined all of them sitting around the dinner table at home that night. I knew I was homesick, but I was too inarticulate to realize I ached with love.

At first I missed my place among the great kids in Montclair and being known the way Betsy or Marcia knew me, but I made some good friends in my dorm, each of whom at one time or another invited me to her home for a weekend. I was the only girl in my dorm who had to have written permission from her parents to leave campus overnight. But by the time I wrote home and got a letter back, the weekend would have come and gone. And I wasn't so sure my father would have let me go, anyway; I was supposed to be studying. But Mrs. Rogers, the tiny woman who was housemother of our dormitory, went out on a limb to permit me to go away on those weekends without my parents' permission.

The school had no social sororities. The fraternities held dances and parties to which I was invited, but my heart wasn't in it. What had I expected of university life? All the accouterments that I had imagined were present—the classic red brick buildings and stately white columns, the giant oaks overarching the campus, the library bulging with knowledge. I guess I thought at university you'd study books about truth and beauty, about good and evil, the soul, life after death, the personality, and whether or not there was a God. You'd write papers and have meaty discussions about the meaning of life.

But from the first week, when freshmen were required to wear DU "dinks," or beanies, and we broke up into little groups with our Big Sister at the freshman orientation picnic, and the hot topic of discussion was what to wear homecoming weekend, I knew I did not really belong. Dubbed the Silent Generation, my cohort could just as well be called the Shallow Generation. Homecoming would turn out to be one of the loneliest nights of my life. Even though I had a date with a cute boy for the football game and fraternity parties afterward, I ended up with the flu in my empty dorm, vomiting into my wastebasket. I missed my mother bringing me broth.

When I had attended a big bonfire pep rally for the football game the previous day, I, too, heartily sang all the old school songs the freshmen were required to learn. I stole looks at the happy, flushed faces in the flickering firelight around me and thought I was the only one pretending to be having fun.

A strange thing happened in our large, mandatory gym class. We female freshman students lined up in rows to await the latest installment of our instructions in tap dancing. The teacher announced that when we reported to class the next time, we should expect to be photographed in the nude for a posture study.

A posture study? In the nude? To me, still modest and self-conscious about my body, this was an excruciating prospect. Who knows what my peers were really thinking, but they seemed to accept our fate; they did not find the nude posture study worthy of conversation. I must have appeared just as unquestioning, for I did not raise the subject, either. Maybe the Silent Generation *is* the appropriate label.

Consider what my mental cultural anthropology field notes of those times reveal: Without our consent and without a peep of protest, young women in 1957 did what we were told. When the designated day arrived, we lined up in the gym, reporting individually to the gym teacher's office. There, a photographer had set up his camera on a big tripod. Against my own private wishes, I removed my clothes and allowed myself to be photographed nude, front, back, and sideways. Untrained in questioning authority, I think we would have all made good Nazis.

Forty years later, I read a cover story in the *New York Times Magazine* by Ron Rosenbaum called "The Great Ivy League Nude Posture Photo Scandal," about the pseudoscience of E. A. Hooton, a physical anthropologist at Harvard, and W. H. Sheldon, who "directed an institute for physique studies at Columbia University." Nude photographs of both male and female students, many of whom became prominent as adults, had been taken over the years, mainly in the Ivy League schools. Should we have been flattered they included the University of Delaware? According to the article, Sheldon "held that a person's body, measured and analyzed, could tell much about intelligence, temperament, moral worth and probably future achievement." Sheldon divided body types into ecto-, meso-, and endomorphs, words that made their way into our dictionaries, the article observed, but not into our science books.

I was considering running for class secretary when Jean Ashe contacted me. I knew who Jean Ashe was. Her photo was in the student handbook distributed to freshmen. She was president of the Student Government Association at the university, but I didn't think she knew me. Jean was a big-wheel senior, and I was a little-cog freshman. When Jean asked me to come see her on a specific day at a specific time, I had no idea why.

Jean lived opposite my brick dorm, in a big white clapboard house across a green lawn; these were the privileged accommodations for female seniors, who shared suites. It was a beautiful fall day, with still-green leaves gently moving in a pleasant breeze and the sun dappling the shadows beneath her open windows.

I don't know how Jean knew I was thinking of running for secretary of the freshman class, but she said to me that it would be a waste, though in my experience in high school, the office of secretary was the only one a female could win. Jean didn't think I should run for president, though, because that was a long shot against male candidates. But she advised me to run for vice president, an office higher than secretary—and one she thought a girl had a chance of winning.

This was the only conversation I remember ever having with Jean. Thanking her, I took her advice and ran for vice president. I put my high school campaign experience to work by folding colored paper and cutting out four-inch-high paper T's that advertised *Tooni fits the job to a T* on one side and *Suzy Tooni for Frosh V.P.* on the other. I propped them up on all the tables in Kent Dining Hall. And I won.

Jean was right that a male freshman would be elected president, but before the end of the first semester, he withdrew from the university. There were rumors that he had quit before he flunked out. Thus I became president of the Class of '61, all because of Jean's counsel.

It was common knowledge that Jean was pinned to a boy in Sigma Nu, one of the social fraternities on campus. The next step after wearing a boy's fraternity pin in those days was wearing an engagement ring. Before the end of the second semester, I heard that Jean had won a Woodrow Wilson Fellowship to do graduate work, but in the culture and parlance of that time, she opted for her Mrs. instead of her MA.

I have not said anything about my academic experience at Delaware, but a little poem or aphorism I wrote years later, after I was married, sums it up:

> Only a committed heart
>
> can possess
>
> a clear mind.

For the Thanksgiving holidays, I made my first train trip on my own from college into Newark, New Jersey, where my father drove by himself to meet me at the station. After my first months away from home, I was feeling pretty grown-up. When I walked in our front door, I was happy to see my mother, who was fixing dinner, and my younger brothers and sister, who gathered grinning around me before they dispersed to leave me standing alone with my father.

"Sit down." He motioned me to the wing chair opposite his. I was still seventeen, but I felt he was treating me as an adult, especially when he suddenly asked, "Would you like some sherry?"

"Really?" I smiled, as the drinking age in New Jersey in 1957 was twenty-one. As a freshman, I did not even drink at college fraternity parties. It was against campus rules, although, of course, some students drank anyway, and those who got caught were suspended. Most of the girls I knew did not drink, and I had no desire to do so at school. The possibility flashed through my mind that my father's invitation was a trick. I took a chance. "Sure, yes, thank you."

My father went to the sideboard in the dining room, poured out two small sherries, and handed one to me. "Well, you're growing up," he said as he settled in his chair, sipping his aperitif. This was new, sitting together, my father asking me what school was like while we waited for dinner. It felt good to be back in the familiar environment, to enjoy my mother's good cooking, to joke around with Frank and hear about all the cute things Neal and Tootie had been doing. Since our family was having Thanksgiving dinner at home the next afternoon, I had planned to go in the morning with a carful of my old high school friends to the traditional Montclair-Bloomfield Thanksgiving football game. The stands for the Thanksgiving game were always packed with high school alumni. The big event at the game was halftime, when everybody poured down onto the path around the field to see everybody else and to be seen. It was a time to feel like a college kid because you had been away. It was a time for squeals of delight and backslapping reunions.

At dinner that night, I mentioned my plans to go to the Thanksgiving game. Unexpectedly, my father said, "*I'll* take you to the game."

My father had never attended a Montclair High football game in his life. I could think of some Montclair families who might actually drive to the football game together, but those kids would sit in the stands with their friends and wander around at halftime while the parents chatted in their seats with their neighbors and other parents. I knew it wouldn't be like that with my father. About the last thing I wanted to do on my first vacation home from college was go to the big Thanksgiving Day game with him.

"That's OK, Dad, but thanks. Gina said I could ride with her."

"Tell her you don't need a ride. I'm taking you to the game."

I could hardly breathe thinking about going to the game with my father, yet I felt so guilty. Hadn't he just made a ritualistic gesture toward recognizing my adulthood by giving me a glass of sherry? Wasn't he trying to improve our relationship by taking me to the football game? What could I say but, "OK, Dad, thanks"?

The next morning, while my mother cooked the turkey, my father and I drove to the Bloomfield stadium. Still in high school, Frank had managed to go with his own friends. I tried my hardest to act as if I were having a good time, but I had run out of things to say before we even got out of Montclair. The stadium in Bloomfield was packed. I craned my neck and strained my eyes trying to see people I knew. As we were borne along the stream of bodies flowing through the stadium gates, my father scanned the Montclair side and said, "It's too crowded over there. There are some good seats up there." He veered to the Bloomfield side.

"But Dad, those are the Bloomfield stands. All my friends are over there." I pointed to the Montclair side.

The incredulity on my father's face bordered on disgust. "Did you come to watch a football game or what?" He had found me out again.

"Wow, that was quite a catch," I said, trying to show some appreciation for the game. During lulls in the action, I pretended to study the program. We were surrounded by strangers, who would every now and then jump up and cheer for Bloomfield. It was hard trying to recognize the dots milling back and forth on the track between the stands and the field on the opposite side of the stadium.

By the end of the second quarter, I had positioned my feet for standing up. "Well, if you don't mind, Dad, I'm just going to stroll over to the Montclair side to see if I see any of my friends."

"Tch. What do you want to get down in that crowd for?"

"Just to say hello." I boldly rose. He remained seated, sitting pathetically all alone, and waited for me to return when the third quarter started, but he might as well have accompanied me as I picked my way through the crowds to the Montclair side, for I felt the tug of his leash.

"Hey, Tooni!"

"Hi, Jack! Eddie!"

"Hey, Suzy, how's it going?"

"Barbara!"

"Toons! How's school?"

"School's great."

I could feel him watching me, spoiling everything. I could hear him saying, "You've got to be kidding. That's what you made all the fuss about? 'Hi?' 'How's it going?'" I hated him. But mostly, I hated myself for hating him.

While I was home for Thanksgiving break, I got to see Sputnik, the world's first artificial satellite, which the Soviet Union had launched. My father knew exactly when Sputnik was going to sail through the night sky over our house. All I knew about what he did when he worked for ITT Federal Labs was that his job had something to do with satellites.

He thought putting a satellite in space had been a great accomplishment. As he was on his way out the front door to spot it, I asked, "Can I come see it, too?"

"If you want," he answered. We stood a couple of feet apart on the short sidewalk, looking up. He pointed to what appeared to be a slowly moving star.

"That's it," he said, more to himself than to me. Rocking on his feet, he clicked his tongue against the roof of his mouth in appreciation. "It circles the earth about every hour and a half."

"Wow!" I exclaimed, more impressed with my father's knowledge than with Sputnik.

"The Russians got ahead of us on this one," he said as I followed him back into the house.

My new friend Bill helped me get through the second semester of my freshman year at Delaware. Bill was older than most of the boys I knew; he had served in the army before going to college and did not live on campus or in a fraternity house. He was in the category the university characterized as "independent men." He had sandy hair, eyelashes to match, and a nice face, and he was kind, cheerful, smart, and well read. I've thought since that if we had had an arranged marriage, we would have continued to enjoy each other's company, and I might have fallen in love with him. He deserved someone who was crazy about him. But Bill liked me, and I felt he actually understood me. We could talk about the meaning of life over coffee and cigarettes for hours. With Bill, I was comfortable being myself. He thought it was great when I had my first poems accepted by *Venture*, the campus literary magazine. Thrilled to see them in print, I wrote home that I had actually been published. My father wrote back, pointing out that I had forgotten to mention how much I had gotten paid. When I replied that the payment was in free copies of the magazine, my father responded in exasperation, wondering when I was ever going to settle down to my studies and stop fooling around.

Although I had my overwhelming doubts, I hadn't completely given up on the possibility of the existence of God and accompanied a friend one Sunday morning to her Episcopal church, whose congregation sat on folding chairs for the service. I found the liturgy comfortably familiar. After communion, my friend introduced me to the priest who greeted us at the door. The priest asked where I was from. Students from out of state were always welcome, he said, as he smiled and shook my hand. And what church in Montclair did I attend? When I replied, "The Montclair Heights Dutch Reformed Church," his face contorted. "You mean you are not an Episcopalian?" The color rose in his face. "And you took communion?" When I nodded yes, he admonished me for all the exiting parishioners to hear, "Don't you *ev*-er do that again." I planned not to. I knew when I was not a member of the club.

If I hadn't written home from the university every week, I would not have had any money. Two of my friends had checking accounts and received ten to fifteen dollars a week as well as a budget for clothes. Their fathers were doctors and deposited the money directly into their accounts. I got four dollars a week in cash, enclosed in a letter. If I wrote home sometime over the weekend giving an account of how I had spent the last four dollars, I would be mailed the next four dollars. If I did not, I would not receive the money.

I tried to get a job, but there were few for freshmen, although I did pick up an occasional evening babysitting. I had taken up smoking at this point and guiltily buried my cigarette expenses in reports of extraordinary numbers of purchases of ballpoint pens, pencils, paper, haircuts, and ice cream cones. I did not have the money when a group of us decided to give a wedding present to one of our pals, Carol, who, though still living in the dorm, had secretly eloped with a senior football player. Earlier in the year, when I had spent a weekend at her house, her German father had reminded me of my father. How could I not chip in? There wasn't time for correspondence, so I gambled by paying for a telephone call home.

"Dad, this friend of mine got married, and a bunch of us are chipping in on a wedding present. Could I ask you to send me some additional money?"

"How much?"

"Ten dollars."

Laughter.

"Dad, they're just starting out, and they don't have a thing. We're just getting them some sheets and towels."

"Who is this person?"

"Carol. Carol Schmid. She's one of my friends I wrote you about."

"I don't even know her. Do I have to support every stranger that comes along?"

"Dad, she's my *friend*." I couldn't remind him that I had spent a weekend at her house and met her family because I had left campus without his permission.

Silence.

"Dad, she's a good friend."

Silence.

"Dad, I can't believe it. Ten dollars for some sheets and towels for a friend who's gotten married."

"*We* need sheets and towels. Do you think I have money to burn? You know how much it's costing me to send you to college, and you're interested in giving showers? What kind of school is this anyway?"

While I was home for spring vacation, my father received a phone call from a woman he had known in Iraq who was divorced and living in New York. She remembered he had a daughter the age of her son and thought it might be nice for us to meet. After my father hung up, I overheard him talking with my mother about the proposed date. My father had had standing and recognition in his society. Among his peers, his family name was known and respected. He nixed the proposed date because he did not feel the son was from a good enough family. But where was his list of good families? Knowing good families was a cultural asset he had left behind in Basra. Then again, what criteria had he met when he ran off with my mother?

Before I returned to Delaware, my father was unusually nice to me. He said he had something he wanted me to think over. I didn't have to make up my mind right away. It was obvious, he said, that with my grades I wasn't going to be able to get a scholarship for next year. He did not have money to waste on me, he pointed out, as he had two sons to send to college who would have families to support. If next year I were to go instead to Katharine Gibbs School, a reputable secretarial school that had a branch right in Montclair, he would not only pay the tuition but also give me the bonus of a trip to Europe to boot.

Hmm. A way to make a living and a trip to Europe. My father's proposal did not sound like such a bad idea, because I had privately determined that I wanted to be a writer, and writers, I thought, needed to be, not in school, but out in life. And so, after I finished my freshman year, I became what was then a newly coined term, a college dropout.

During the summer between University of Delaware and Katie Gibbs, as the secretarial school was dubbed, I remember walking into the kitchen where my mother was preparing dinner to find her standing still in thought in the middle of the kitchen. She looked dispirited. "What's the matter?" I asked.

"They murdered the king and his family in Iraq and hung his body outside," she replied, as if she had known Iraq's royal family personally. "The king was just a boy when we left."

"That's terrible."

My father was home from work and sitting at the far end of the living room on the sofa. I stuck my head in the room. Reading about the details of the coup d'etat in Iraq in the paper, he was *tch-tch*-ing his tongue and shaking his head seemingly in disgust by the barbarity of the attack. What was he thinking? He must have felt lucky and justified that his family had read their future in Iraq accurately and made the wise decision to leave the country. But he must have also been sad that the Iraq of his boyhood no longer existed.

These are my present-day conjectures, because I don't remember my asking him how he felt or his volunteering anything.

My father invented and patented a wireless burglar alarm for safes: when disturbed by thieves, his device inside the safe would directly radio the police. Surely this invention would bring him the million bucks he dreamed about. A picture of my father appeared in the *Newark Evening News* with an article describing his invention, and he sent the clipping to me where I had started a summer job on an island off Connecticut as a mother's helper. Shortly after I received his letter, he telephoned me, a startling thing to do in our family when out-of-state news between relatives and friends was still communicated by post except for emergencies.

"Well?" he said. "What did Mr. Schmid think?"

Mr. Schmid, who came up from New Jersey to his summer cottage on the island to be with his wife and children on weekends, was a jewelry salesman. My father did not know this. I can only guess he assumed that if the Schmids were wealthy enough to own a vacation house, Mr. Schmid would be interested in promoting his safe.

"What do you mean?" I asked.

"What did he say about my invention?"

"I haven't talked to him about it."

"What? You haven't shown him the clipping?"

I felt shame and guilt that my father seemed so hurt I had not been bragging about him: I had blocked his way to fame and fortune.

Patai says that the Arabic language itself, with its emphasis on exaggeration and intensity of expression, predisposes Arabs to equate a verbal statement about a desired event with an accomplished fact. My father had already verbalized in his mind that once Mr. Schmid read about his burglar alarm, he would rush to my father with offers to sell it. But I was not an anthropologist or a linguist. I thought he was clever to have invented an alarm that radioed the police but, of course, I could not possibly have known then how he had amazingly anticipated late twentieth century security systems. At the time, my thoughts were elsewhere. I had just read *On the Beach*, a novel about nuclear war, and was worried about our ruined planet and my early death. My father did not hang up, however, before extracting my promise to show the Schmids the clipping, which all the rest of that day I casually tried to work into the conversation.

After I received my letter of acceptance from the Katharine Gibbs School and the bill for the first semester arrived, my father drew up a contract. Before I started classes, he wanted to make the stipulations of his investment clear. "Read it over, and after you sign it," he said, "your mother will sign as witness."

> I, Suzy Tooni, do hereby solemnly promise and swear that in exchange for their love and care, and over $800 dollars which my parents will pay for my tuition at Kathryn [*sic*] Gibbs in 1958-1959, I will do as follows:
>
> 1. I will conduct myself according to the advice of my parents without "flying off the handle" when some of their advice might not suit me.
>
> 2. I will come directly to my house every day after classes are out at Kathyrn [*sic*] Gibbs. In the event I have to stop at the library after school, I will so inform my mother in the morning and specify the amount of time I will spend in the library. (Such time not to last later than 4:00 P.M.)
>
> 3. I will study at home for at least four hours—such studies not to last later than 11 P.M.
>
> 4. I will not entertain the idea of living away from home until after I reach the age of 21, or after I get married, whichever comes first.

I was eighteen years old, penniless, and paralyzed. I had no choice but to consent to my house arrest. Most of my friends were in college. Except for a flicker of fun with a few female classmates, the year I spent at Katharine Gibbs was mostly a black smudge. It is the year I considered suicide, not so much for suffering imprisonment as for having my plans for escape dashed.

For sad reasons of her own, Marcia, too, had dropped out of college and tried to kill herself again. This time she did not go to a fancy private hospital to recover but to Overbrook, a state mental hospital, just over the mountain from our house. Since I did not have a license, when Gina was home on a school break, she drove me to visit Marcia. I wondered if I could legally adopt her to get her out of the loony bin. When Marcia came home from Overbrook during my second semester at Katharine Gibbs, we conspired to share an apartment together in New York. She was thinking of getting on her feet by going to Katharine Gibbs herself the following fall so that she could also get a job. I was dubious that she could stand the confinement of secretarial school but elated about the prospect of my own liberation.

Before she left for a prolonged stay with her mother in Georgia, Marcia shepherded me into the city for my first visit to the Metropolitan Museum of Art, where we looked at famous paintings by Titian and El Greco we had seen only in a book. And then we caught the matinee of *La Bohème*. We sat in the cheapest seats in the next-to-last row of the old Metropolitan Opera House, both of us wiping our eyes for the "resire" that welled up in us during Mimì's aria. We vowed that whoever got married first would give the one left behind the complete album of *La Bohème*. After the performance, we walked past apartments for rent and imagined what it would be like to live in them. We even took the elevator to one and walked around inside it with a real estate agent, trying to figure out how much we would have to earn at the jobs we didn't have yet to be able to afford it. It had been a long time since I'd felt so happy.

While Marcia was away, we corresponded. But then I got her letter telling me about the wonderful opportunity that had come up she could not refuse. She would not be going to Katharine Gibbs after all. She had landed a job as assistant cook on a ninety-foot brigantine that was going to sail around the world! That was when I wanted to kill myself, both for feeling abandoned and for knowing I had neither the imagination nor the strength to escape on my own. Like Neal's rabbit, George, with all the world before me, I had hopped on top of my cage. My future loomed monotonously dreary and pointless.

Desperate, I sat down at my typewriter, for by then I knew how to type. I was going to give free rein to my suicide letter, although I had yet to determine by what method I was going to end my life. But then a strange thing happened. I typed "Dear Paper" and began to tell the paper, as honestly and precisely as I could, why I was feeling so suicidal. My new friend, the paper, interrogated me: If you were trying to persuade a friend why not to kill herself, it asked, what reasons for living would you give? And I labored over this list of mysteries for consideration: curiosity, beauty, resire, laughter, music, and love. Over the years to this list against despair I would add the mysteries of talent and interest, sleep and dreaming, tears, language, friendship, marriage, giving birth, learning, eating, sex, nature (particularly fish breathing water and birds flying), energy and light, the existence of the Jews (among the reasons I read somewhere Frederick the Great gave for his belief in God), the cells in our bodies, the stars, and the universe. But where had my draft that night come from? It gave me so much to think about, I decided I wanted to live. Importantly, I learned that I did not *have* to live: I *chose* to live.

A vivacious representative of Time Inc. came to talk to our class at Katharine Gibbs about job opportunities in publishing. Before she even spoke, just from the way she bounded up the stairs to the stage, I knew immediately that her company in New York City was where I wanted to work. I wore the Katie Gibbs required hat and gloves on my first interview there and was hired as a secretary in the advertising sales department of *Time* magazine—the last time I wore a hat. I was nineteen years old.

Out of my first sixty-nine-dollar weekly paycheck, twenty dollars went for bus commutation, twenty dollars went to my father for room and board, and what was left was mine to keep. My wanting to work in Manhattan instead of closer to home in New Jersey caused a battle with my father. He thought I was foolish to accept a salary smaller than I could make in New Jersey—not to mention the fact that if I had a job in New Jersey he could drive me to work and I would save the expense of commuting.

After I got my first couple of paychecks, he was also annoyed that instead of buying a frilly dress I could immediately afford, I preferred to purchase at Hahne's, on installment, a smart and expensive subtle pink-and-aqua tiny plaid wool suit made in England. His making me feel I was wasting my money on books did not stop my growing synchronistic relationship with them: titles seem to fall into my hands just when I needed them. One of the first wise people to speak to me was Victor Frankl in *Man's Search for Meaning*.

Every morning I arrived in Midtown Manhattan via the No. 66 bus and walked from the Port Authority Bus Terminal to Rockefeller Center. Some days the city seemed exciting, an architectural glory of beautiful buildings filled with beautiful people doing important things. But there were other days when, feeling like an invisible spectator, I saw the city as though it was swathed in dirty gauze, and all I noticed was the spittle in the gutter or the man whose legs were stumps, propped on a dolly on the sidewalk, extending an empty cup. If a gust of wind picked up a piece of abandoned newspaper and blew it along the street, I felt sick from identifying with it. With nothing to hold onto, like my childhood pet goldfish, I felt the vortex of the big drain. How could it be that one day the city was exhilarating and the next, dismal? I knew no one rearranged the city each night while I slept.

But doubting my own perception gave me a new glimmer of hope. Perhaps it was not life that was awry, but just the way I looked at it. I discovered for myself what the Talmud then unknown to me already said: "We do not see things as they are; we see them as we are."

After I started working, the letters from Marcia began to arrive, enclosed in blue onionskin airmail envelopes pasted with exotic stamps. The dispatches in her muscular scrawl reported skin diving in the Red Sea, climbing to the top of Kilimanjaro—things I thought a writer should be doing. And what was I doing? Relentlessly shuttling back and forth on the No. 66 bus to a secretarial job in New York. I felt inferior that my climbing and diving were done invisibly in my own interior. I read *Lady Chatterley's Lover*, camouflaging its cover in plain plastic. I did not yet know Hemingway's advice: "In order to write about life, first you must live it."

One Sunday afternoon, I took a walk near our house in the bird sanctuary at Mountainside Park. A secluded bench at the top of the park rewarded climbers with a view of New York, its skyscrapers miniaturized in the distance along the curve of the earth. Sitting on the bench, I smoked a cigarette while contemplating the skyline. I had a vision of a gigantic carving knife peeling off the bumps of buildings like a rind. I thought, *what short work we could make of everything that is important to us!* Normally that thought would have depressed me. But that spring afternoon, it did not, for then I argued with myself that even if a gigantic knife could pare the skyline, *it could not touch anything that was really important, like love, for instance*. For some reason—maybe the wind bending the grass and stirring the leaves; maybe the squirrels scampering and the birds chirping around me, like the little animals who came to keep Snow White company—I did not feel alone.

Marcia returned to Montclair with one tale after another of adventures on exotic islands and the high seas, stories that could have been spun by Herman Melville. And while it was still a secret, she confided in me that she was going to marry a boy she had met on the boat. "And how are *you*?" she finally asked.

"It's possible—I mean I've had just a glimmer—but I'm beginning to think that maybe there is a God," I said.

She smiled, I thought, patronizingly. She said she could understand why I would think that. We had always been honest with each other. I had not been anywhere, and I did not have a boyfriend. My belief, she felt, was *compensation*. Not trusting my own feelings, I thought she had a point. But what was I trying to say when I offered, "Maybe there is a God"? The word *God* does not mean "Santa Claus in the sky": it is code for the mystery that cannot be said. Any definition that *God* could fit into would be too small. In their own way, feelings have eyes, and my feelings had glimpsed something: that my life might have meaning.

I don't know if my father quit his job or his job quit him. With a dearth of electrical engineering jobs in New Jersey at the time, he had found a new job—his first "people job," my mother called it—as director of electronics at the Institute for the Crippled and Disabled in New York. Part of his duties was finding electronic piecework for the disabled to do, an assignment that I think put a lot of pressure on him, for sales were not his forte. I was touched by the only remark he made about his new job that I can remember. He said at the dinner table one night that he could not help but admire the people he was hired to help for their eagerness to work with so much against them.

I ended up commuting with my father after all. Finding myself alone with him in the car, riding back and forth to the city each day, I discovered my interest in my Iraqi heritage waking up. At home, the only ties my father retained with Iraq were gustatory and occasionally exclamatory, with his invectives not always aimed at us. When he read in the paper that Fidel Castro, slated to speak at the UN, and his entourage had allegedly brought live chickens with them to stay at the upscale Shelburne Hotel in New York City, he let loose a string of Arabic words I didn't recognize. I asked him what they meant, and he replied, "I'll tell you when you are twenty-one." Roughly translated, I would later learn, he had said about the Cuban leader, "Even the flies are farting."

I began keeping a little spiral notebook in my purse in which I jotted down Arabic phrases. As I sat alongside my father in the front seat, I would pull out my notebook and ballpoint pen and ask, "How do you say, 'Would you like to have some coffee?' to a woman?"

Grudgingly, my father would divulge the Arabic, but I could sense his impatience: "*Tree-deen ga-wha?*"

"*Ga-wa?*"

"*La* [No]*! Wh-a! Ga-wha!?*"

As best I could, I would record this information phonetically in my little notebook, which vibrated in my grip as we sped along Route 46.

"And to a man?"

"*Treed ga-wha*. Why do you want to know all this Arabic for anyway?" He took his eyes off the highway long enough to shoot me a look that told me my project was pointless.

"I don't know. I just think it would be fun. I wish now I had never stopped speaking it."

This exchange was followed by a long silence, which I dared break by interviewing him: "Did you play any games like we did when you were a boy in Iraq?"

"Of course." He pursed his lips. "We had something we played with a stick and a ball."

Prying in this way, I found out that he had been an altar boy. As he warmed up a little, he even volunteered that as an altar boy, he had often gotten the giggles. The giggles? My father! He had certainly never revealed any sympathy with my attack of the giggles the day of my confirmation. Why hadn't he told me this before? He volunteered additionally that he would be a Roman Catholic if the Mass were not in Latin and he could understand what they were saying.

Another time, I asked him, "What exactly *is* electricity?"

"We know how to use it," he answered, "but we can't really say what it is."

I think he must have heard something on the car radio that made him say the next thing, as he delivered his words spontaneously, with lively interest. "They're building an antenna in West Virginia that can receive messages from space," he said, not taking his eyes off the highway, "so they can listen for other intelligence in the universe."

"Wow!" I exclaimed. "That's neat!" My enthusiasm was genuine. I felt I had just received a blip from outer space myself. It was the closest I ever felt to my father.

Ten minutes late, I hurried out the revolving door of the Time & Life Building on 50th Street. My father's Buick was parked at the curb, waiting for me in front of the entrance.

"Hi. I'm sorry I'm late," I said, flinging my purse onto the back seat and sliding into the front alongside my father. Just as the heat distorts the air around a car that has been baking on a hot parking lot, the waves of frustration and rage undulating around him were palpable.

"All day I have done nothing but buck traffic," he said, "yet I manage to be on time, and then I have to wait for you."

"Oh, Daddy..." In my mind I could hear my friend Gina's voice as she had said those very words to her father in my presence. She asked him for money to go to the movies, and with a little smile on his face, her father pulled out his empty pants pockets and shrugged his shoulders.

"Oh, Daddy..." Gina playfully attacked him, digging her hand into his jacket pocket. Laughing, he hugged and tickled her, and laughing herself, she said, "C'mon, Daddy, don't be so mean!"

"OK, OK, you win," Gina's father said, reaching into his back pocket for some bills. Handing the money to her, he gave her a kiss and told us both to have a good time.

"C'mon, Daddy," I said in the car, "don't be so mean."

Wham! My father's arm slammed like a gate across my face. Tears sprang to my eyes, but all I could think of was whether anybody from my office had been coming out the revolving door or walking along the sidewalk. I wanted to disappear like loose change down the crack in the seat. The light on the corner turned green, and my father turned with a jolt into the traffic going up Sixth Avenue.

As soon as I could get my wits together, I gasped, "What did you do *that* for?"

"You call your father 'mean,' huh?"

"But Dad, it's just an expression."

"Oh, yeah. We'll see. I want you to look up the definition of *mean* in the dictionary. Call your father 'mean,' huh?" He shook his head as if he couldn't believe it.

Now my own rage was simmering, and I slouched in the seat as close to the door as possible. The silence encased us like cement for the rest of the commute.

When we walked in the door at home, he had not forgotten. I wasn't halfway up the stairs to my room when he called up after me to look up *mean* in the dictionary and bring it down to read to him.

I opened the dictionary on my desk and was surprised when I read the definition. Loosely closing the book covers over my finger to mark the place, I carried the dictionary downstairs.

My father was in the living room, settling himself in his chair and about to open the evening newspaper. "This isn't what I meant," I said.

"Read it. Out loud."

I read: "1. Lacking distinction or eminence: Humble 2. Lacking in mental discrimination: Dull 3.a. of poor, shabby, inferior quality or status b. worthy of little regard: Contemptible." I looked up.

He was nodding with satisfaction. "Go on."

"4. Lacking dignity or honor: Base 5.a. penurious, stingy b. characterized by petty selfishness or malice." I looked up.

"Go on."

The definition continued, showing the shared meaning of *mean* with words like "ignoble, abject, sordid—so low as to be out of accord with normal standards of human decency and dignity," all of which he made me continue to read out loud.

"'The lowest of the low.' So this is what you think of your father, huh?"

"No, it's not what I meant at all."

"Do you think calling your father 'mean' shows respect for your father?"

"No, but I was only kidding around."

"Oh? A joke? I don't find anything funny in that definition, do you?"

"That's not what … "

"Do you still think it was nice to call your father 'mean'? Hmm?"

"No, I guess not."

"Well?" He waited. I knew what he was waiting for. Nothing would cut the tension, wipe the slate clean, until I said it.

"I'm sorry."

Was he crazy? Or did he have a more educated grasp of the English language than I? Or, having lost control over his own destiny, was he hanging on as the respected king of his own house who could at least control his family? His self-esteem seemed so fragile.

Or maybe I was the crazy one. Had I not insulted my own father by tossing around a word whose meaning I didn't even know? Didn't I therefore deserve what I got?

⁓

My father rented a cottage on Long Beach Island on the Jersey shore for two weeks in August for a family vacation. I went along for my first extended holiday from my new job. I was still nineteen, and Frank, who had recently finished his freshman year at the University of Michigan, was seventeen.

Dressed only in his swim trunks and an unbuttoned matching shirt flapping in the breeze, my father seemed happy. Almost daily he went surf fishing, standing calf deep in the ocean to cast his lure into the waves. After a week of not catching anything, he learned from the fishermen around him that bluefish were running. My father booked spaces on a charter fishing boat for himself, thirteen-year-old Neal, who loved to fish, too, and Frank, who did not but went for the fun of it. I joined my mother and Tootie at the beach. Tootie had just turned nine, and I benevolently rode the waves with her, or body surfed, as the activity is called today.

Afterward my father said Neal and Frank had been a little seasick, and since no fish had bitten their hooks, the captain gave them two big freshly caught bluefish to take home. My father said the bluefish were fierce and were known to bite back. As my mother cleaned them, she couldn't help commenting that she wasn't having a vacation. We ate the bluefish for dinner. None of us was too keen on the taste, which seemed heavy after the lightness of shad.

Most nights, I went up to the unfinished attic room in the cottage—I was glad to have it to myself—and read *The Brothers Karamazov*. I had asked my sociology professor at the University of Delaware what important book about life I should read, and he had recommended it. Determined to learn, I made myself look up every word I did not know and write its definition in a little notebook I kept just for vocabulary. The task constantly interrupted the story and reminded me how little I knew about anything, but by the time I finished, I felt I had really read *The Brothers Karamazov*.

I don't remember much more about that vacation except that one night, driving her little Hillman, my mother dropped Frank and me off at the movies in Beach Haven, where we joined the long line of people waiting to buy tickets to see the new Alfred Hitchcock movie *Psycho*. I also remember the morning we packed up the cottage to go home—and for my father and me, to return to work—because my father was standing in front of the refrigerator, cleaning it out by eating all the leftovers. He grinned guiltily as he stuffed his mouth with giant romaine lettuce leaves, pickles, whatever he found, as one would feed branches into a wood chipper.

That early evening, back in Montclair, after participating in loading and unloading two cars, making the hundred-mile drive, closing up and reopening two different dwellings, and weeding his flower garden, my father complained of indigestion. While I had never seen him lie on the living room rug before, I figured firm support was part of his finding relief. (Long ago, he had sandwiched a big piece of plywood between the mattress and box spring of his and my mother's bed.) I had made plans to see my friend Betsy before she headed back to college. When she tooted her horn outside, I had to get down on my knees to reach my father on the rug to kiss him good night. We children kissed him; he didn't kiss us. Not kissing my father before I left would have been like leaving the period off a sentence.

I returned around eleven thirty to learn that my father's indigestion had gotten so bad my mother had called the doctor, who instructed her to drive my father to St. Vincent's Hospital, where he would meet them. "Do not take time to get him dressed," the doctor had cautioned her, "but bring him as he is in his pajamas."

To go out in public in his pajamas and to be forced to ride in my mother's car, not as the driver, but as the passenger, established my father's errand as a frightening emergency. The destination of the hospital, a place he abhorred, added panic. In the hospital elevator, my father died of a massive heart attack. My mother said he was scared to death.

That night, my mother, Frank, and I numbly sat down, got up, sat down, and wandered around the downstairs, trying to absorb the stunning fact of my father's death. To be sitting around the living room in what he would have called "dirty play clothes" filled me with almost wild abandon. I felt vaguely lightheaded and exhilarated from relief, yet the latter was a sensation I did not allow myself to name. What I could experience clearly was terrible guilt, anxiety, and fear. What I could name was the sadness for my father's truncated life, cut off at forty-nine, when I thought he was just starting to show signs of mellowing. Hadn't he seemed almost tenderly vulnerable when I had kissed him goodbye earlier that night? Hadn't we almost had a real conversation recently in the car when we commuted together to New York? Who knows how things might have turned out?

That was the way I felt then. It took me many years to be able to acknowledge the possibility that had my father lived, our relationship could have grown more difficult. For example, he might, have interfered in my choice of a partner when I married and have been critical of what my husband did for a living. But speculation either way is only fantasy. The reality is that he died.

―

I did not find it strange when my mother said, "I am going to have a drink." Was this not exactly what the characters said when they received a terrible shock in every detective story and family drama that ever passed across our movie and television screens? "What I need is a good, stiff drink!"

"Here, take this, dear," the movie star doctor would say, handing our wobbly-kneed protagonist a brandy. "It will calm your nerves."

For my mother, that drink signaled a slight shift, a barely perceptible shudder along a fault line. After years of increasingly worsening tremors, that fault line would eventually gape into a chasm as large as the one caused by my father's death. I did not understand at the time that the fault had been there invisibly all along.

When we finally decided to go to bed and I was alone in my room, it started to rain. As I watched the rain out my window, I cried realizing that my father didn't even know it was raining. I felt sorry for him.

―

My mother had an open coffin at the funeral home. Before visiting hours began, she gave each of us in our nuclear family a few minutes alone with my father to say goodbye. The wax replica lying in the satin-lined box looked like my father. My brothers, sister, mother, and I all agreed he had that little smile on his face that we would see when he had just caught a lot of fish. But I knew my father was not there. I knew this was the end all right, the end of something that had never begun. When I told the mannequin in the coffin goodbye, I cried for the waste of it all: we had never really said hello.

―

Bebe Therouza openly sobbed in our living room on Highland Avenue. Uncle Kamil, whose cheeks were also wet with tears, brought his mother to Montclair to see my father, her second son, in the funeral home. It's the painfully wrong order of things for a parent to bury a child. Arabs are supposed to show their emotions, to weep and exhibit their pain and misery. A man lamenting is not considered unmanly; nor is a woman emitting loud cries considered unseemly. The whole Arab contingent that showed up at the house and funeral home snorted and sniffed and wiped their eyes. Their demonstrations threatened the floodgate holding back years of my mother's unwept tears. She was especially impatient with Bebe Therouza for carrying on and being so dramatic.

Bebe Lorene arrived from Missouri. She told Bebe Therouza that she was sorry for her loss. When Bebe Therouza did not understand her, Bebe Lorene shouted, "I'M SORRY FOR YOUR LOSS." Bebe Lorene expected my mother and us children to go back to Missouri to live with her. My mother made it clear to her that Montclair was our home, and this was where she was going to stay. And she made it clear to Uncle Joe, who was between wives, that she was not interested in him.

My father had faithfully attended the Montclair Heights Dutch Reformed Church and was invited to be an elder there —an honor he declined because he saw it as a fundraising job for which he had little time. Nonetheless, out of respect for Bebe Therouza, to whom the Catholic Church meant so much, my mother offered to give my father a Catholic funeral and burial. But St. Cassian's Parish in Upper Montclair would have nothing to do with the idea. My father was no longer a member of the club.

Standing in front of my father's bureau, where he had emptied his pockets for the last time, I felt strange knowing there was no possibility he would walk in on me as I looked at his wallet, his money clip, his watch, his diamond ring, and the linen handkerchief he had left on the doily beneath the mirror. Something had mysteriously departed even these inanimate things. Their importance seemed to have evaporated.

My memory of the visiting hours at the funeral home and the funeral service for my father at our packed church is of one big blur of people. Sweet Bill from University of Delaware, who was by then also working in New York, came on his own to be with me. He was at my side for the short service at the cemetery after the funeral. When my father's coffin was lowered into the grave, I lost whatever composure I had and bawled like an Arab—the gift of tears. My mother's eyes were watery, but she kept her tears in, as if doing so would somehow get her around the painful truth.

I thought of a girl in my class at the University of Delaware who lived in another dorm and whom I did not know except to exchange hellos with. She had stopped me on campus one day to ask if she might drop over to my room sometime to talk about poetry. Sure, I had replied. Not long thereafter she came by. She said that she had read my poems in *Venture* and liked them. She was trying to write some poems herself. After we talked in this vein for a few minutes, she revealed what I thought was her real reason for coming: there was a prayer group in her dorm, and wouldn't I like to join them for prayer some morning? I began to see her interest in poetry was just a wedge to get in to proselytize. I told her flat out that I was an atheist and was trying to be a good sport about it and didn't need her crutch. (Years later when I went back to college, I had a religion professor who asked, "What's wrong with a crutch if you have a broken leg?") But my rude response irritated my classmate, and as she stood up to go, she said angrily, "You just wait! Someday something terrible will happen, and you'll be down on your knees."

I thought my father's death qualified as that terrible event that was supposed to bring me down to my knees. But all it did was make me think that life was senseless. If God did exist, I thought as I considered my mother, a widow at forty with three dependent children, God was a rat. Ironically, I felt my father's death had brought me *up* to my knees. Although math was never my forte, when my eighth-grade math teacher, Mr. Barheit, introduced negative numbers, I readily understood them. My father's death had hoisted me up to zero.

I've known people born in my cultural era who, even though their parents never articulated their love for them, were confident that they were loved. I was not one of them. But one important thing death taught me was that if you love someone, you should tell them so while you have the chance, for I was as sorry that I never told my father I loved him as I was that he never told me. I vowed that I would never again let down my side of the equation.

I did not understand then what many years later I would learn in therapy. In the experience of transference, the client often projects the movie of his or her parents on the blank screen of the therapist. After successfully being helped to become him- or herself, the client begins to see the screen as screen and the therapist behind it as a person with individual struggles and talents and interests. Similarly, I found that when I projected my atheism on the screen of the universe, I was really saying that there was no one there for me. When I recognized the screen as screen, I found the universe behind it full of mystery and wonder and myself full of awe.

Two mornings after my father died, my mother sat at the kitchen table, absently stirring a cup of coffee.

"I had the craziest dream last night," she said. "It was a parade, and most of the people were colored. They were all marching and laughing, but it was a funeral. They were all happy and playing music and singing."

Her description made me think of the song "When the Saints Go Marching In." "As the procession marched under the arch of the cemetery gate," she continued, "I could read the name of the cemetery on the arch."

"What was it?"

"Done Rovin'. That's odd, isn't it? Done Rovin'."

———

After my father's funeral I made an appointment for my first complete physical examination as an adult. I felt that, like my father, I was going to die young, for didn't I deserve to? I wanted to know two things: if my heart was all right and if I was normal. I didn't look like the women walking on the sidewalk who caught my father's eye when he stopped his car for a red light. Was something wrong with me?

After my exam, I dressed and sat in the doctor's office to hear his verdict. "You're a young woman," the doctor said. "Your heart is fine. You are in excellent health."

"But am I normal?" I asked.

"What do you mean?" The doctor gave me a quizzical look. I looked down at my lap.

"I mean ... down there."

Suddenly understanding me, he grinned. "Quite."

But I had no confidence in his examination. What had a doctor known about my father's heart? My heart might behave well for an electrocardiogram, my hypochondriac reasoning went, but a doctor couldn't be with me all the time to detect the sudden twinges and irregular palpitations that only I could feel. How did I know that something within me was not going to turn on me when I wasn't looking—the adult version of my childhood prayer "If I should die before I wake"? And what was that unnamable guilty feeling I labored under?

Years later, a passage in a book on psychology helped me connect my deserving- of-death feeling with my father's shrieking at me that I was killing him. It was also many years later before I understood that in thinking there was something wrong with me, I had "taken up the wrong cross," as the psychologist and theologian Ann Ulanov might put it. I thought real girls don't like to shovel snow (as I did), girls don't do sports (except maybe tennis), girls don't like to mow the lawn, girls don't whistle. Real girls wear frilly dresses and makeup.

Culture, both Iraqi and American, was to blame for making me think there was something wrong with me. Culture interfered with my experience of the sacred. Our ability to make culture comes in our genes, but culture itself does not come in our genes. Culture is something we contrive and learn and pass on. Coming from a different culture, it's easier to recognize a certain immaturity in the Arab culture of my father, for example. Lest anyone feel superior in recognizing the immaturity, however, think in Western culture if we can call mature telling our children to use their words instead of fists, while raining down bombs on our perceived enemies. Culture is something we can change.

―

My mother came in the front door from doing errands one afternoon. She seemed bothered. She said that an elderly woman had come up to her in Kings Market, someone who looked familiar but whose name she could not remember.

"Weren't you married to the man who just died?" the woman had asked my mother. "He was that foreigner, wasn't he?"

―

Nejib and Doris with friends at the Casino Russe in New York.

Grandfather Lloyd Hisaw, Bebe Lorene's former husband.

Grandmother Bebe Lorene.

Suzy holding little brother, Neal, with Nanny in Neosho.

Kamil and May touring the Statue of Liberty.

Suzy (front row, first on left) with Ricky Crane (front row, third from left), in Miss Liebold's fourth-grade class at Edgemont School.

Doris in the kitchen on Brookfield Road.

Nejib on family vacation one summer in Maine.

Suzy (back row, third from left), chair of the Dance Committee at the Girls Club of the Women's Club in Upper Montclair.

Frank, Doris, and Suzy pose in front of the family Buick before going to church.

Frank with Neal and Tootie, who are ready for church, too.

Suzy (on left), as the maid of honor at Marcia's wedding, admiring her new ring.

PART THREE:

IN VINO VERITAS

***T**HE CHRISTMAS AFTER MY FATHER DIED*, I wracked my brain to think of a present for my mother. She was only forty years old, and I thought she needed to be involved in something, preferably something fun where she could meet new people her own age. She'd always liked music. She could play the piano, although I hadn't heard her sit down at ours in a long time. Summers in Neosho, she had taught Frank and me how to read music and coached us through a beginner piano book on Bebe Lorene's piano. She still used her clear soprano voice in the church choir every Sunday. I could imagine my mother well and happy, intelligent, talented, funny, and looking pretty—as if her potential were a kind of hologram that walked along beside her. It was the hologram I addressed rather than her reality when I pondered what activity would fit her talents and interests and hit upon what I thought was a brilliant idea.

There was an organization in town called the Montclair Operetta Club. The club's productions ranged from *The Student Prince* to *South Pacific.* While I understood that some roles were filled by paid professionals, local amateurs auditioned for its chorus and orchestra. Wouldn't this organization be a great place to revive my mother's love of playing the violin?

The first violin Doris learned to play was an inexpensive one from a music store in Neosho. When her mother saw that she was practicing four hours a day, she agreed to buy her daughter a better instrument and drove Doris to Joplin to the tiny second-floor shop of an old German violin maker. He had the construction of two violins under way but agreed to accept the order for another. The violin cost two hundred dollars, a sacrifice for Lorene, whose salary as a junior high social studies teacher was sixty-five dollars a month. Doris proudly played her new instrument in the fifty-piece Neosho High School Orchestra. Coming in third in a county contest, she also performed with her violin on the radio at the invitation of a station in Joplin.

One afternoon my mother was out. I opened the door to her closet and took down the black violin case we children were forbidden to touch and opened it. The instrument, richly reddish brown and gleaming, was lying on the blue velvet lining. The bow was in the case, too, but its strings had rotted.

I was not so naïve as to expect that after all these years of inactivity, my mother would be able to simply pick up her violin and play it. A new music store and school had just opened in Upper Montclair, and my Christmas gift was going to consist of not only having her bow and violin restrung and ready to play, but also presenting her with a gift certificate for three brush-up lessons. When I explained everything to the man in the music store, he thought my idea was excellent.

Christmas morning came. The bathrobes, pajamas, and sweaters were summarily opened. Finally, chomping at the bit, I ran upstairs to get my wrapped gift, which I had not dared leave under the tree for fear its shape would be too revealing.

"What in the world?" My mother smiled, arching her eyebrows.

I could hardly contain myself. Would she ever get the wrapping paper off? When she finally exposed the violin case, my mother's mouth was still smiling, but her eyes were not.

"What have you done?" she asked.

"Well, open it! Open it!"

"My violin," she said flatly. "What have you done?" She lifted it out of the case and turned it over to inspect it.

"It's all ready to play!" I was spilling over with excitement. "Here, open this, too. It's part of the present." I handed her the envelope containing the gift certificate. "It's for brush-up lessons. I explained to the man in the music store how you haven't played in twenty years, and he said he'd bet you'd be playing in no time. Maybe you could play in the Montclair Operetta Club orchestra," I added, in case she hadn't thought of it.

Still holding the violin in her left hand, my mother looked down at the case and frowned as she reached for the bow.

"Try to play," my brothers and sister and I urged her. "Come on, Mom, play something!"

My mother rose and walked over to the piano, hit the A key, and plucked the violin strings, listening as she tuned them. (She was the one to whom Frank and I had taken our plastic ukuleles, gifts of Bebe Lorene, to have the "My Dog Has Fleas" put back in the strings.) She flipped through the book of elementary all-time favorite songs for the piano Tootie had left propped open on the rack. Settling her chin on the rest, she began to play "Jeanie with the Light Brown Hair." Her playing sounded fine, a little scratchy, but for someone who had not picked up a violin in twenty years, I thought she did amazingly well.

We applauded and whistled and cheered.

My mother frowned. "This isn't my bow. Mine was irreplaceable. They've substituted an inferior one."

"Oh, no," I groaned. "I'll take it back to them. Maybe it's just a mistake, and they just got it switched around."

"Don't bother. You'd never be able to identify it, and it would be just your word against theirs. This is why I didn't want you touching my violin," she said irritably.

"I'm sorry, really. It's too bad this happened."

"But thank you," she added, noting my crestfallen face. "I don't want you to think I don't appreciate your thought." She laid the instrument back in the case. "This violin was made from one-hundred-year-old wood."

"Wow," I said, thanking my lucky stars the man at the music store had not stepped on it.

My mother did use the gift certificate for the lessons. The afternoon she returned from the last one, I asked her how it went, and her answer got my hopes up.

"Fine. He didn't really give me lessons. We just spent the whole time playing our violins together. He said there wasn't anything he could teach me I didn't already know and that all I needed to do was play."

But my mother shut down something in her soul as surely as she snapped down the lid of her violin case that day for the last time.

When my father died, my mother did not know how to write a check—how bills got paid before online banking. My father had handled all the household business, telling my mother where to sign only as occasion necessitated. She must have been overwhelmed to be suddenly thrown into responsibility for everything—a passenger, untrained in navigation, thrust into the wheel room of a foundering ship.

I encouraged my mother to go back to college, but she was quick and firm with her "No." She did not want to be a teacher, the only purpose she could imagine going to back to school would fulfill. Instead, she studied to become a real estate broker and earned her license. She started showing houses at the beck and call of prospective buyers, with the added pressure of having to leave her young children at home alone to do so, especially on weekends. After a year of this, with no sale panning out, she took a job as a secretary in the same real estate office, with a reliable albeit small paycheck.

My mother's alcoholic deterioration did not happen all at once but in stages over the years, taking her in a direction from which it became increasingly harder for her to return. In the beginning, for a while, I told myself everything seemed OK, even while my gut told me it was not. Remembering my first suspicion, I can't believe I puzzled over it. I discovered a whiskey bottle in the broom closet instead of in the liquor cabinet, where it belonged. Was my mother hiding it? And if so, why?

Sometimes I came upon her in her bathrobe, sitting yoga style on the Persian rug in her bedroom and watching television as she rolled up her hair. I would observe two little juice glasses beside her. One was filled with water into which she dipped her comb to wet her hair, which she then twisted in little coils and secured with two bobby pins. In the other was whiskey to sip while she performed this nightly chore. By then she was open about her little bit of drinking. She was, after all, an adult. She looked nice for her job and got to work on time.

I kept my promise not to move to the city until after my twenty-first birthday. But when the time came, I hesitated, feeling the responsibility of not abandoning ship, of staying to help my mother with Neal and Tootie and contributing my financial share for room and board. In the kitchen, my mother said to me what I felt at the time were generous words: "You are not my friend. You are my daughter. I do not want you to stay here for me. Go. Live in New York." And so, without guilt, I did.

I wonder now if she did not simply want me out of the house so she could drink in peace.

After living in New York for more than four years, I met Tom, the man I would marry. We were dating but not yet engaged when I went home to Montclair one weekend. While I was visiting, my mother received a phone call. I watched as she hung up, obviously shaken.

"Who was that?" I asked, curious to know who or what had nonplussed her.

"That was Grace Hisaw."

That was a new one on me. "Who's Grace Hisaw?"

"My stepmother."

"Your *stepmother*?"

"Yes, my father married again. Grace called to tell me that my father is very sick and in the hospital. He has emphysema."

"You mean your father is *alive*?" I couldn't believe it. "Where do they live?"

"Pierce City."

"*Pierce City*?" This was too much. Pierce City was less than a half hour's drive from Neosho. "You mean he's been alive and living in Pierce City all these years?"

"Yes. Grace said he asked for me. She told me he said, 'I want to see Doris.'"

"Are you going to go?"

"I don't know. I'd have to fly." My mother had never been on an airplane before.

"You'll like flying," I assured her. But she was nervous about more things than flying.

Once she made up her mind to go see her father, I wondered whether she would pack a bottle in her suitcase. How was she going to handle her need to drink?

From the airport in St. Louis, my mother took a puddle jumper to Joplin, where a cousin whom she hadn't seen since she was eight years old met the plane. He drove my mother straight to the hospital. But by the time she got there, her father had died.

I don't know how my mother handled what happened. I think that basically she didn't. At least she knew that on his deathbed, her father had wanted to see her. But I was involved in my own happiness with Tom, and it took me a long time to understand that the pain of my mother's loss was not just from her father's absence all those years, but also from his rejection.

Tom and I married and, after a year of living in Manhattan, moved to northern Westchester County in New York, commuting distance from the city. We lived a little over an hour's drive away from my mother in Montclair. Still secretly drinking, my mother met Carlton, a divorced man who played the organ in her church, where she still sang in the choir. They married, but when her new husband realized how far beyond social drinking my mother's habits had gone, he threatened to leave if she did not stop. She quit cold turkey, but nothing changed; her behavior was still dysfunctional. By not examining why she drank so much, by not being able to name the pain she had been trying so hard to medicate, she turned into a dry drunk, slang for "untreated alcoholism."

But my mother's having a husband who cared about her gave me respite from worrying about her. She began sending birthday cards again, which she signed, "Luv, Mom."

My mother and Carlton came to us for holiday dinners. I loved living in our little rented cottage in the woods. Tom's brother called it a chicken coop. For the first Thanksgiving we hosted, I was on the phone a lot with my mother, getting answers to questions about cooking my first turkey. (This was before recipes came with video instructions on the Internet.) My siblings had standing invitations to holiday dinners at our house, too, and would join us when they were available.

———

Three times in my mother's childhood in Neosho, the morticians parked their combination funeral coach and ambulance in front of her family's home at 303 West Spring Street and carried a casket up the porch stairs and into the middle of the front room. There, they opened the lid and displayed the deceased for three days. The first to die, when Doris was nine, was her great-grandmother, Nanny's mother, whom Doris called Granny Shearer. The second, when Doris was twelve, was her great-grandfather, Nanny's father, whom Doris called Grandpa Shearer. And the third, when she was sixteen, was her grandfather, Nanny's husband, whom Doris called Granddaddy Fowler and who was like a father to her.

Each time the black satin ribbon was nailed to the door, the dining room and kitchen tables groaned under hams and fried chickens and cakes and cobblers that thoughtful friends and relatives brought. My mother helped carry plates of food to the visitors, who sat in the folding chairs arranged around the casket. The bodies were all embalmed, and the smell of formaldehyde in combination with the oppressively heavy odor of the flowers made it hard for her to sleep just a room away. To escape all the people filling the house after Granddaddy died, she climbed into the mulberry tree in the backyard where as a little girl sequestered in its branches she had read *Treasure Island*.

After eight years with my mother, Carlton died suddenly one night of heart failure. To her list of childhood losses could now be added not only her first husband but also her second. She was sad, but she stoppered her tears.

———

"Now don't you worry about me," my mother assured me after Carlton's death. "I'll be fine." But she went back to drinking again, proving the psychologist Carl Jung's observation that "neurosis is a substitute for legitimate suffering." Yes, my books are wise friends.

A living friend of mine put it this way: Sometimes a car part breaks—say, the mirror—and when you replace it, the car looks as good as new. Sometimes something more serious happens, like the transmission goes. The repair is costly and may take time, but it puts the car right again. But if you open the hood and slam a sledgehammer down on the engine over and over, you will most likely damage your car permanently.

My mother became a sledgehammer-to-the-engine kind of drinker.

My mother didn't want any of us children at her house. I was busy raising my own children, and when both of them were in school full-time, I went back to school, too. I kept in touch with my mother by telephone, imagining the line stretching for miles between our houses like an umbilical cord. Who was the mother? Who, the daughter? Limited to a telephone relationship with my mother, I took advantage of her lubricated tongue to find out about her, to learn what kind of childhood she had had, and to ask her questions about my own childhood.

One day on the phone, I asked my mother if she remembered the black eye she had when we got back to Montclair from our trip to Neosho after Neal was born.

She knew exactly what I was talking about and replied without hesitation, "Yes. Your father had given me money to get a new dress, shoes, and purse for a dinner at a restaurant with the people from his office. I had never met any of them before, and I thought I looked nice. I don't know where your father had disappeared to, but his secretary, Dotty, took me around and introduced me to everybody. I was beginning to get the idea that everyone knew your father and Dotty were having an affair. All through dinner, your father was giving me *those looks*. In the car going home, he accused me of being a tart for having his secretary take me around to introduce me to everybody. That's when he gave me the black eye."

How mixed up is this? Socking my mother for what his secretary did? Punishing my mother for what *he* did? Culture? Gender? Crazy? Or all of the above?

———

Sometimes in our telephone sessions, I misguidedly thought that the "talking cure" might bring my mother some relief, maybe even insight. But I began to realize that she was not paying attention to what she herself said. The experiences she had buried because they were too painful to bear were simply leaking out as she recounted them in a flat way. I think about George Santayana's aphorism "Those who cannot remember the past are condemned to repeat it." We can say about personal history that those who cannot remember how the past *felt* are condemned to repeat it.

"Mother was a real disciplinarian," she was telling me another day. "I always say she killed five peach trees on me."

"What do you mean?"

"She'd cut shoots from the peach trees out back to switch me with."

So that was why my mother had spanked me so hard. I wondered why, when she took the back of her hairbrush to me, she didn't remember how much it had hurt and humiliated her to have her legs whipped with a switch from a peach tree. I mulled over this information.

She misinterpreted my silence as a negative judgment of Bebe Lorene. "Now don't get me wrong. Mother always kept me with pretty clothes and pocket money, but I never slept alone in my life. She'd even read my mail. I'd get clobbered if the envelope said SWAK, you know, 'Sealed With A Kiss.' I think she thought sex was dirty. If a date kissed me good night, she would take a board to me. Just a couple of weeks before I was married, I got it with her shoe, only I laughed because she broke the heel off. I'd go to Nanny, and she'd say, 'Lorene, what are you doing?' And Mother would say, 'She's *my* daughter!'"

I took in *I got it with her shoe*, but *just a couple of weeks before I was married* sailed right by me. I was thinking of my mother as a child, not as the young woman who was going into her sophomore year of college when she ran off to get married. I also missed *I never slept alone in my life.* What did she mean by that? My own unconscious had its listening limits. I was definitely not her therapist. (The time I told her that I was seeing a therapist, she responded, "Good! You're crazy.") I think my mother felt guilty that she had revealed too much, because she suddenly changed course. "Mother could be real nice, though. One time she drove a whole bunch of us out in the country to see a will-o'-the-wisp that bounced right on the hood of the car."

As I slowly assembled the parts of the puzzle of my mother's experience of childhood, I found there was no piece too small. In one conversation she said only, "My father sent me bloomers and a doll for my birthday one time. I know because my mother opened the box, but when she saw what was inside, she wrapped the package up again and sent it back."

"I had to go to all the teachers' conventions with Mother," she answered in response to my questions about what her summers were like. If you did not know her well, you might not have been able to tell she had been drinking. "So I got to see personages like Admiral Byrd and Eleanor Roosevelt. But they didn't impress me as much as getting the free pencils and Crayola crayons.

"Mother was paid sixty-five dollars a month to teach school and not paid in the summer, yet she was expected to keep going to school for her degree. I had to go to college with Mother every summer. When I got older, I'd just wander around the campus and go into an art class if I felt like it. Mother was a plodder. I saw her graduate from college when I was nine. When Mother started her Master's work at University of Missouri, I played my violin in the summer orchestra."

Sometimes, as my mother rambled on, I would forget she was drunk. Mainly, I got into her tales about what life was like in a different era. Especially since I knew Neosho and had spent so much time in the big house her great-grandfather had built, I felt I could put on her shoes and walk around in her stories.

"Nanny and Granddaddy thought I should have chores," my mother recounted. "Every day after school I had to haul in an armful of wood and a bucket of coal. I had to help on washday too. You know, the old washing machine and wringer, two rinse waters. I was hanging out the whole wash and bringing it in by the time I was nine or ten. One time we had a whole baseball team boarding with us, a farm team, and I had to wash all the sheets and make the beds. Mother made the starch and starched the pillowcases. I ironed. You folded up a sheet on the bottom and ironed everything on top of it, so that when you were through, the sheet was ironed too." This was the experience that had come in handy at my father's Royal Palm Hotel back in Basra when she pitched in to iron sheets.

"Mother and I might be all set to have a little spree in Joplin, and Granddaddy would come in and drop down a basket of peaches. We would have to get on our old clothes and peel peaches so Nanny could can them. I could pluck a chicken and cut it up. Granny Shearer was still alive, so I must have been less than eight.

"We got mail-order chicks. We had to put them next to the stove to keep them warm. When I was three or four years old, one rooster didn't like me and would always attack me. The family said it was because of my red dress. Mother always wanted to dress me up in red because it put a little color in my cheeks. People often said how pale I was. One day we went for a picnic in Baxter Springs, and they told me we were having that old rooster for lunch. I didn't care; I was glad to be rid of him."

～

During a hot spell on Brookfield Road, I remember my mother acting silly when she kicked off her shoes and walked around the living room barefoot, something my father did not approve any of us doing. In Iraq in his era the only people who walked in bare feet were those too poor to own shoes, and they ran the risk of contracting hookworm.

But that day my mother had jokingly reminded my father that he had married a hillbilly from the Ozarks. She laughingly validated her authenticity with the tale of her distant cousin in the mountains who hid a still for making whiskey in a grave and stirred the mash with an old shinbone. I knew she was having fun entertaining us with a tall tale.

Would my mother ever have told me the stories from her childhood if she had not been drinking?

"Granddaddy could do carpentry. When he took down the smokehouse, he made a playhouse for me out of the wood, with miniature furniture. He didn't talk much; he was very quiet. He had a red mustache." She said he let her dig a big hole in back of his grocery store and put a chair in it so that she could sit in the hole to read.

"But Granddaddy was always disappointed I never learned to fiddle," she said. "My violin teacher was Italian, and we did all classical music. She was wonderful."

Years later Bebe Lorene explained that Granddaddy never complimented Doris on her violin because he didn't like classical music. He wanted her to play "Turkey in the Straw." He and Nanny always listened to "Grand Ole Opry" on the radio.

Freely associating, my mother segued into how Granddaddy happened to get her her beloved dog.

"He was a little black fox-terrier mutt whose tail had been cut so short," she said, "it looked like a button wagging. Did he howl when I practiced my violin! The migrant workers they call Okies [probably fleeing the Dust Bowl in Oklahoma] and gypsies, too, would come into Granddaddy's grocery store and look around at things, especially during the picking season. Strawberries were a big crop in that part of the country. Granddaddy was real kind: He'd take a paper sack and fill it up with cheese, bananas, bread, or maybe some crackers and go outside and slip it into their car.

"One time an open touring car pulled up, and while Nanny waited on the Okies inside the store, Granddaddy went outside to talk to the little boy who sat waiting in the car holding his dog."

"'Mister,' the little boy said to Granddaddy, 'I don't have anything to feed my dog. Do you think you would take him?'"

"'What do you want for him?'"

"'I'll let you have him for a dollar. But Mister, he's got to be called Fido.'"

"I ran all the way home with Fido under my arm. He was about the first thing that really belonged to me. I barely had a drawer to call my own."

"Doris loved that dog," Bebe Lorene later told me. "The day she got him she tore up the stairs, shouting, 'He's mine! He's mine!'"

It can't have been easy going through junior high school when your mother was Mrs. Hisaw, the social studies teacher who had a reputation for being strict, and you would overhear fellow students refer to her as Old Lady Hee-Haw. For two years, my childhood friend Judy taught colonial American history at the same junior high school in Neosho. She told me she called on my retired grandmother in hopes of gleaning some wisdom from her experience of teaching for forty-five years. How did she keep forty-five students under control, Judy asked her, when she herself had so much trouble with thirty?

"Well, my dear," Judy reported my grandmother answering, "you can't *hit* them anymore." My grandmother was referring to the outlawing of corporal punishment in public schools in most states, although, ironically, as of this date, Missouri hasn't officially banned the practice.

Even though Doris felt like her mother was "watching me like a hawk even in school," she did get away with playing hooky once. "I was a sophomore in high school, and it was during the harvest show. They closed off the square for it every year, and there was a carnival."

"In Missouri in those days there was a 3.2 beer called Mule Beer. Our family were real teetotalers. Nanny wouldn't have liquor in the house. But Mule Beer had a promotion at the harvest show that year that I just had to see—a real mule drinking beer."

A Missouri mule drinking beer. What irony! Was the attraction a premonition? Fellow feeling?

"It was a big ol' mule," my mother said, "and he would just pick those bottles up and guzzle them. But Granddaddy spotted me."

"'Oh, please don't tell,' I begged him." "Granddaddy winked. 'I won't if you won't.'"

"I won't!"

"'I ain't seen nuthin',' Granddaddy promised me, and I ran back to school."

My great-grandmother Nanny had always been subject to "female trouble." But since in Neosho I was regarded as one of those little pitchers with big ears whose entry into a room reduced a conversation to silence, I never learned what affliction she actually had. When Nanny was a young woman, maybe whatever she suffered affected her ability to care for her new baby son and her two-and-a-half-year-old daughter, Lorene, at the same time. But Bebe Lorene told me that after her brother was born, she felt she had been given away.

At her grandson's birth, Granny Shearer asked her daughter, Nanny, "Is there anything I can do to help? Could I take Lorene?"

According to Bebe Lorene, her mother answered, "I sure wish you would." Bebe Lorene's grandfather Shearer had quit farming and built the big house in Neosho after he lost his left hand to a steam thresher. However long she actually stayed at her grandparents' house, Bebe Lorene spoke of this separation from her parents as an abandonment. After finishing the lower grades at a local one-room schoolhouse near the farm, anyone in the rural districts who wanted to continue the higher grades had to board in the closest town with a high school, which was why Bebe Lorene went back to live with her grandparents to attend Neosho High School. In later years before her parents had stopped farming and moved to town to start their grocery store, Bebe Lorene would always refer to her home with her parents as "the farm" and her grandparents' house in Neosho as "home."

As I continued to sift through the dust of family history in search of clues to what secret pain my mother's drinking was masking, I unearthed a hard wad of old, chewed gum from Nanny's past.

"I had to dust every day," my mother said, "but one day, when Mother was still at school, I said to Nanny, 'Do I have to dust under this thing?'"

"What thing?" I asked.

"Willie's chewing gum. Nanny's brother, Willie, died when he was just a boy, and his mother saved the gum he was chewing the day he died."

I hadn't known Nanny had a brother. "You mean she kept the gum on the table in the living room?"

"His mother kept it on the table in the living room and wouldn't let anyone throw it away. Nanny had to dust under it, and then I had to dust under it. But one day after Granny Shearer had died, I said, 'Can I throw this thing out?' and Nanny said, 'I sure wish you would.'"

The last time I visited Bebe Lorene before she died, she gave me a clipping of the obituary of her adolescent uncle Willie, whom, of course, she never met:

> Once more in His all surveying wisdom God has seen fit to call from our midst Willie Oron Shearer .... He was a good and obedient boy always ready to do whatever his parents told him to do.
>
> On Monday, the 18th, in the afternoon he was suddenly attacked with congestion and in a short time he seemed to lose his mind and his speech.
>
> His funeral was preached at the Baptist church on Saturday evening ....

The last song that Willie was known to sing was "What can wash away my sins? Nothing but the blood of Jesus," which was a favorite song of his, and which he often sang and played on the organ for his ma. Willie is gone.

In my search for explanations for my mother's behavior, for the chain of cause and effect, I read the obituary and thought about what that piece of petrified chewing gum might have meant. I tried to empathize with Nanny, Willie's older sister, whose mother idealized her son so much she saved the wad of gum he was chewing before he died. I wondered if Nanny experienced herself constantly compared to that ideal and if she felt she measured up. And I wondered how much attention she would have been able to pay to her daughter, my dutiful grandmother, Bebe Lorene, who also had a younger brother.

Maybe the chain of abandonment that passed down from my great-great-grandmother to my great-grandmother to my grandmother is why my grandmother clung so tightly to her own daughter, my mother. Maybe rebellion against clinginess is why my mother kept me at arm's length. It was a possibility, but it didn't give me that "a-ha!" understanding. I knew there was a father-shaped hole in my mother's life, but why did she fend off her own mother, too? I still felt something was missing.

───

Telephoning my mother gradually became more unpredictable: I never knew what I'd find. Once I was greatly relieved to learn that she had lost her driver's license. For some time I had been afraid she was going to cause a serious accident in which she would either be killed or kill somebody else or both. She had already had too many little accidents in places like the Kings Market parking lot. They were always, of course, the other person's fault.

"Honestly, the way people drive today," she would complain.

The day I called, she didn't tell me what had happened right away. (In later years she would cagily not tell me anything at all, and I would discover each disaster obliquely, after piecing together little pieces of information she dropped.) When she finally got around to mentioning what had happened, her story was feebly veiled. She was, however, her usual galled and indignant self.

"How can they concoct a case for drunk driving when I wasn't even on the street?"

"What do you mean?"

"I was in my own driveway, minding my own business."

"Had you been drinking?" Very daring of me to ask.

"A body can have a little drink in her own house every now and then, don't you think?" It was the closest she had ever gotten to admitting she drank.

"Well, what happened?" I asked.

"I had the car parked at the top of the driveway, as I usually do, and the gas pedal stuck."

"What do you mean?"

"I tried to stop the car with the hedge, but the car just kept going. I finally got it to stop just before that little white picket gate. Remember it?"

Of course, I remembered the gate. What had happened was that my mother had driven through the tall hedge bordering her steep driveway, traversed her neighbors' long, sloping backyard, and come to a halt on the *inside* of the little white picket gate leading up to their front door. Indeed, she had not been driving in the street.

———

In the 1987 movie *Ironweed*, based on the novel by William Kennedy, who also wrote the screenplay, a profound moment occurs that I think is communicated more successfully on the screen than in the book. It is a moment in which I recognize my mother. Meryl Streep inhabits the alcoholic character Helen so masterfully that her performance earned her an Oscar nomination. Managing to scrape together money for drinks, Helen and her alcoholic companions, in their soiled and shabby clothes, go to the Gilded Cage, a saloon in 1938 Albany, frequented by both "bums" like them and "swells." When the bartender and owner, a former singer, learns that Helen used to sing on the radio, too, he escorts her to the floor microphone on the little stage at the far end of the saloon, where he asks his piano player to accompany her.

It's been so long since Helen sang professionally that at first she is shy standing on the stage, but taking the leap, she gives her all to "He's Me Pal." Her voice is clear and energetic, and she holds the last note for an exceptionally long time to thunderous applause from the well-dressed audience sitting at candlelit tables under sparkling chandeliers. She breaks into a big, gratified smile, but her bad teeth remind us of reality; the scene is repeated, with Helen's voice wavering and unable to sustain the last note.

The thunderous applause at the song's end is really only a stray clap. She looks out at an audience sitting at tables without candles, giving her odd looks—if they are noticing her at all—and Helen unsteadily descends the stairs to return to her companions at the bar. It was the hologram of her best self who sang so well.

I made a date for my husband and me to take my mother to lunch in Montclair at the Marlboro Inn. Although Tom knew beforehand we could not know what to expect, he was surprised by my mother's deterioration. After we pulled up to her house, he waited in the car while I got out and rang the doorbell. My mother opened the door buttoned up in her soiled coat, ready to go. When we entered the restaurant and the maître d' showed us to our table, I could feel the heads turning. The bright white tablecloth contrasted sharply with my mother's dingy coat, which she kept on. She read the menu almost haughtily, as if everything were fine. She was Helen in the movie, belting out her old number and caught up in the fantasy that she was singing to thunderous applause, when the truth was that we had brought a bag lady to lunch, and she did not smell good.

Did she believe that she had successfully pulled us into her fantasy and that we thought everything was fine too? Had we done her a disservice by taking her to a nice restaurant as if everything were normal? We could see she was suffering without a drink, so we told her to order whatever she wanted. All I thought we were doing was trying to be kind, stay connected, and let her know that we cared about her. But by the time the meal was over I was emotionally exhausted, because in truth I was trying to save her, and I was totally unsuccessful.

We pulled up to my mother's house, and Tom again waited in the car while I walked her to the front door. I stood by her on the little brick porch as she fumbled with the key to let herself in. After she closed the door behind her, she probably breathed a big sigh of relief that at last the charade was over. She had pulled off what *we* wanted. Now she could live the way *she* wanted.

―

My sister, Sally (she no longer wanted to be called Tootie), and her husband, Ray, a preacher, were living in Bullhead City, Arizona, where they had started from scratch a Foursquare Gospel church. Their denomination would next send them as missionaries to Toowoomba in Queensland, Hobart in Tasmania, and Manila in the Philippines, and it would be another ten years before we saw them again. I joked that if they got any farther away, they'd be closer. But before setting off on their international travels, Sally came east from Arizona to visit us with their firstborn child, my almost-two-year-old nephew, Ben.

Sally and Ben stayed with us at our house in New York, but my sister understandably wanted to see our mother. I arranged to drive us to Montclair and take our mother out to lunch so that she could especially visit her daughter who lived so far away and meet her grandson. I had warned my sister what might happen. We agreed beforehand that if things did not look good when we went to pick up our mother, we would simply leave and go to the restaurant without her.

As Sally hefted Ben in her arms, we stood facing my mother's front door for what seemed like a long time, waiting for her to answer the doorbell. We finally heard her making her way downstairs from the second floor. She opened the front door and stood unsteadily in her slip, annoyed at us because she wasn't ready. Like a bad actress, she flashed Ben a big, fake smile.

"This is Ben, Mom," Sally said. "Ben, this is Bebe." The name "Bebe" had been passed down to the next grandmother.

I could see this was not going to work. My mother was in no shape to go to a restaurant. "I'm going to take Ben to the park," I said to Sally, who wanted to talk to our mother. When Ben and I returned from our recess, we went straight into my car to wait. Sally shortly came out of the house by herself, and we drove to the restaurant for a bite to eat before heading back to New York.

At our house that evening, Ben toddled into the living room, where my children, his older cousins, were watching *Bewitched* on television. Ben pointed his finger at the image of a woman in a cape and witch's hat that was filling the screen. "Bebe!" he called out. He had been in his grandmother's house for less than two minutes.

―

While Sally was on the other side of the globe, my brothers Frank and Neal and I attempted a family intervention with our mother. We arrived at her house together one Saturday afternoon to tell her that we knew she was drinking and were worried about her and wished she would get some help, go to Alcoholics Anonymous. My mother did not receive our concern graciously. She later said, "You turned on me like a pack. I'll forgive but I'll never forget. Why do you always think the worst of me?"

―

I became an investigative reporter delving into my mother's case because it was my case, too. I wrote and telephoned all my mother's long-lost relatives, most of whom I hadn't previously known existed. Our sons were teenagers when Tom manned the fort while I went to visit Bebe Lorene in Neosho; I planned to talk with her in a way I had never talked with her before. I also made arrangements to meet my mother's stepmother, Grace, whom I never knew existed but lived in nearby Pierce City; I would stop there on my way back to the airport before returning home. There was something I needed to ask her.

Now it was I who was taking Bebe Lorene for a mystery ride, only the mystery was her relationship to my mother. We drove out to see the renovations on the Jolly Mill; in 1845 it had belonged to a Hisaw forebear, and it was now in the Register of Historic Places and surrounded by an inviting park. We drove past a neat, rectangular acre of dark-chocolate earth that had been cut out of the burgeoning verdure of Capps Creek valley. When Bebe Lorene said, "That was our farm," I felt a great connection with the land.

I boldly asked my grandmother if she had been in love with her husband, Lloyd, when she was first married—the husband we had never before mentioned. She answered, "Why, yes. I was crazy about him. There's our house over there."

I thought of their young love, of spring, as I scanned the landscape for the dwelling in which my grandmother and Lloyd began their marriage and had a baby daughter.

"There. It looks awful rundown now. The family we sold the house to had six kids. I don't know how they did it."

My eye had passed over a weathered gray wooden shed but returned to it as I realized it was indeed the house of my mother's birth and my grandmother's short marriage. Now the little structure listed, abandoned, and the yard around it was overgrown, but my imagination cleared away a kitchen garden in which I could see my grandmother working.

"Four rooms and a privy," Bebe Lorene said. "One bedroom for Lloyd and me, kitchen, dining room, and living room. The hired man had to sleep on the couch in the living room."

"The hired man?"

"Lloyd didn't want to work. He was so lazy, he hired a man to do the farming, and he didn't even have any money to pay him."

So much for the romance of the land.

"I had to pick blackberries on that hill yonder to pay for Doris's layette. Lloyd did take them into town for me to sell them. I had some chickens, and I heard some noise out there one day, and I know he took one or two of my chickens into town to sell and kept the money for himself. I thought Lloyd was grand until I married him."

My grandmother remembered that before her marriage, her friend Gene Henry had taken her to a pie supper and bought her pie. "He asked me not to marry Lloyd," she said. "Gene Henry thought Lloyd was a playboy." I wish I had asked if Gene Henry had been interested in her.

I learned from my grandmother that the culture of her time and place dictated that pregnant women stay home. I knew that while she was still single, she had taught at the nearby one-room Ross School, but she told me the law prohibited her teaching after she was married. And because she was pregnant, the cultural norms did not allow her to attend the annual Jolly Mill picnic, so Lloyd took two other women with him. When he drove the hired man home on Friday nights, he stayed out all night partying, she said.

My grandmother thought Lloyd had been expelled from the University of Missouri, but she said he gave the excuse that he had to quit school because of his eyes.

I asked Bebe Lorene about her in-laws' farm. She said that her father-in-law had put up his house and farm to pay for Lloyd's house and farm as well as some whiteface Hereford cattle. She didn't know what had happened, but she thought they had gone in over their heads and lost all their money. Bebe Lorene said Lloyd sued her for divorce because she wanted to live in their own place and not in the Hisaw house with his parents. His parents and her parents were on opposite sides of a split in their church— some "Baptist fuss," as she put it.

Did she remember returning any gifts Lloyd had sent to my mother? She answered no, but that's not what my mother had told me. The only thing he gave his daughter, my grandmother recalled, was a gold Eversharp mechanical pencil when she was graduating from high school. "He bought it at Foster Evans Drug and had it delivered to her right in the classroom. She was thrilled with that."

After the divorce, when my mother was only about two years old, Bebe Lorene said, "Lloyd came and took Doris right out of the yard and took her to his parents'. He kept her for two weeks, and his parents wanted custody of her. I had to go to court for that. The court said that he could get her two days a month, and then he had to have her back." Divorce was so scandalous that my mother had told me she always felt like a bastard growing up.

"Why did Lloyd stop visiting his daughter?" I asked Bebe Lorene.

She answered, "One day Doris said to him, 'You was mean to my mother, and I am not going with you.'" I told Bebe Lorene that my mother claimed she had instructed her to run away from her father, but my grandmother denied it. I don't think Bebe Lorene was purposely lying. I think she had convinced herself that what she was saying was true.

The reason I believe my mother's version is twofold: first, if she told me a story about her childhood and I waited a few weeks and asked her to tell the story again, she would tell it verbatim. Somebody who makes up stories may forget what they said the first time or even contradict herself. Secondly, the pain embedded in my mother's childhood stories authenticated them for me. Hadn't she said how much she loved her father's coming to pick her up?

"Since you had to go to school every summer," I asked Bebe Lorene, "why didn't you let Lloyd have Doris for the summer? Wouldn't it have been easier for you, too?"

"Oh, no, I couldn't do that," she replied. "Doris would come back from the farm with chiggers. They didn't take good care of her."

Bebe Lorene had been nothing but generous and kind to me as I was growing up.

I liked her sense of humor; it came out in little things you didn't expect her to say. For instance, one time she was flipping through her mail and remarked, "The only person I ever hear from is bill." I thought she was funny. She treated me differently than she had her daughter. But it helped that I was not hers to hit.

Grace had been married to Bebe Lorene's ex-husband for thirty-five years.

Nonetheless, I felt I was betraying my grandmother when, as I packed to go home, she asked me why I was leaving so soon for the airport. I answered that I wanted to give myself plenty of time to get there. She understood that perfectly.

Highway 60 from Neosho to Route 97, where I would turn to go to Pierce City, winds through some of the most beautiful rolling farmland in the world. At least, that is what I felt my genes declare. I had one last thing to do. Since Grace had established contact with my mother as Lloyd lay dying, I knew where she lived. I had introduced myself to Grace through unashamedly gratuitous notes, telephone calls, as well as flowers at Christmas. I think I was trying to prove to her that she could have had this nice granddaughter all along if she had wanted to. I had gotten cheated out of a grandfather.

I had plenty to think about on the drive. The farm on which Lloyd and his brother were born and grew up did not go to them. There weren't many people left who could remember why their father, Fred Hisaw, had lost it. Everyone I'd dug up to ask was of the old school belief that "if you don't have anything nice to say about somebody, don't say anything." The records simply showed that Fred had borrowed $4,500 against his farm and couldn't pay it back.

"Many farmers lost their farms like that during the Depression," said one cousin. His father was the director of the bank that foreclosed on Fred's mortgage, and he had snapped up the farm at the auction. His father had also been appointed administrator of Fred's estate. "There was talk about our family after we got the Hisaw farm," the cousin admitted, "but you know how people are," intimating the unfairness of scuttlebutt. One thing I've learned: we all want to look good.

After Lloyd's brother, Lee, the Harvard professor, and his wife died, their adult children never spoke to their uncle Lloyd again. The history of their estrangement is so convoluted it's difficult to follow. They had always heard the loss of the farm was Lloyd's fault. They understood that Lloyd had talked his father, Fred, into mortgaging the Hisaw farm so that Lloyd could buy cattle. But when Lloyd sold the cattle, instead of paying back his father, he bought a house for Grace, his second wife. They'd also heard that Lloyd had taken his late mother's jewelry and furniture from his father's house to give to Grace.

To top off the trouble, to keep the Hisaw farm going, Lloyd's brother, Lee, a struggling biologist with a young family at the time, scraped together $2,300 to lend his father, which, of course, he never got back. According to Lee's daughter, her mother had a vehement, lifelong hatred of her sister-in-law, Grace. Animosity does not rise out of a void, but all I had was hearsay to account for it.

Maybe Lee's parents thought he would come home from studying biology in college to run the farm and would be a better farmer for his education. Maybe Lloyd felt that when his brother continued on to graduate school, he got stuck with all the responsibility for the farm. Maybe Lee thought that while he was working so hard in school, the least Lloyd could do was take care of the farm.

Mulling over these thoughts, I sailed right past Grace's tidy, white-frame house. It was so little and close to the ground I missed it. Had I been expecting a grander dwelling, stuffed with underhandedly acquired family heirlooms? I turned the car around to go back, pulled into her driveway, and stood on her tiny front porch next to a wooden chair swing suspended on chains from the ceiling. I half expected to be greeted at the door by a short witch with beady black eyes set into a shriveled face, like the apple dolls we used to see as kids at the Ozark souvenir stands. Her dress would be floor-length, like the ones in the sepia-colored photographs she had sent me of my grandfather's parents.

Grace, nearing ninety, was indeed diminutive, but when she opened the door, I was surprised by her attire—gray slacks, a blue-and-white-striped blouse with a bow, and a blue woolen vest. Her eyes were not beady, but big and blue, made even bigger by the magnification of her glasses. Her modest house was immaculate. She told me she had a neighbor girl come to clean it once a week.

Grace had baked muffins to serve with tea, but I was the only one who ate and drank anything. What gave away Grace's age, as it did Bebe Lorene's, was how she got out of her chair. She made a top-heavy effort whose momentum propelled her forward in an involuntary trajectory of quick, tiny steps to gain her balance. But once stabilized, Grace had no trouble showing me around. She took me into her dining room to see several framed photographs of my grandfather Lloyd as a handsome young man, as well as a photograph of her only child, Bill, dressed in his uniform as a second lieutenant in the US Navy, who was lost at sea during World War II. Grace's first husband was only twenty-seven years old when he was electrocuted doing his job as a lineman for an electric company. Their son was the Billy my mother had played with when she visited her father, the red-haired, freckled-face boy she said was like a brother. She had not told the whole truth: when she was ten years old, Billy was her stepbrother.

Grace had put aside some mementos to give me: a little album of postcards my grandfather had collected as a boy and a large photograph of a reunion of Lloyd's mother's side of the family, the Cumminses. "I want you to have this too," she said as she handed me the strange souvenir of a marble jar with a chipped lid; it had contained the ointment for a bad burn my grandfather had suffered as a little boy. She told me that my grandfather was a fine man. When I asked her what he liked to do, she said he liked to read. I guess his eyes were not so bad.

I have no memory of this, but my mother had told me that when we first arrived in Missouri from Iraq, she drove with my father, Frank, and me out to the Hisaw farm to meet her father. But Lloyd—by then married to Grace—had been away that day. As an alcohol tax agent for ten years, he often traveled to inspect bars and restaurants for liquor licenses. Did Grace tell him that we'd been at their house? Did she look over us grandchildren and decide one visit was enough? Did she intercept my mother's letters and Christmas cards, which my mother finally stopped sending?

But I wasn't there to blame. "Grace, there's something I've been wanting to ask you. Why didn't Lloyd get in touch with my mother, his only child, all those years?"

After a long silence, she said, "Well, I don't know. Maybe ... " She paused to find the words. "Maybe it was because he was hurt."

"Hurt? By what?"

"Maybe because your mother ran off to get married without telling him."

I stood up, thanked her, said goodbye, got in the car, and bawled all the way to the Joplin airport. That was the stupidest thing I'd ever heard! My mother did not have a father because *what*? A father abandons his daughter because *his* feelings are hurt? Or maybe he was embarrassed to have made a fool of himself calling the FBI. And wasn't he even curious about his grandchildren? I thought of the wreckage. What a total waste! I wanted God, the director of this movie, to boom out of the clouds: "*CUT!*" And then we'd all pile into a trailer on the set for coffee, saying things like, "Boy, Lloyd, you were terrific the way you rejected your daughter, playing the immature father to a T. And Nejib, you've got that Arab thing down pat, keeping the women in their place. How's the harem? Ha-ha! Lorene, I was so persuaded by your suffocating possessiveness. Your touch of sadistic disciplinarian was brilliant. And Doris, what can I say? Your wounded witch—a touchstone performance." And we'd all hang up our costumes, hug and joke around, clap one another on the back, and go back to being our real selves, all smiling and relaxed.

But that is not what happened. That is why I was still crying when I reached the outskirts of the airport in Joplin, trying to find the entrance to the rent-a-car place.

After I got home, my mother telephoned me to freely associate while I listened. She was repeating herself about having nothing but a drawer of her own as a child when a light went on in my brain. My mother had spent most of her childhood in a thirteen-room house. Granted, those rooms were often occupied by tenants, but there was enough space for her to have had a bedroom. She'd always made sure her own children had rooms of their own.

"How come you never had your own room?" I asked. Why hadn't I thought to inquire before?

"Are you kidding?" my mother answered. "I only had a drawer of my own."

"I know," I said, "but why?"

Then a question that in all those years had never occurred to me began to assemble itself in my mind. If she did not have her own room and if she barely had her own drawer, did she have her own bed?

"Did you at least have your own bed?" I asked.

"Are you kidding?" my mother answered.

"You mean you slept in the same bed as your mother?"

"Yes."

"Did you ever ask her for a bed of your own?"

"Yes."

"What did she say?"

"She said, 'What for?'"

I boldly asked, "Did your mother sexually abuse you?"

"No, it was nothing like that. But she would cuddle up in bed and put her arm around me. What do you call it? Spooning. I had to sleep with my mother until the day I ran off to get married."

There was my answer. My mother had mixed me up with herself. She always said that I never wanted to be held, but it was she who didn't want to be held by her mother, at least not the way her mother had held her. She was the one who didn't want to be touched in the inappropriate way her mother had touched her. She made sure all her children had their own rooms because she had never had one. In *Into the Woods*, Stephen Sondheim's musical adaptation of Grimm's fairy tales, a wicked witch steals a girl, Rapunzel, to raise as her own daughter and locks her up in a tower. When Rapunzel wants to leave her to marry her prince, the witch sings the song "Stay with Me." Bebe Lorene sang her own version of "Stay with Me" to her daughter, Doris: "Who out there could love you more than I?" Love does not imprison.

During my final visit with Bebe Lorene before she died, she had told me that not long after my parents had eloped, a young man she did not know had knocked on her front door. He said, "I won't be needing this now" as he handed her a manila envelope. Opening the flap, she pulled out a formal black-and-white photograph of my mother that she had never seen before. The young man said that he and my mother had met at Southwest Missouri State Teachers College where they were both music majors and that they were engaged. Doris had not told her mother about her engagement. I'm sure she was afraid that her mother would have found a way to break it up. Would my mother have had the strength to stand up to her mother's interference? Would that young man have had the strength to pack his visiting mother-in-law's clothes back into her suitcase and drive her to the train station to send her home?

How alone, ashamed, and crazy my mother must have felt to have not been able to tell someone what was happening in her house, to have to constantly swallow her anger, fend off her grief, and pretend that everything was all right. But the only way to the other side of pain and suffering is *through* them. To remember what happened but not how she *felt* about what happened only indicated what terrible pain she must have been in. She did not live in an era or culture where the common man recognized and accepted the benefits of therapy.

Was my mother's elopement rebellious? Yes, but thanks for her rebellion, or I would not be here to tell the tale. Do I think my parents' elopement was romantic? Yes, maybe a little wild, certainly risky, but isn't falling in love a kind of temporary insanity? American culture supports Cinderella's infectious "Someday My Prince Will Come" syndrome. But for my mother he really did: my father might just as well have charged in on a white steed to sweep her off her feet and into the saddle as they galloped off. I give my mother credit for trying to save herself by saying yes to my father. She had not hopped on top of her cage.

～

"Hi, I just wanted to see how you're doing." Once again I was checking in on my mother by phone.

"Oh, fine, I guess," she answered in a normal voice, "except I've been pretty annoyed by all the singing in the neighborhood."

"What do you mean?"

"It's a group," she told me, "and they apparently get together at various houses in the neighborhood"—I'm wondering what singing group could be practicing at someone's house—"and they either sing until 3 a.m. or chant."

Until 3 a.m.? "What do you mean by 'chant'?"

"Oh, they take a word like *peanut butter*, and they chant it over and over." Peanut butter? I tried to keep her talking. "Any other words?" I asked. "Sometimes *sauerkraut* or *wiener* or *ham 'n' eggs*."

"What kinds of songs do they sing?"

"All kinds. Oldies, some folk songs. I expect they'll be getting into Irish songs this week," she said, sanely acknowledging the upcoming St. Patrick's Day. "But one song they sing all year."

"What is that?"

"'Jingle Bells.'"

"I can see where that would annoy you," I said as the terrible seriousness of her alcoholism sank in. I was frantically trying to think of what I could do to help.

"No, I don't mind; it's just the chanting that gets annoying. One time the bass singer did scales up and down until I thought he would never quit. It drove me crazy."

My mother was all alone in a world inside her head, and I could not think of what to do. I had already researched the possibility of hospitalizing her to dry out and had learned that the alcoholic has to give her own consent to go to the hospital.

―――

It was one of those times when she was not answering her phone at all. I went through the phase of letting it ring not fifteen times, but fifteen *minutes*. When she did not answer after fifteen minutes, I suffered the torment of a kind of paralysis. If she was dead, I guessed it would not matter, except dead for how long? But what if she was injured and could be helped? Should I call the police? But if I called the police and she was only drunk, she would be madder than hops and never forgive me. Or should I just get in the car and go see for myself what was going on?

This time, after fifteen minutes, she answered, "Hello."

"Mom! I've been trying to get you at different times, all day and night. I was worried about you."

"You always suspect the worst."

"Mother, I let the phone ring fifteen minutes each time."

"Well, I could be out in the backyard."

"At ten thirty at night?"

"I could be looking at the moon."

There was something about her answer that touched me—there was a certain innocence, even beauty, in thinking of looking at the moon. But it did nothing to make me feel better about her downward trajectory.

I was touched another time I called and she said, "You know that streetlight in front of my window? That seems to be where everybody stops to fix their cars. Two fellows stopped there the other night, working on their car, and I could hear them talking. The next thing you know, two more fellows joined them, and guess what?"

"What?"

"They all had Ozark accents! I almost yelled, 'Where are y'all from?' But it was three or four in the morning."

"What were they saying?"

"I didn't get out of bed, so I couldn't tell. But I could hear them talking. They must have been from that group on the hill, because what do you suppose they started singing?"

"I don't know."

"'That Ozark Smile.' Why, I haven't heard that song in years, since I was a girl! Neosho was the county seat, you know, and the Ad Club—that was like the chamber of commerce—used to have contests for 'That Ozark Smile Girl.' They'd take them around and bring them on stage at the Orpheum so you could vote. They've been singing 'That Ozark Smile' up there all week now. That and Christmas carols, but they sing those, I've told you, all year."

It made me so sad to listen to my mother's delusions because they revealed things she genuinely loved—music and her hometown.

Unable to drive, Doris called a taxi to take her to the bank, to buy booze, and sometimes to make a stab at selecting groceries at Kings Market, which she had delivered. If I had been a stranger walking past her down one of the store's aisles, would I have had a clue about the universe of singers and chanters who inhabited her? Tormented by hallucinations, how did she function? Who could comfort her? But maybe her need for comfort was my own projection.

Each time the operator reported that my mother's telephone had been disconnected, I always panicked that this was it. The telephone bill was usually the first bill my mother paid when she came to after a siege of letting her mail mount unopened.

One time, after neglecting her oil bill too long, she ran out of heat, and the pipes burst. How long had water been pouring through the downstairs ceiling into the hall and living room before she did something about it? How long had she been without heat? She told me that a cup of water in her bedroom had frozen.

"Now don't get all excited," she said that time. "The insurance man has been here already, and they are going to pay to have the damage repaired. They are even going to pay for painters, who are coming next week, and a man came yesterday to take the rugs away. Tend to your own business. I'm managing fine."

But I worried. Had a reputable rug dealer picked up her valuable rugs for repair, or had someone ripped them off? Would they disappear, the way all her jewelry had vanished? Or the silver dollars her great-grandpa Shearer had given her every birthday as a little girl? Or the prize Revolutionary War musket her second husband, Carlton, had mounted on the dining room wall? Who was coming into her house?

After two days and two nights of letting the phone ring for fifteen minutes at a time, I had been unable to rouse her. Then her last friend in Montclair, a woman she knew from church, called me to say my mother had not telephoned her in an oddly long while, and she, too, had been unable to reach her. Maybe this time, she suggested, I had better come to Montclair.

Trained in making a molehill out of a mountain, I foolishly set off for the hour drive alone. Entering Montclair, I stopped at a deli and bought coffee and Danishes for my mother and me. I parked in front of her house, leaving my purchase on the floor of the car until I could see what was what, walked up to the porch, and rang the doorbell.

My mother did not answer. Was she acting out of peevishness, or was she passed out or, worse, dead? I tried the front door, but it was locked. All the windows were fitted with combination storm windows and screens; fat chance I would get in one of those unless I broke the glass, which I did not want to do. I walked down the driveway. Both the back door and basement doors were locked. I walked back up the driveway and, parting the ivy, pushed against one of the basement windows, but it seemed sealed. I tried another, and it easily swung open. So much for the impenetrable fortress, I thought, and wondered who else had been in and out.

With my purse slung over my shoulder and wishing I had worn jeans instead of a skirt, I backed in through the window. Wriggling on my stomach feet first, I touched down on a two-shelf bookcase, from which I hopped to the floor. I frantically rifled my purse for a tissue to put over my nose. The smell of decomposition was overwhelming. At least I thought it was decomposition. I had never smelled a dead person before, so I couldn't be sure.

I looked around. Everything in the basement was useless, the flotsam of a now receded tide—the few volumes in the bookcase hopelessly mildewed, the bookcase itself buckled, our old Ping Pong table warped, the studio couch steeped in dankness. As I made my way to the stairs, I reckoned I had better announce myself. If I found her alive, I didn't want to be accused of scaring her to death.

"Mother!" I called loudly as I ascended to the kitchen, hoping the door at the top, which was closed, would not be locked. It opened. But when I stepped into the little back hall by the broom closet, the stench and the sight of the kitchen propelled me backward.

"Mother!" I called again, breathing through the tissue I held to my face. The front hall was packed with bulging brown paper bags from the supermarket, crowded together like a stand of tree stumps. She had apparently not taken out the garbage in months, yet there was an eerie logic to the bags I could not grasp.

"Mother!" I called again as I slowly rounded the banister and faced up the stairs.

Where was her tomcat? What if my mother was dead and the cat had not been fed in days? Would it have been as resourceful as my surviving white mouse?

Mounting the stairs, I called one more time, "Mother!"

When I reached the doorway of her bedroom, the cat bounded off my mother's body on the bed and thumped to the floor, slinking under her dressing table. Had it been gnawing on her face? My peripheral vision took in her room, a shambles of beer cans and bottles, a compost of dirty cups and crumpled paper bags. I tried to get my breath as I started for the bed and hoped I could keep from fainting.

"Mother."

As if in rigor mortis, my mother's torso reared up stiffly from under the rumpled spread.

"Who's there?" she demanded, looking stunned and trying to focus her eyes.

I gasped, incredulous at the phoenix arising from its ashes. "Hi! It's me. Suzy. Your daughter, Suzy."

"How dare you come into my house like this?" Her eyes flared, and her chin jutted out.

It was such a relief to be on familiar ground again. "I've been trying to get you on the phone for two days, but you didn't answer."

"You have no right to come barging in here like this." She swung her legs around to the side of the bed and dropped her feet to the floor, where they searched futilely for her slippers.

"Go downstairs. I'm coming down. Go on." She swept the covers back.

"Listen," I said, "I brought us some coffee and Danishes so you wouldn't have to fuss." (Was *I* nuts?) "I'll go get them. They're out in the car." I ran down the stairs, brought in the bag from the deli, and set it down on the coffee table in the living room. And then I just stood there, waiting for my mother to come down.

Next to the couch, cat feces were piled on a stain on the floor, but they were pretty dried up. Small pools of water stood in the creases of the plastic sheets that covered Carlton's grand piano and Hammond organ. The ceiling had been recently plastered and painted. The Persian rugs, rolled up and tied in brown paper, leaned against the wall and had apparently been cleaned and returned. I peered into the paper bags crowding the hall. Their content was not garbage but groceries: putrefied chicken and pork chops still neatly wrapped from the meat counter, broccoli and lettuce decomposing in their packages. Groceries she had ordered and had delivered, but which never made it to the kitchen. The bags made me so sad, for they seemed proof that my mother wanted to take care of herself and just couldn't. But what could I do to save her? The house was cold; I was freezing and nervously shaking.

"How did you get in the house?" my mother demanded, coming down the stairs in her bare feet and filthy robe. I explained about the basement window as I took the paper cups out of the deli bag. She planned to have the window repaired right away, she said.

She unsteadily approached the table and stirred her coffee with the plastic stick, but then left the cup on the table and took a seat on the piano bench, pulling one of her bluish feet up under her. I sat in a wing chair and took one sip of coffee, which, of course, was stone cold, but it gave me something to do. I became conscious that the upholstery underneath me was soaking wet and leapt to my feet.

"I feel like we're in a Bette Davis–Joan Crawford horror movie," I blurted out. My mother laughed and nodded. "I know what you mean," she said.

Huh? She knew what I meant. She knew the difference. Then why didn't she do something about it?

"I choose to live the way I please," she continued. "I sleep late if I want, read or watch television whenever I want. I don't interfere in your life," she pointed out. "I'm independent. I don't ask anything of you." I found her words confusingly true.

"Yes, but ..." And so, picking the card she had chosen, I entered her world. "Well, I was worried about you. I just wanted to see if you were all right."

"I'm fine."

When I left, I was glad to have the long drive ahead of me. I had seen the world so thoroughly through my mother's eyes, suffered so keenly the pain she fended off, that I was disoriented, doubting from her reactions what I had seen and felt myself. I did not have enough skin to keep from flowing out of myself or to keep my mother from flowing in. Driving north up the Garden State Parkway, it dawned on me that the whole time I had been downstairs with her, I had not held a tissue to my nose. I had gotten used to the smell.

⁓

A fireman from the Montclair Township Fire Department called me at home and wanted to know if I knew a Doris Tooni.

"Yes," I answered, bracing myself to hear that the phoenix had finally gone down. "I'm her daughter. Is everything OK?"

"Her daughter? We asked her if she had any relative we could telephone, and she answered, 'What good would that do? My daughter lives in Tasmania.'"

"That's actually true. My sister does live in Tasmania. But I am Mrs. Tooni's daughter, too, and my two brothers and I live only about an hour or so from one another. You mean she didn't mention us?"

"We looked around the phone for names we might call."

"What exactly happened? Was there a fire? Is she all right?"

"She's all right. I mean she's not hurt or anything like that, but …" He paused. "She has some serious problems."

No shit, I thought, but said, "Yes, I know; she's an alcoholic."

"We just thought the family should know, so they could help her. We just want to prevent a tragedy from happening, you know."

A little late for that, I thought. "We've been trying to get her to go to AA for years," I said defensively, intuiting his opinion that we were rotten kids for having abandoned our lonely old mother. "But she insists she doesn't have a problem. Please tell me what happened. How did you get involved?"

"A neighbor called the police. They noticed the basement door swinging open, and they thought something might have happened to her."

"They did the right thing to call," I said. "Did you have to take her to the hospital?" I hoped he would say yes, hoped that my mother would finally be detoxed with medical supervision, that people besides her children, authorities of some kind, would tell her she had to stop drinking.

"We found her sitting up in bed, knitting. She was drunk. You wouldn't believe the place. I've never seen anything like it," he said, as if his observations would come as a surprise to me.

My mother's nightmare had come true. Strangers had forced their way into her house. Strangers had stood around looking at her in bed. Strangers must have scared her out of her skin: big policemen and firemen, clomping up and down her stairs, observing her behavior, while she was cornered like a hunted animal.

"It had to be bad," I said. "I haven't been inside her house in several years, and it was so bad then I had to put a handkerchief to my nose." I could feel my defensiveness rising. "There's not much we can do. Her children are all willing to help her, but she doesn't want to see any of us. She's ashamed." I hoped to transmute his disgust to compassion. "She's really a very nice, bright person. Are all those bags still in the hall?"

"Lady, you can barely get in the door." He hesitated, as if he was withholding even more information, but finally all he did was repeat, "You wouldn't believe the place."

"It's very sad really," I said. "You see, what she would do is order groceries— fresh vegetables, meats … " What was I trying to do? Convince the fireman, or myself, that my mother was someone who used to know about well-balanced meals, that we should at least give her an A for effort? "The delivery man would pass the groceries to her through the door, and she would just set the bags down in the hall. The smell is the groceries decaying." Was I trying to persuade him, or myself, that there was a distinction between decomposing groceries and garbage?

"The place is a fire hazard," the fireman said. "She doesn't smoke, does she?"

"No, luckily, she doesn't smoke."

"Yeah, she said she didn't. We've issued her seven citations for safety violations and given her a week to clean up the place." He gave me the date she was scheduled to appear in court.

"What if she doesn't comply?" I asked, thinking if she couldn't do any better before, how could we expect better now? It would take at least a month to clean up her house, even if we all pitched in.

"That's up to the judge. She might want to have her evaluated."

"You mean for competence?"

"Yeah, the judge could do that. She could send her to a state hospital for a couple of weeks to be tested."

This was great news, I thought. If we stayed out of it, she would never be able to get the place cleaned up and get herself to court in time. The judge would *have* to put her in the hospital.

"Well, I just thought you would want to know when she had to be in court, so that someone from the family could be there. We're just trying to prevent an accident."

"Yes, thank you. I appreciate your calling. Did this happen today?"

"No, yesterday."

After lengthy telephone discussions with Frank and Neal, who could not get away from work, we decided it was a good opportunity for me to let her know the fire department had called. A good time to confront her again not only with the knowledge that she drank but also with the fact that none of this would have happened if she did not drink. A good reason to get herself to AA and get help.

I telephoned her. She did not make excuses for herself. She was quiet. She just listened.

The next morning I called the judge's office to tell her about my mother. My mother's court appearance would be a great opportunity for the community to intervene, I suggested to the clerk I spoke with. A two-week psychiatric evaluation and detoxification might be just the thing to turn things around.

"You wouldn't believe the place," the woman said. "I've never seen anything like it in my life."

"You mean you were in the house, too?"

"Yeah," she said, "but I couldn't take it. I had to wait for the judge out in the van."

"The judge, too?" Had all of Montclair been milling around inside my mother's house?

"Yeah, but the smell was too bad for me."

I felt myself readying to launch into my grocery/garbage explanation, but she kept right on going. "I've seen some bad cases," she said, "but not like this, with feces on the floor."

"Feces?" I was sure she hadn't cleaned up the cat feces I had spotted the last time I was in the house. Then I remembered that she'd told me her cat had disappeared many months before. "Could they be old cat feces?"

"They didn't look that way to me."

"God. Well, you see what I mean about her being a sick woman? My brothers and I have agreed that we think it's important that we not protect her from the consequences of her actions. She told me she hired somebody to clean up the mess for $800. I'm a little concerned because he's already taken her Hammond organ in part payment and is interested in her car."

"I saw a dumpster parked outside her house when I drove by today."

"Really? Huh. Well, my brothers and I just want to convey our hope that the judge will take advantage of this opportunity to have her evaluated in a hospital. This whole incident could turn out to be the best thing that could have happened to her."

When I learned the trial had been postponed a week because the judge was ill, I felt even more confident that my mother would not be able to stay sober that long or actually get herself to court. I called the following week to find out what happened. This is what the clerk in the judge's office brusquely told me: "Mrs. Tooni complied with the citations. The fire department reported the place was cleaned up. She paid a $350 fine and agreed to install fire alarms."

I was stunned. "That's it?"

"Yes."

"You mean the subject of evaluation never came up?"

"No."

"It was such a great opportunity … "

"She was sober. She had her hair done. She looked nice."

"But the judge saw her house."

"That's it."

"Yes, well. Well, thank you. It's too bad it didn't turn out differently."

I was so angry. This was the way it was going to be—up and down and up and down, crisis after crisis, and back to the same old thing. My emotions were played out. Always I had tried to be compassionate, to try to understand that her anesthetizing herself was because of the pain of a past over which she had no control. I had tried to stay unhardened to her sickness. Wasn't it a sickness? Was she free not to be sick? So sick, perhaps she couldn't be responsible? Yet look at what she had just been able to do: clean up her house, appear in court at the appointed hour, look presentable, and comply with the citations. If she could be clever enough to save herself so that she could continue to destroy herself in her own way, why could she not be clever enough to just plain save herself?

It was in this period of having fooled the judge that my mother told me on the telephone she thought she should sell her house and live in an apartment. I responded that I thought it was a good idea. She did not invite me to help, and privately, I once more doubted she could get her haunted house in shape to sell. Neither did I think she was well enough to hunt for an apartment or arrange to have her things moved into it. But in seemingly no time, she accomplished exactly all those things.

Not knowing how much or how little money she had—she had told us it was none of our business—I was incredulous that she rented an apartment in the nice Valley Road Garden Apartments, adjacent to the Montclair Operetta Club and within walking distance of shops in Upper Montclair. Unknown to her four children, she had also smartly arranged with her lawyer to sell her house for her, and he did. She had the Valley Road place ready for herself when the house sold. I found out about the sale by chance, when I called to see how she was doing just days before she was supposed to move. I asked if she would mind if her children walked through the house to see if they had left anything behind they might want, and she said OK; she had bought new furniture for her apartment and was basically going to vacate the house as it was.

It was obvious the house had been stripped. Her violin was gone, but I comforted myself thinking that maybe, like the red violin in the movie of the same name, it had moved on to its next episode and owner. Frank wanted the Persian rug that had been in the living room and was still wrapped up from having been cleaned after the water damage. The other rugs had rotted in their wrappings. In my father's near-empty desk, I discovered a scrapbook of newspaper articles he had amassed about robberies to show the need for the radio alarm he had invented. In the basement I found silver mementos from Iraq that had not been stolen because they were wrapped in yellowed newspaper in a dank cardboard carton and were so blackened they were no longer recognizable. Neal wanted nothing. Sally was in Australia.

After my mother was settled in her apartment, she telephoned me. In the neutral tone of voice one might use to talk about the weather, she told me the woman who stopped her car to help her up from where she lay in the middle of Alvin Place said it was a good thing she had not been going any faster, or she would have run over her. Say what? My mother had been lying in the street near her apartment? And a woman who could have run over her got out of her car to help her? Had my mother passed out? Was she drunk or weak from not eating? Had she tripped on something? Or all of the above?

I was further confused when she said she could hear the singing again, but now it was coming from the direction of the nearby

Montclair Operetta Club. I didn't know whether the singing was in her head or really emanating from rehearsals.

No, she didn't want me to come. She could take care of herself. Everything was fine.

But *I* wasn't fine. Every time my mother called, I learned disturbing information that was burdensome because I could do nothing about it, and it was hard not to carry it around. I also felt guilty that I wasn't doing anything to help her, but I didn't know what to do.

That night I had a dream that seemed like a breakthrough. It taught me something I not only did not know but, more importantly, had not *felt* before. In my dream, I was in a hotel that looked out over a great expanse of water. Standing at the window of my room, I observed a huge passenger plane take off from dry land. It was a heavy plane, a transport plane of some sort, but I could see passengers' heads behind each of the little round windows along its side. Suddenly, I was shocked and horrified to see the airborne plane flip over on its back and struggle to turn over. In the dream, I knew I was helpless to save the plane; nonetheless, I bent my knees and prayed as hard as I could that it would right itself before it was too late. But it fell on its back in the middle of the placid bay and sank, instantly disappearing.

I knew the minute I awoke that the dream was about my mother. Talking to my mother was like my dream—witnessing a catastrophe and being helpless to do anything about it. Like the plane, my mother was going to crash. In the dream I did not blame myself that I could not stop the plane from crashing. I had to stop blaming myself that I couldn't stop my mother from crashing.

My sister, Sally, and her family were back in the States. She and I drove together to our mother's apartment in Montclair. The kitchen door was unlocked, so we let ourselves in and called out to her. The apartment stank. She was upstairs in her bedroom, sitting up over a hole in the mattress big enough to allow me to glimpse the springs inside, but she quickly moved her body in such a way that she covered the hole. She said she was not feeling well enough to go out with us to lunch, but accepted our offer to bring some food in to her. This was a new attitude. She also agreed to my buying her a new mattress. In an advertisement on the radio about Dial-a-Mattress I had heard that the store could deliver a mattress and dispose of the old one on demand. She also listened when we asked her to think about our finding a nursing home for her to live in, somewhere she could get help. When we returned with her lunch, we told her we'd come back the next day to let the Dial-a-Mattress people in.

On the way out of the apartment, Sally and I opened a closet door onto what looked like a geologic column—smelly trash stuffed in strata to the top. Looking in the refrigerator too, we found the expected decaying contents. We agreed that my mother had descended to a new low; she was not even up to pretending she could take care of herself. At lunch my sister and I discussed our telling our mother that we would like to help her but would not attempt to find a nursing home for her unless I had power of attorney. If she did not agree, I was going to stop trying to help her. Sally supported my resolve.

Before we headed for home, we looked at two nursing homes in Montclair and picked up their brochures. Both were expensive but did not pass our sniff test. Even if our mother agreed to my terms, the prospect of our finding a proper place for her care loomed depressingly. And what were we going to do if she had no money?

The next day, Sally and I arrived at our mother's apartment in time to let the two men in who were delivering the Dial-A-Mattress. We hurried up the stairs ahead of them to be with my mother when they carried the mattress to the second floor and into her bedroom. We helped get her out of bed and found that she was too weak to stand by herself. With no chair upstairs, we held her up between us as the men propped the new mattress against the wall and commenced to pull the old mattress off the bed.

"What the …!"

"Oh, my God!"

The men discovered that the mattress was full of excrement. Because our mother could not get out of bed by herself, she had resourcefully made the hole in her mattress to serve as a toilet. How long had she been in her bed? How long had she gone without food?

To the credit of the deliverymen, they said not one more word as they propped the old mattress against the wall and slid the new mattress onto the box spring. I fumbled in my purse for my wallet. I wanted to give them a huge tip, but I had only eighteen dollars. I gave it to them, apologizing that I did not have more. They took the money and left. I felt shame to imagine them swapping stories with their buddies over a beer: "I thought I'd seen everything, but you won't believe what happened ... "

I had bought new sheets and pillowcases and quickly made the bed while Sally continued to hold up our mother. I noticed a big patch of black skin under our mother's arm. Before we got her into bed, we walked her to the bathroom, where, sitting on the toilet lid, she actually let me wash her. I wondered if the patch was cancerous, but it turned out to be a treatable fungus.

After we had made her comfortable in bed, I calmly gave her my spiel about needing power of attorney in order to help her. As unexpectedly as she had arranged with her lawyer to sell her house, my mother said, "I can't live like this anymore" and agreed to give it to me. She was sober. She had probably just survived the frightening experience of going through the DTs, delirium tremens, drying out in bed alone.

Sally and I went straight to her lawyer's office. I explained our situation to him, and the office prepared the necessary papers for my mother to sign. A kind man, the lawyer said some of his clients were well satisfied with Green Hill in West Orange and that my sister and I might want to look into it. A women's residency, Green Hill offered independent apartments, assisted living, and a nursing facility. And what a relief to learn that, yes, our mother had the money to pay for it.

Sally and I made a beeline to Green Hill. We became giddy as we drove up the driveway, which artfully curved through the landscaped property surrounding the building that looked like a grand hotel with its porte cochere. The interior was well appointed, clean, and odor free. After discussing the benefits of living at Green Hill and coming to an agreement on the finances, the man in admissions advised us to call an ambulance to take our mother to the hospital. He said a doctor from Green Hill would come to the hospital to evaluate her for what level of the facility she should enter. With the inability to care for herself and a certain amount of alcoholic dementia, our mother went straight into the nursing unit. And there ended her children's dread of one day finding our mother dead and decomposing.

As Sally and I waited in the emergency room with our mother during the process of admission to Mountainside Hospital, a nurse opened the curtain of our cubicle to see how we were doing. I guessed what she must have been thinking and cracked, "Dysfunctional family!" It was shame speaking.

The nurse looked at Sally and me protectively flanking our mother. "Not dysfunctional," she said. "You're here, aren't you?"

ACKNOWLEDGEMENTS

Over twenty-five years ago, my first draft of this book was entitled *Riding Backwards*. When my mother saw how much as a child I enjoyed riding backwards on the train, she joked it was because I like to see where I've been. That first draft was 783 pages long and included the Louisiana Purchase and academic Endnotes. Identifying with the definition of writer as "someone who stares at the blank page or computer screen until little drops of blood form on her forehead," I thought because I had remembered everything I could possibly remember and written it down, I was done. In short, I didn't know that my first draft was a confusing mess. The reason I am saying this is because that was the draft I foisted on my first readers, heroes all for plowing through it.

To my siblings and first-draft readers Frank, Neal, and Sally, their confidence in me and making me feel I got it right meant a lot.

Thanks to first-draft readers, Paul and Ellie Becher, Barbara Cavalieri, Evelyn Dunphy, Aziza Ellozy, David Friedson, and Kevin Roche.

Thanks to writer Linda Donn for telling me my typewriter was passé and persuading me to buy a computer. Yes, it was that long ago. Thanks to our nephew William Kane, who then working at IBM, kindly ordered and delivered my first personal computer. Thanks to my brother Neal for his infinite patience and good humor in teaching me how to use a pre-Word writing program.

Thanks to Rhoda Gushue, then library director, and Eileen Baer, librarian, at the Bedford Hills Free Library in Bedford Hills, NY, for helping me find the kind of details that make a story come alive.

To all the cousins on both sides of the family, many of whom I had never met, thank you for answering the questions in my letters and telephone calls and the pleasure of talking with you, ranging from Hisaw and Cummins cousins in Missouri to the Issa/

Al-Khouri cousins in the US—Albertine, Fikrat, Hekmut, and Farid, the latter then still in Baghdad who translated my letter to his mother, my Great Aunt Therouza, and translated her answers in his response. Thanks to cousin Robert Nipp, in Houston, Texas, who I learned is the great grandson of Chief Green Feather of the Shawnees: the Native American in the family finally met the Arab. Or as Alex Shoumatoff concludes in *The Mountain of Names*, we are *all* cousins.

Thank you to Kathryn E. Jones, for confirming my research that I am a descendant of Robert Crockett, Davy Crockett's brother, through his daughter, Jane Crockett, Davy's first cousin, who married George Hisaw in a line down to Lloyd Hisaw, my maternal grandfather to my mother and me. Jones documents all this in her letter and book, *Crockett Cousins* (Graham, Texas 76046: 1419 Crescent Drive, 1986).

Special thanks to cousin Lois H. Crockett (her husband was not related to Davy), the daughter of Dr. Frederick Lee Hisaw, my grandfather Lloyd's brother. Although estranged from my mother, her first cousin, Lois generously extended her family photographs and history as well as her friendship to me.

Thanks to Robert G. Tucker, PhD. and Certified Genealogical Record Searcher, based in Noel, Missouri, for locating and copying for me deeds, probates, wedding and death certificates, and other research that helped establish a timeline for my mother's forebears and helped me understand their relationships.

Thanks to Arthur M. Bixby, historian for the National Railway Historical Society (Roanoke Chapter), who helped me name the trains we took from Newark to St. Louis and from St. Louis to Neosho.

My gratitude to the Sisters of St. Mary's Convent, then in Peekskill, NY, for the gift of silence. Thank you for their hospitality and friendship and for providing me solitude in community as I finished my first draft. Special thanks to Sister Mary Angela, who having once worked in publishing, said after reading it, "It has more about penguins than I wanted to know." Thanks to Joan Murphy, a fellow retreatant and writer for reading it later, too.

Thanks to feminist Jane Gould, for her helpful criticisms, especially to cut the manuscript in half, and to Drs. Marlene Fisher and Cora Brady, RSCJ, professors at Manhattanville College, for the generosity of their time and attention in reading the first draft.

Thanks for the chain of kindness generated by a fellow singer in the Master Singers of Westchester, writer Steve Lesher, who gave me the contact information of his agent, Gerard McCauley, whom I queried about my book. Mr. McCauley forwarded my letter to the publisher Henry O. Houghton, Jr., and asked me to send him a copy of my manuscript and one to Mr. Houghton as well. My letter was better than the manuscript. Mr. Houghton sent a nice note returning my manuscript and said that Mr. McCauley would put me in touch with editor Ellen Joseph, "who I hope may guide you in the right direction. Mr. McCauley will no doubt keep me posted on whatever may develop." Sending my manuscript to Ellen Joseph, she read the mess and returned it with some notes. She did not charge me. Then I put my draft in a drawer to work on my graduate degree.

The first US-led war with Iraq under President George H.W. Bush that began in January 1991 disturbed me greatly, and I began writing letters and articles about the war, which I continued doing through President George W. Bush's invasion of Iraq in 2003 and which are collected on my website at www.suzytkane.com. It would be twenty years before I pulled the manuscript of my memoir out of storage. By then, I was not the same person.

To the No Coast Writers group in Taos, NM, thanks to Bunny Eggborn, Martha Grossman, Janet Majerus, Susan Mihalic, Penny Semi, Brian Tacang, and Susan Washburn, for being grammar mavens and literarily astute and for providing a safe and caring place to reveal ourselves without judgment. I'm grateful for both the laughter and the tears. You taught me the difference between writing family history and writing creative nonfiction.

Thank you to Daniel M. Klein, co-author of *When Plato and a Platypus Walk into a Bar* and author of *Travels with Epicurus* as well as a shelf of additional titles. A friend since junior high school,

Danny, too, was an encouraging reader of both my first and fifth draft and an invaluable publishing mentor.

When Margaret (Maggie) Hinck McClure, also a friend since junior high school, was administrator of the Lake George (NY) Historical Association Museum and Book Store, she chatted one day with a museum-goer who introduced himself as Chuck Gosselink. He told her he had written a history about the properties and their owners in the Benjamin Van Buren's Bay area on northern Lake George. He said he spent the summers on the Penfield property there with his wife, Charlotte, who was a Penfield, explaining that *he* did not spend summers there in his youth as she did because he had grown up in Iraq. "I know only one Iraqi," Maggie commented, "a friend whose father was from Iraq who went to the University of Michigan. "Oh," he replied, "you must mean the Tooni brothers." Maggie was stunned. What are the odds of such a coincidence?

In synchronicity within synchronicity, Chuck turns out to be the son of my father's English teacher in Basra, George Gosselink! As a missionary, Chuck's father wrote weekly letters from Iraq to his parents and siblings back in Pella, Iowa, that Chuck collected with some commentary in the book *Dear Folks at Home, 1922-1925* (Silver Bay, New York: Boat House Books, 2008). The book offers a peek into the world of my father and his family. Looking like an Iowan but born and raised in Iraq, Chuck, of course, spoke fluent Arabic and called Basra home. He introduced me to the concept of the "third culture kid." As an English teacher himself, his reading of my section on Iraq was a big help: he translated Arabic words, confirmed the culture, answered my countless questions, and shares my love of Iraqi cuisine. Any mistakes the reader might encounter, however, are my responsibility.

Thanks to fifth-draft-reader friends Evelyn Dunphy, Elizabeth Ohlson, and Marge Reading for donating their precious time, especially since they are each engaged in their own projects as artists.

Thanks to friend since childhood Judy Haas Smith and her husband, Bill, for their hospitality in Neosho, MO, and to Judy for helping track down a family document at the Newton County

Courthouse and for taking me to visit Fredine Haddock, my mother's high school friend. In her nineties and with a clear mind, Fredine not only knew my mother but was present when my father was in Neosho looking for a wife. Six years later, Fredine and her husband spent an evening with my parents when they returned to Neosho from Iraq. Her husband was my mother's boy friend who never got to be alone with her.

Thanks to library director Ginny Raye at the Neosho/Newton County Public Library, Rilla Scott, head genealogy librarian, and librarian Mary Roundtree—all for their help in finding local details.

Thanks to Susan Mihalic with appreciation for her thorough initial editing and for teaching me to ask the question of every scene, "Does this contribute to the storyline?"

Thanks to editor Diana Rico for her astute and perceptive questions whose answers when I dug for them gave the story the coherence and layering it needed. While I'm no Wolfe, Fitzgerald, or Hemingway, Diana is my Maxwell Perkins.

I am grateful for the expertise of Debra Gallek and her essential contributions in both website and book design.

It is my privilege to be the mother of two fine sons, Tom and Peter, who, with our also fine daughters-in-law, Samantha and Tanya respectively, are all good parents—a love fest.

Lastly, thank you to my good-humored husband, Tom. You are the King of Common Sense and the Yes in my life. I am grateful for your support of both my writing and late-blooming education. You know how much I love you.

BOOKS THAT HELPED

Balian, Basil. *Once Upon a Time in Iraq* (self-published, BookSurge Publishing, 2008).

Barker, J. *The First Iraq War: 1914–1918, Britain's Mesopotamian Campaign* (New York: Enigma Books, 2009).

Campbell, C. G. *Folktales from Iraq* (Philadelphia: University of Pennsylvania Press, 2005).

Hoffman, Ruth, and Helen Hoffman. *We Married an Englishman* (New York: Carrick & Evans, 1938).

Irving, David. *The Trail of the Fox: The Search for the True Field Marshall Rommel* (New York: E. P. Dutton, 1977).

Jackson, Iain. "The Architecture of the British Mandate in Iraq: Nation-building and State Creation." *Journal of Architecture* 21, no. 3 (2016): 375–417. https://doi.org/10.1080/13602365.2016.1179662.

Kilmarx, Robert, ed. *America's Maritime Legacy: A History of the US Merchant Marine and Shipbuilding since Colonial Times* (Boulder, Colorado: Westview Press, 1979).

Memmi, Albert. *The Colonizer and the Colonized* (Boston: Beacon Press, 1967).

Morison, Samuel Eliot. *The Two-Ocean War: A Short History of the United States Navy in the Second World War* (Boston: Atlantic Monthly Press, 1963).

Patai, Raphael. *The Arab Mind* (New York: Charles Scribner's Sons, 1973, 1976).

Radi, Nuha al-. *Baghdad Diaries* (London: Saqi Books, 1998).

Rejwan, Nissm. *The Jews of Iraq: 3000 Years of History and Culture* (London: George Weidenfeld & Nicholson, 1985; Louisville, Kentucky: Fons Vitae, 2009).

Solh, Raghid El-. *Britain's 2 Wars with Iraq, 1941, 1991* (Berkshire, England: Ithaca Press, 1996).

Stokesbury, James L. *A Short History of World War II* (New York: William Morrow and Company, 1980).

Van Ess, Dorothy. *Fatima and Her Sisters* (New York: John Day Company, 1961).

———. *Pioneers in the Arab World* (Grand Rapids, Michigan: Wm. B. Eerdmans Publishing Company, 1974).

Van Ess, John. *Meet the Arab* (New York: John Day Company, 1943).

Wallach, Janet. *Desert Queen: The Extraordinary Life of Gertrude Bell, Adventurer, Adviser to Kings, Ally of Lawrence of Arabia* (New York: Nan A. Talese, 1996).

Warner, Geoffrey. *Iraq and Syria, 1941* (Newark: University of Delaware Press, 1974).

Made in the USA
Monee, IL
29 June 2021